CONTENTS

DEVELOPMENT, LEARNING AND TEACHING IN THE EARLY YEARS: A COGNITIVE PERSPECTIVE

Gillian Boulton-Lewis

The aim of this book is to provide a review of recent research and theories of development and learning in the early childhood years and to draw from them the implications for effective teaching. Where possible and appropriate the perspective is Australian, particularly in the discussions of families, social competence and socialisation.

This work is unique for at least two reasons. First because it deals with all aspects of development and learning in the early childhood years, and second because it presents a cognitive interpretation of most aspects of development. Children are described as extremely competent learners from very early in life. In a favourable social and physical environment they take in and process information to the best of their developmental capacity, and construct a knowledge base consisting of information, skills and procedures which allows them to rapidly become proficient in most areas of their world. Children's development and learning will be described in these terms for professionals who work with children since effective care and education of young children demands a full appreciation of such capacities.

Each chapter presents its author's perspective on the topic at hand, which is shaped by that person's reading, research and beliefs. However, all the authors but one originally worked in the same department which was concerned with child and family development, and are familiar with each other's work. We believed when we proposed the book that our views were compatible and that together we would present an interesting and coherent perspective on children's development and learning. There is some overlap in the authors' viewpoints and even in some of the research described, but this is advantageous because it invites you to consider some aspects of what is being said from a slightly different perspective. The first chapter will describe the organisation, content and objectives of the other chapters.

Chapter 2 is concerned with the origins of thinking and, in particular, with perception and cognition in infancy. The chapter presents an overview of the emergence of cognitive functions, and draws on a number of contemporary models and recent research to describe the development of basic processes such as sensory perception, attention, representation, memory and categorisation. Thought is defined as the establishment and activation of networks of information derived initially from the child's sensory experience of the world.

The general themes are that the basic cognitive processes are in operation in early life, that children deploy these competently to appraise the world around them, and that the efficiency and wider application of these processes develops with experience, knowledge and maturational change. The links between perception and cognition in early development are explored in a discussion of cognitive processes as apparently driven by or derived from perceptual processes. Subsequent development of cognitive functions is then considered with an emphasis on conceptualisation, reasoning and problem solving.

Finally, the impact of caring and educational environments on early cognitive development is explored. This includes a discussion of practical matters such as strategies for developing children's knowledge bases and appropriate ways to observe and interpret children's responses and behaviour in naturalistic settings, for example by running records.

After studying chapter 2 you should be able to:

1. Describe the basic processes that children exercise to derive sensory information;

2. Discuss the operation and development of these processes;

3. Present arguments on the question of whether infants and young children perceive the world in a coherent and meaningful way;

4. Describe the links between perception and cognition in early development;

5. Discuss subsequent development of cognitive functions and in particular the relationship between these and conceptualisation, reasoning and problem solving;

6. Describe effective ways of facilitating cognitive development and learning in early childhood;

7. Describe and apply the above information in observing and interpreting young children's behaviour.

Chapter 3 is concerned with memory, cognition, learning and teaching from three years to about eight years. It is divided into three main sections. First the relation between cognition and the development and operation of children's information-processing systems will be looked at, then theories that explain how cognition develops, and finally the implications of the preceding sections for learning and teaching in the early years.

The first section is a discussion of how children process information. Specifically it includes a model of the information-processing system including storage of sensory information, short-term memory, working memory, long-term memory and metamemory (knowing about memory). The function and development of each of these aspects of memory in children is described, then the implications for learning and teaching in early childhood are considered.

The second section looks at the neo-Piagetian theories of Biggs and Collis (1982, 1989), Case (1985, 1988, 1991), Fischer (1980; Fischer & Farrar, 1988) and Halford (1988, in press) compared with Piaget's classic stage theory of cognitive development. It attempts to bring together these theories, it considers the effect of knowledge on development and learning, and it summarises Case's proposal for a theory that occupies a middle ground on the general and specific aspects of development.

The third section of the chapter considers the implications of the above for learning and teaching as well as some of the procedures that teachers can use to maximise learning in early childhood. There is discussion of learning in and out of school, scaffolded instruction and reciprocal teaching, computer-assisted learning, the phenomenographic approach to teaching, assessing and controlling the processing demand of learning tasks, situation-specific learning, and concept mapping.

With regard to teaching the argument is that the child's own construction of knowledge is crucial in meaningful learning. It is important for teachers to find out what each child knows and is interested in as well as to consider the developmental constraints that exist in the early years and their implications for teaching. It is suggested that teachers should be metacognitive about their own teaching.

After studying chapter 3 you should be able to:

1. Describe the function and development of children's information processing systems;

2. Describe and compare contemporary theories of cognitive development with Piaget's theory;

3. Discuss learning and development in terms of the interaction between a child's capacity to process information, prior knowledge, and environmental factors;

4. Describe the procedures and strategies, derived from the above theoretical perspectives, that can be used to facilitate and enhance learning for children in preschool and the first years of school.

In chapter 4 language acquisition in the early years is taken to be the origin of a process that continues well beyond these years. The links between linguistic and cognitive development are made clear. The chapter begins with a brief discussion of the nature of human language, contrasting the concepts of language and communication. This is followed by consideration of the prerequisites of language acquisition, including pre-linguistic phonological abilities such as discrimination and control of speech sounds, non-verbal communication, and mental representation. From here the relationship of speech with early cognitive development is discussed, as is the transition from vocables to symbolic word usage. The one-word stage is explored in some detail, including the structure of children's early vocabularies and vocabulary development.

The next section deals with phonological development, and includes consideration of normal articulation milestones and phonological processes which result in articulation errors. The discussion emphasises the fact that

articulatory control takes some time to develop and that many speech errors can be considered 'lawful' developmental phenomena. This should provide a basis for preschool teachers and parents to make judgements about when a child may require speech therapy.

The discussion of grammatical development centres primarily on its interaction with conceptual and phonological development. A semantically based approach to the acquisition of grammar rules is emphasised.

Some suggestions for teacher strategies to encourage language acquisition are made based on recent work on preschool adult–child interaction. The evidence that some types of modified language input may facilitate children's language growth is also considered.

After studying chapter 4 you should be able to:

1. Discuss the nature of human language as opposed to communication;

2. Describe the prerequisites of language acquisition;
3. Describe children's early vocabularies and vocabulary development;
4. Discuss phonological development;
5. Outline the interaction of grammatical, conceptual and phonological development;
6. Describe ways in which parents and teachers can actively encourage language acquisition.

Chapter 5 focuses on the development and learning of movement skills in early childhood. It provides a comprehensive description of children's progression from fundamental movement patterns to complex everyday and, finally, skilled movement. It begins with a discussion of the processes that underlie motor development on a continuum from involuntary, automatic and reflex movements to the cognitively controlled skilled movements that require planning and practice.

The reflexes of the newborn child are described as an example of involuntary movements. Other basic involuntary processes such as postural stability and sensory integration are discussed and illustrated using developmental milestones such as sitting and crawling, and fundamental movement patterns such as walking, running, jumping, throwing and catching, as examples.

The general argument is that both normally functioning involuntary processes and cognitive processes, defined as the ability to voluntarily learn and control movements, are necessary for the development and learning of skilled movements. Such cognitive processes consist of information-processing components including aspects of memory, and the ability to learn about and control movements with regard to force, timing and spatial parameters.

After studying chapter 5 you should be able to describe:

1. The reflexes of the newborn as an example of involuntary movements;
2. The progression from fundamental to skilled movements;
3. Developmental milestones and fundamental movement patterns;

4. Fine motor development;
5. The relation between cognitive processes and skilled movement;
6. Age appropriate activities that will facilitate gross and fine motor development.

Chapter 6 is concerned with the development, encouragement and integration of the processes of artistry in early childhood. The introduction discusses the value of the arts in society, how they have been important since humans first gathered in groups to live, and how they allow people to express their thoughts, perceptions and feelings. The arts enhance the quality of life and constitute a unique body of knowledge, skills and ways of thinking.

The arts are then explored as an alternative way of knowing and representing the world which involves cognition through the senses. Knowledge of the arts is not always expressed in words because what we understand from a work of art is often a personal interpretation. Metaphor is used extensively in all art forms and the arts have the capacity to link the cognitive and emotional domains. The theory of multiple intelligences proposed by Gardner (1983, 1988) acknowledges musical and spatial intelligences as distinct. Finally, we know that young children interact with their environment through non-linguistic as well as linguistic forms of knowing and that many of these experiences occur as forms of play and involve representations.

The next section is a discussion of symbols used by children in play and especially in drawing. This is followed by a more detailed discussion of the role of objects and scripts in young children's artistic experience and the need for children to scribble and experiment. Child-centred arts education is proposed and such issues as philosophical justifications, the importance of play and the way the approach fosters open-ended discovery and autonomy in learning, and the use of open-ended resources, are considered. A guide for teachers is provided to give examples of the ways in which teachers' behaviour can influence and assist children in artistic development and learning. This is followed by a section concerned with cultural influences and play. The chapter concludes with a section on the implications of the development of artistry for early childhood education.

After studying chapter 6 you should be able to:

1. Describe how the arts have different language forms and provide alternative ways of knowing;
2. Discuss the use of symbols in the arts as ways of developing and communicating meaning;
3. Understand why these forms of meaning are important in early childhood;
4. Describe the developing processes that children engage in when they are involved in artistic experiences;
5. Discuss the implications of development of the arts for early childhood education.

Chapter 7 looks at young children's peer relationships and the development of personal and social competence. In the first section of the chapter psychoanalytic, biological, social learning and social cognitive approaches to describing and explaining social development are outlined. The usefulness of each approach is illustrated with reference to encouraging sharing behaviour.

In the following section the social development of young children is viewed as encompassing the processes of individuation and socialisation. Individuation is the development of a unique self-identity depending on temperament in early infancy, personality traits, development of sex roles, gender concepts, self-concept and self-esteem. Strategies for helping children to develop competent and resilient personalities are discussed.

The final section is concerned with children's developing social competence with peers. Both social behaviour and social problem-solving skills are identified as important components of competence. The skills of friendship, the determinants of peer acceptance, and children's understanding of the nature of friendship are addressed. The roles of parents and educators in helping children to develop social competence are discussed. The long-term problems that are experienced by children who are rejected by their peers is highlighted and methods for facilitating the development of social skills in children are briefly reviewed.

After studying chapter 7 you should be able to:

1. Describe the theories that contribute to understanding social development and behaviour;

2. Discuss the social development of young children in terms of individuation and socialisation;

3. Describe the origins of individuality;

4. Discuss the features of personal identity and strategies for fostering competent and resilient personalities in children;

5. Consider the implications of the development of social competence for early childhood environments for young children.

In chapter 8 the socialisation of children within their primary social context, the family, is examined. Socialisation is defined as the process by which individuals acquire the ways of behaving within a society, that allows them to function successfully within it. The multi-disciplinary research perspectives supporting this chapter include a sociological view of family, systems theories of family development, findings from developmental research, attachment theory and social cognitive theory. The focus is on the reciprocal influences of biology and environment on individual development.

The first part of the chapter discusses general systems theory and then its application to human development; as in Bronfenbrenner's ecological theory of human development. The family as a microsystem is considered, including basic organisational patterns, functions, and characteristics that influence socialisation such as the child's development and behaviour, socioeconomic status, and cultural background orientation.

The next section looks at the influence of temperament on social-emotional development and describes how the effects are dependent on the interaction of the characteristics of the parents with the characteristics of individual children. The development of attachment is then considered as a relational concept which is dependent on caregiver-child interaction.

Dimensions of parenting behaviour and their association with desirable socially competent behaviour in children are discussed. The research into outcomes of different types of parenting styles are described, including children's contribution to the socialisation process. Parental characteristics, resources and beliefs about parenting are considered. This is followed by a discussion of the intergenerational transmission of parenting behaviours, which concerns the extent of the influence of childhood experiences of parenting on subsequent parenting behaviours in adulthood. The final section discusses parental support systems.

The chapter concludes with the proposal that human development is understood best when research systematically compares the environmental systems in which children develop. From this ecological perspective the most important findings are likely to be related to how the interactions between people and settings develop and function.

After studying chapter 8 you should be able to:

1. Describe the multi-disciplinary perspectives of research on families and socialisation;
2. Discuss the organisational patterns, functions and characteristics of families that influence socialisation;
3. Describe the effect on social development of the interaction of child and parent characteristics;
4. Discuss the development of attachment;
5. Summarise the research in the outcomes of different types of parenting behaviour on children;
6. Consider the effects on parenting of parental characteristics, resources, beliefs and social factors such as support systems.

In conclusion, chapter 9 reviews and draws together the general issues and themes of the preceding chapters to provide a broad framework for considering development and learning in early childhood. A dominant principle of this framework is viewing young children as active information-processors, engaged from birth in the task of 'knowing' all aspects of the world around them. From this general framework, some implications for caregivers, educators and other professionals who deal with young children are brought to light.

THE ORIGINS OF THINKING: PERCEPTION AND COGNITION IN EARLY CHILDHOOD

Di Catherwood

The changing picture of cognitive development

This chapter covers the emergence of thinking, or cognition, in the first few years of life. Cognition is the capacity of the human mind to store and use information about the world. Such information initially arrives via the senses (of vision, hearing and so on) and can consist of sensory impressions such as colours or sounds, or of input that has some wider, perhaps symbolic meaning, such as words or numbers. Although both kinds of information are used in early cognition, sensory or perceptual information is initially relied on, so here we will consider the close relationship between perception and cognition in early life. The current view of cognition emphasises the everyday nature of thinking. Cognition enters into all our experiences, from deciding what to eat for breakfast to reading the latest book on early development. It is constantly used to guide and filter our experiences. Cognition can be fairly aimless, with one thought tagging along after another, or it can be specifically directed to some goal or problem. All of this remarkable activity depends on the capacity of the human brain to store and later reactivate information when it is required. All of these aspects of cognition will be covered in this chapter.

The development of this impressive capacity begins very early. In fact, it now seems probable that infants begin to use cognitive abilities from the earliest moments after their entry into the world. In the past few decades, there has been a remarkable change in our understanding of early cognitive development. It was once thought (Piaget, 1953) that in the early years of life, cognition was relatively restricted and consisted mainly of fleeting and disconnected sensory impressions (images, etc.), or only memories of movements or actions. On the other hand, the cognition of older children and adults was said to consist of more orderly and logical manipulation of symbolic or abstract information. From this perspective, children did not begin to engage in genuine cognitive activities until aged six or seven. Prior to this, their thinking was seen as being composed of 'egocentric' views of the physical world. It was described as 'animistic', or incapable of distinguishing reality from fantasy, and as only able to fix or centre on one aspect of a situation at a time.

However, research from two different directions has altered this picture. Research with infants and very young children has indicated that early cognitive abilities have been seriously underestimated in the past. Procedures for assessing cognitive responses even in newborn infants have shown that many of the basic cognitive processes used by adults are available in the first moments of postnatal life (Haith, 1990). And at the other end of the developmental scale there has been a reappraisal of adult cognition. Recent findings suggest that adults do not always use the logical, abstract style of thinking attributed to them in past accounts (Martindale, 1991). Adult thinking appears to involve basically the same kinds of processes as those used by young children. The main developmental difference lies in the efficiency and flexibility with which these processes can be applied. This general theme will be apparent throughout this chapter.

To begin this revised story of cognitive development, it is first necessary to consider the recent findings on sensory or perceptual abilities in early life. It is obvious that the senses of vision, hearing, touch, taste and smell are the first avenue for collecting the material or information that lies at the basis of all of our cognitive processes. Of course even adults use such information, and sensory features often enrich adult experience. However, in early life, this information is by necessity of greater importance. Without access to language or cultural symbols, infants must somehow begin the task of investigating and understanding the essential properties and principles of the world around them. By and large, all infants apply their senses to this challenge with a vigour and single-mindedness that seems unparalleled in later learning activities. The suggestion that the senses are the first tools of cognitive development is not new (Piaget, 1953). However, over recent decades, there has been a dramatic re-evaluation of the quality of this early sensory activity. Past views suggested that infants experienced an overwhelming or disorganised sensory universe, comprised of fleeting, vague impressions with neither structure nor order, and with no connection to each other or to any enduring knowledge or understanding of the world (Piaget, 1953). It is now clear that this is far from the truth.

First knowledge: using the senses

To begin with the visual system, it was once considered that infants were capable of registering only very poor or degraded visual impressions in the first year or so of life. But more recently developed methods for assessing vision in pre-verbal infants have confirmed that even in the moments after birth, the visual system is capable of conveying rich and coherent information about the visual world.

Infant visual 'acuity' (or the ability to see visual detail) cannot be measured with the Snellen charts of alphabetical letters used to assess adult acuity. However, another method called the Forced Choice Preferential Looking Procedure, can be used instead. Essentially, this involves presenting two circular patterns of equal size and overall brightness for the infant to view. One pattern is a blank grey patch, while the other consists of black and white stripes. If the infant can actually see (i.e. distinguish) the stripes, it is expected that she or he will turn towards or fixate the striped pattern (because this is more interesting than the plain grey patch). The tester continues to present the infant with such pairs of patterns, but with the striped pattern becoming progressively finer and finer. At some point, the infant will not show a preference for this pattern: the stripes can no longer be distinguished so this

pattern now also appears as a plain greyish patch. This indicates the limits of visual acuity in infants in a similar way to that for adults trying to read the progressively smaller rows of letters on the Snellen charts. Using such procedures, it has been shown that while newborn infant visual acuity is considerably poorer than that of adults, it is more than adequate to see the main details of important objects in the visual world (such as the facial features of an adult cradling the infant). Moreover, the development of visual acuity is so rapid that infants approach 20/20 vision by nine to ten months of age (Rosner & Rosner, 1990; Teller, 1979).

It is thus clear that babies are by no means blind, but do they see the features of the visual world in a coherent or 'sensible' way, or are the features merely a jumbled disarray, without clear structure or definition? The answer to this important question has been provided by many experiments using a procedure known as the 'habituation' method. Here, infants are repeatedly presented with an item, for example a coloured light or a pattern on a screen. In the first instance, the infant will probably show considerable interest in, or fixation to, this item, but will eventually become more and more reluctant to look at it for any length of time. At this juncture, a new or different item is presented for the infant's scrutiny. If the infant now shows interest in this new item (while continuing to show a lack of interest in the old or familiar item when it is presented), then this can be taken to imply that the infant sees the old and new items as different or visually distinct in some way. By carefully varying the differences between the items, it is possible to assess an infant's ability to see a whole host of visual features. (See figure 2.1.)

This basic procedure has been employed in many studies over the past few decades and has shown that even at birth babies are able to visually distinguish between different shapes (e.g. circles and squares), between objects of the same shape but different size, between different numbers of items and even between different orientations (i.e. vertical from horizontal) (Slater & Bremner, 1989). Moreover, newborn babies can even distinguish most of the main

HABITUATION PARADIGM

Habituation phase

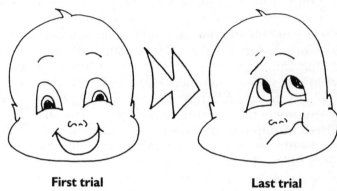

First trial   **Last trial**

Test phase

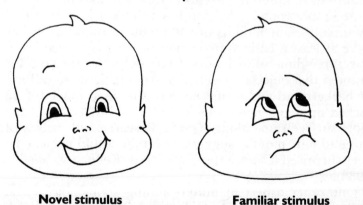

Novel stimulus   **Familiar stimulus**

Figure 2.1: The habituation procedure.

colours, with colour vision being essentially mature by three to four months of age (Teller & Bornstein, 1987). It was once believed that such abilities required assistance from language, but it is now apparent that the visual world is perceived in a well-structured and clearly defined manner long before a child uses or comprehends language.

In addition to these basic visual capacities, it has also been confirmed that the infant visual system allows the processing of qualities once thought to be well beyond the abilities of pre-verbal babies. For example, it was considered that infants were unable to make any connection between one view of an object and a different view of the same object (from a different distance or viewpoint). It was even proposed that infants may believe that they have hundreds of different parents (since each new view of the parent would mean a new or different parent!). However, research which observes infants' reactions to different views of the same object has shown that even in the first months of life they respond as if they perceive objects to remain the same or 'constant' when seen from different distances (size constancy) or viewing angles (shape constancy) (Bremner, 1988). In other words, it is most unlikely that infants suffer from the misconception that they have hundreds of different parents of different sizes or shapes.

At a more complex level, it has also been suggested that by three to four months of age infants respond as if they have at least a basic appreciation of what an 'object' is in our three-dimensional world. For example, we take for granted that objects are separate from their surroundings or background and would be very surprised indeed if we picked up a cup from a table and found that part of the table surface came along with it. Research with babies of three to four months suggests that they would likewise be very surprised if such a thing occurred (Kellman & Spelke, 1983).

One other aspect of understanding about objects also seems to develop much earlier than formerly expected. This concerns our acceptance of the idea that objects continue to exist or have 'permanence' regardless of whether we are observing them. Infants younger than about eight months often will not search for a toy that is hidden under or inside another object and this was taken as evidence of a lack of such understanding (Piaget, 1953). However, more recent studies have shown that even 3- to 4-month-old babies act surprised and interested when an object concealed behind a screen subsequently disappears alto- gether (Baillargeon, Spelke & Wasserman, 1985). There is some suggestion that an understanding about object per- manence develops early for objects concealed *behind* other objects, but that more experience of the world is required for a full understanding about objects hidden *inside* other objects (Harris, 1983), possibly because the world is full of contradictory cases where objects do indeed seem to cease to exist when they are hidden inside another object (e.g. food in the mouth). In any event, all of the research on infant understanding of object permanence shows a fasci- nating picture of the young child attempting to come to grips with the 'rules' of our physical universe through the interaction of innate perceptual capacities and experience.

This portrayal of a sensible or coherent visual world in early life is echoed by the findings for the other perceptual systems. The habituation procedure has been adapted to examine these other systems, with comparable results. In regard to hearing or audition, it has been shown that in the earliest months of life infants are able to distinguish between different volumes, pitches and rhythms (Brem- ner, 1988; Dowling & Harwood, 1986; Werner & Lipsitt, 1981), and actually show superior abilities (relative to those of adults) in distinguishing the range of sounds used in human speech (Eimas, 1975). This same general pattern emerges from studies of touch ('tactile' and 'haptic') per- ception (Ruff, 1984). Young infants actively employ touch with the hands or mouth to explore objects and it is now clear that they are capable of distinguishing the shape, size, texture or temperature of objects on the basis of touch alone. Likewise, for the senses of taste and smell, even newborn babies respond as if they can distinguish between different tastes (showing a preference for sweet tastes over others) and different odours (preferring pleasant odours such as vanilla to unpleasant ones such as rotten fish) and are even capable of distinguishing a sample of their own mother's milk from that of another mother (Macfarlane, 1975; Werner & Lipsitt, 1981).

Furthermore, infants appear to be capable in the first months of integrating or combining input from the different perceptual systems. For example, contrary to past speculation, it has been shown that newborns act as if they have an expectation that the sight and sound of the same object (such as the sight of a person speaking and the sound of that person's voice) will occur simultaneously. Just as adults become disturbed if the sound of a movie is out of step with the visual action, so too do infants become distressed under similar conditions (Broerse, Peltola & Crassini, 1983), showing a preference for watching puppet displays that move in synchrony with music rather than in different rhythms (Spelke, 1979). In short, there is now good evidence that the various sensory or perceptual systems do not operate in isolation from each other, presenting the infant with a strangely disjointed set of impressions. Rather, there is every indication that the perceptual systems present the infant with a well-coordinated experience of the world.

Overall, then, it is now clear that even from birth infants are remarkably well prepared for processing sensory or perceptual information in a structured or coherent fashion. This is not to suggest that early environment or experience plays no role in the emergence of these capacities. On the contrary, there is clear evidence from studies with other animals (Held & Hein, 1963) that even innate sensory abilities require stimulation from the environment to be sustained during early development. However, provided such basic requirements are met, infants appear to be fully equipped to begin the lifelong task of exploring and sampling information about the world. But acquiring sensory information is only the first step on the road to understanding. If knowledge is to be generated and retained on any permanent basis, further 'cognitive' processes must come into play. In the remainder of this chapter the development of these processes in early life will be explored.

Overview: development of basic cognitive processes

There are numerous ways of describing the basic processes used in cognition but, in general, cognition is described in terms of the interplay of the processes of 'attention', 'encoding', 'representation' and 'memory', with the latter involving the establishment and activation of networks of information or knowledge within the brain or mind. All of these essential processes are used in the more complex cognitive activities of 'conceptualisation', 'reasoning' and 'problem solving'. It is now generally considered that these basic capacities are in evidence even in the early years of childhood and do not change in terms of their essential nature, or manner of operation, over the lifespan. However, there are important developmental differences in the ease with which these processes can be applied. These general themes will be explored in the following sections.

To illustrate these issues, the following example may be useful. A child goes to the circus for the first time and sits inside the big top to watch the performance. Several acrobats and clowns enter the ring to begin the show. The clowns initiate a mock argument over the possession of a small bicycle. Such antics are routine fare for circus performances, but as the child observes the proceedings, it is likely that all of the cognitive processes listed above will be engaged. The manner in which this occurs is explained below.

Attention in early development

As the child at the circus watches the performance, he or she will undoubtedly process the available sensory

information, such as the colours, shapes, sounds and smells inside the tent. Some of these impressions, however, may be sufficiently powerful or salient that further cognitive processing is initiated. The first such process may be that of 'attention', the selective or heightened processing of a particular aspect of the available information. In turn, this will probably result in a re-direction of sensory or motor responses, so that all available resources are now attuned to the selected information. The preliminary phase of attention may be an 'orienting response' (a reflex reaction in which heart and breathing rate are slowed and the senses are 'oriented' towards the stimulus). This may then be followed by a more sustained attentional phase.

Our attention can be guided by simple sensory stimulation, so that the child at the circus, for example, might attend to the clown making the loudest noise or wearing the brightest costume. In addition, attention can be directed because of the degree of similarity between present and past experiences. The child might attend to the clowns because they are so novel or different to past experience or, alternately, because they are very similar to clowns seen previously in books or on television. Attention serves a useful purpose by concentrating our cognitive resources on the most salient or useful information available. Without this capacity, cognitive processing could be overwhelmed by the vast array of stimulation potentially available from the senses and within the mind itself.

When does attention first develop? Attention is evident in newborn babies. Even at this time of life, infants display an 'orienting response' to salient stimuli and then, if the item warrants further processing, will continue to show more sustained or prolonged attention (Campbell, Hayne & Richardson, 1992). Moreover, infants' attention is not helplessly at the mercy of any and all stimulation available to them. On the contrary, it has long been known that when shown a variety of visual patterns, infants demonstrate clear preferences, directing their attention to particular or favoured patterns (Fantz, Fagan & Miranda, 1975). It is also the case, however, that certain types of stimuli are more likely to attract attention than others. For example, in regard to visual stimuli, infants appear to prefer the human face over other patterns of similar complexity and contours (Dannemiller & Stephens, 1988). It is also known that infants attend to strong (saturated) colours

(Teller & Bornstein, 1987) and to shapes of moderate rather than low or high complexity (although the latter may be due to the acuity level of the child's vision). In regard to auditory stimuli, infants show greatest attention to the human voice (even though this is not within their most sensitive hearing range), and to rhythmic and complex or rich sounds (such as music), rather than to other kinds of sounds (Dowling & Harwood, 1986). Overall, it has been proposed that infants prefer to attend to stimuli that are 'moderately discrepant' from their current knowledge or understanding, rather than stimuli that are very different or very similar.

Although newborn babies are capable of showing attention, it is often asserted by parents and early childhood educators that young children are 'easily distracted' or have a 'short attention span', implying that they rarely stay tuned to one item or task for any protracted length of time. Indeed, it may well appear to be the case that in many situations children's attention can be described in this way. However, before concluding that this implies some kind of cognitive deficit two issues should be considered.

First, as discussed above, attention is driven to a large extent by knowledge and interests. This applies equally well to all age groups. It would be a rare adult who had not allowed her or his attention to wander to other things during some long speech or lecture on a subject irrelevant to her or his concerns. This same proviso applies to children. Thus, if a child's attention is not on a task, the first possibility to explore is that the task is simply not perceived as interesting, useful or salient by the child. In other words, it is unlikely that for most children there are *never* periods of sustained attention. The challenge (for parents and professional educators alike) is to engage a child's attention through the medium of his or her own interests.

Second, even if young children do appear to flit from one item to another, this tendency can be viewed as a positive attribute in early life rather than as a drawback. The inescapable fact is that the world is simply a more novel place for young children than it is for adults. There are therefore many times more things that seem worthy of attention and exploration for young children. An adult entering a room for the first time does not need to investigate the power sockets or the pot plants, since these items have long been established for the adult as minor and incidental for most of life's activities. But for the young baby, crawling into this same room, there is a wealth of detail to be legitimately explored — power points and pot plants included. This can be seen as a necessary precursor to further learning. Indeed, without such preliminary investigations in early life, it is conceivable that even adults would have to explore such 'incidental' items. In fact, adults could empathise with the infant's situation when beginning some new occupational position or attempting some new skill such as learning to drive. In such situations, adults too may find that their attention is scattered in all directions, without the necessary knowledge regarding what is important and what can be ignored.

In sum, then, attention emerges early in life and is influenced both by salient physical stimuli and by knowledge and interests. Young children may appear to have a shorter attention span, but this can be seen as a necessary precursor to learning what is important within a particular context, and what can be ignored. In any event, attentional persistence is likely to be affected by the child's interest in the available tasks or items.

Encoding and representation

To return to the child in our circus example, the next cognitive processes likely to be engaged in, once attention has been directed to the clowns in the circus ring, will be the functions described as *encoding* (taking in the information being attended to) and *representation* (forming some kind of cognitive impression of the information being attended to). Both of these activities are selective in so far

Figure 2.2: Babies are capable of directing and maintaining their attention to features of the world that provide 'information' or offer a problem to solve.

photo: Petra Skoien

as the end product is likely to differ from one person to the next. The child in our example may well encode only some particular aspect of the clowns' performance, such as their colourful costumes, or perhaps the costumes will be overlooked in favour of their behaviour. In any case, the end product of the encoding process (i.e. the resulting cognitive impression or 'representation') will probably be a unique cluster of qualities or aspects of the information available to the child.

It was previously thought that children's representations consisted wholly of sensory or motor impressions (i.e. records of features such as colour or movement routines) whereas adults' representations were essentially abstractions or symbols that were one or more steps removed from actual experience or sensory impressions. For adults, then, thinking consisted of manipulating or moving around these symbols, much like the pieces on a chessboard, whereas children's representations were simple reflections of sensory experience. But the situation is more complex than this. In contemporary models of cognition, it is considered that, even for adults, representations (of objects, events, features, etc.) are probably comprised of a *cluster* or *network* of many different kinds of information and may well include a web of sensory or perceptual features, symbolic or abstract information and other aspects of psychological response such as associated moods or states.

It is obvious that children's earliest representations will consist primarily of perceptual impressions, since cultural or symbolic information is more likely to require further experience. Recent research using the habituation procedure has established that even newborns are able to selectively represent perceptual or sensory features, such as colour or shape (Haith, 1991), rather than just movements or motor routines, as once suspected (Piaget, 1953). However, young children also begin to include more abstract information such as culturally defined features or symbols (like words) as part of their representations, as soon as these become available. In other words, the extent to which representations of items or events involve symbolic aspects may depend on experience with, or knowledge of, such aspects, rather than age per se. Adults are likely to have richer or more embellished representations of a particular item than young children, but only in areas of greater experience. Thus, for the child in our circus example, the representation being established during the clowns' performance may well include a network of information such as perceptual features (colours, smells, sounds, etc.), as well as feelings (such as happiness or sadness) and possibly 'symbolic' attributes (such as the spoken or written word 'clown') if these are available or had already been acquired by the child.

Conceptual representation

In another sense, it was also once proposed that young children's representations were less 'abstract' than those of adults or older children because of young children's inability to think in general terms or go beyond specific examples to form general impressions or understanding. It is true that adults are more likely to have more 'abstract' representations, because such general knowledge comes from repeated experience of different examples in one area. But this process *begins* in early childhood. Such general impressions of objects, events, etc. are often called 'concepts' (or 'categories', when referring to the group of things that can be classified together on the basis of a concept). For example, our concept of 'entertainer' may include such information or attributes as 'someone whose occupation involves the amusement of others' and, based on this *concept*, we might include in our group or *category* of 'entertainer' such examples as musicians, actors, clowns, and so on. The basis for concepts can be perceptual features (such as shape), culturally defined features, or some blend of the two. The concept or category of 'clown', for instance, could probably be readily formed on the basis of perceptual exposure to different clowns, since in general they share similar perceptual features such as bright colours, outsized clothes and so on. On the other hand, the concept or category of 'entertainer' can include a range of items that bear little or no perceptual resemblance to each other at all (e.g. a clown, a concert pianist, a magician). To detect or form the latter category or concept, it is necessary to have access to information other than perceptual or sensory features. This distinction has obvious implications for the development of conceptual representations.

Children's earliest concepts and categories are formed on the basis of perceptual features such as shape, since these are the most readily accessible or conspicuous. As noted, this process begins much earlier than previously suspected and, likewise, children are able to form concepts based on 'non-perceptual' features at a younger age than that suggested in previous accounts.

There is evidence that even within the first few months of life, infants are capable of processing categorical similarities among items on the basis of perceptual features such as colour and shape. This has been shown, once again, with a version of the habituation procedure. For example, the classification of shapes by infants has been demonstrated in the following way. Infants were habituated to a series of shapes from the same category (e.g. different triangles), and were then presented with two new shapes to inspect. One of these shapes was from the same category as the familiar shapes (in our example a new triangle) and the other was from a different shape category (e.g. a square). If the babies could detect the similarity between different triangles (i.e. could effectively respond as if they could group or classify 'triangles' as being alike), then it would be expected that they would be less interested in the new triangle than the other new shape (because they had already seen 'triangles'). Of course, such studies controlled for natural preferences for one shape over another. In general, babies of three to four months of age respond in this way, suggesting that they do indeed perceive 'categories' of shapes of similar nature to those of adults (Bomba & Siqueland, 1983). The same kinds of experiments have been conducted to show that babies of this age also perceive categories of colours much as adults do (i.e. babies act as if they see similarities among different shades of blue, etc.) (Teller & Bornstein, 1987).

Moreover, similar procedures have been used to show that by seven months of age, infants are able to classify more complex perceptual patterns such as human faces. For example, 30-week-old infants respond as if they discern a category or class of 'female face': in other words regardless of the particular examples involved, the babies act as if they can detect similarity among female faces (Cohen & Strass, 1979). In another example, 7-month-old infants responded as if they could categorise the facial expressions of 'happiness' or 'surprise': that is, as if they could see similarities amongst different examples of each of these types of expression (Ludemann & Nelson, 1988). And such capacities do not appear to be limited to facial patterns. Babies nine months old respond in habituation studies as if they can perceive categories of other complex shapes, such as 'birds' (Roberts, 1988). For instance, if babies are habituated to a series of pictures of different birds and then shown a picture of a new bird and one of a horse, they will show more interest in the latter, suggesting that a similarity between the new and familiar birds has been detected. (Such studies have ruled out natural preferences as an explanation for these results.)

These remarkable capacities for categorical response emerge well before the acquisition of language to assist in the categorisation process and very probably arise out of natural or inherent perceptual abilities. Indeed, the tendency to categorise objects on the basis of perceptual features such as shape is so strong that young babies will even attempt to classify drawings of make-believe 'animals' into groups (Younger, 1985). However, it does not take much longer before children begin to show signs of categories or concepts based on less obvious perceptual features or even on non-perceptual features. It was previously considered that children younger than six or seven years of age did not classify items at such an abstract or 'superordinate' level. This conclusion rested largely on studies which required children to sort items into categories or to indicate which of two items matched or belonged with a third item. For example, they may have been asked to select between a white cat and yellow flower as the matching item for a yellow dog. Younger children typically select the so-called 'perceptually' matching item (in this case, the yellow flower) over the 'conceptually matching item' (in this case, the other animal, the white cat). Alternately, when asked to choose between, say, a cat and a bone, to match a dog, younger children (and coincidentally, older adults) select the bone. Such evidence was for a long time considered to show a 'shift' in the basis for categorisation from perceptual (or in the case of the bone example, from 'thematic') to conceptual (occurring around school entry age).

But more recent assessments of category development

indicate that this is an oversimplification. Studies using the habituation procedure (e.g. Ross, 1980) have shown that infants of 12 months of age have already begun to form or respond to such broad, superordinate categories as furniture, animals and food. Furthermore, recent studies which have re-examined the standard matching tasks used to assess concept development have shown that children as young as 16 months will choose the 'conceptual' item most of the time, provided that the task instructions and goals are clearly explained to them (Bauer & Mandler, 1989). It would thus seem that past failure to obtain evidence of conceptual response in children under six could have been due to their lack of understanding of the task requirements rather than to a complete absence of superordinate concepts. Obviously children will continue to extend and enrich their concepts with increasing experience and knowledge. However the process of general conceptual representation clearly begins in early childhood.

In fact, much of the apparent failure of young children to show evidence of conceptual representations can be traced to difficulties with the language to express these concepts, rather than to a lack of concepts as such. The representation of colour is a case in point. Even babies respond as if they see the main colour groups as adults do (Teller & Bornstein, 1987). However, it may be a number of years before children are able to attach the correct names to each of these colours. In other words, one of the challenges for early development is this task of matching language with the already formed concept or representation. In general, most languages make this a difficult task for young children because of the often idiosyncratic use of words. A clear example here is children's understanding of the concept and word 'alive'.

Animism?

One of the strongest misconceptions about representations or thought in early childhood is that young children have an 'animistic' view of the world (Piaget, 1929), implying that they believe that inanimate things are 'alive'. One of the classic ways for assessing this belief was to simply ask children questions like: 'Is the wind alive?' Children younger than six or seven may well answer 'yes'. However, more recent studies (Carey, 1985) have indicated that this is due to a lack of full understanding about the meaning of the *word* 'alive', rather than to a lack of understanding about the *concept* that underlies the word. This was shown by presenting four year olds with a clockwork toy monkey that could move and make a noise and then asking the children whether such a monkey could breathe, eat, have babies and so on (all the defining qualities of a living animal). The same children were asked the same questions in regard to a real monkey. The results were clear. Children said that the real monkey had these qualities, but that the toy monkey did not. In short, the children indicated a clear conceptual distinction between the animate and inanimate objects. But when the children were asked if either monkey were 'alive', they answered 'yes' to both monkeys. This clearly suggests a confusion over the *word rather than the concept*. One possibility is that the English language uses the word 'alive' rather loosely to refer to inanimate parts or entities (such as car batteries, parties, etc.) and it may simply take some time for children to work out its full meaning (Carey, 1985). In any event, this example highlights the gap that can exist between children's early conceptual and language development. Clearly, one of the primary tasks for early childhood education is to facilitate this mapping of language onto concepts which may already be fairly well-formed.

In regard to conceptual representation then, it could be expected that the preschool child would (a) already have developed most basic categories founded on perceptual features, (b) be developing superordinate categories, (c) would know many more categories than could be verbally defined, and (d) would probably know more categories in areas of personal interest, since experience leads to further development of conceptual networks.

Scripts

One other kind of general representation that emerges in early life is that of 'scripts' — that is, general knowledge about routine events or sequences. These play an important role all through life in helping us cope with new situations. If the latter bear enough resemblance to our past scripts, we can adapt more easily and readily to the new circumstances. Children too develop 'scripts'. For example, just as adults have a script for activities such as eating out in a restaurant, three year olds who have experienced several trips to McDonald's restaurants have clearly defined representations or scripts for the sequence of events in such an outing (Nelson, 1978). Likewise, children who are accustomed to preschool routine will have clear scripts for the preschool day (Myles-Worsley, Cromer & Dodd, 1986). The child in our circus example would undoubtedly be developing some kind of script for the activity of going to a circus, or even more generally, for going to any kind of entertainment event.

In summary, recent research has made it clear that from the earliest ages, children engage in active and rich representation of their experiences, involving any features or qualities within the realm of their knowledge or experience. Although the primary content of representation in infancy is necessarily perceptual in origin, it seems likely that representation based on non-perceptual features begins to develop within the first year of life and is in evidence by 12 months of age. However, children's language may be out of step with their conceptual capacities in this regard.

Memory: storing and retrieving information, and building our knowledge base

It is not enough simply to be able to form representations from our experiences. We also need to be able to store this
children

information and retrieve or reactivate it at some future time. Without this capacity, we would be limited to an immediate experience of the world, without the ability to learn or adapt our behaviour, or to build up a reservoir of knowledge or understanding from our experiences. Our memories hold information relevant to every aspect of our lives, from knowledge about how to walk or talk, to recognition of our family and friends and even to our values or learned attitudes towards the world.

The storage of information in memory is usually described in terms of three phases or aspects. To begin, there is a fleeting or momentary period (less than a second) in which nearly all the details of an item are faithfully recorded (sensory memory). However, much of that detail is lost as we try to further deal with or process information in our 'short-term' memory. This aspect of memory processing is limited, being able to handle only five to seven items at a time, unless we use techniques or strategies to increase this capacity. If the information is important enough or has been experienced often enough, it will probably pass into more permanent storage in our long-term memory, where it will remain until it is retrieved or called back into short-term memory at some later time. The information in this permanent storage can theoretically remain there for our lifetime and makes up the sum of our experiences, our knowledge base. It is believed to resemble 'clusters' of perceptual and more abstract or symbolic features that are our representations of items or events. These clusters are joined to each other in 'networks' across the brain so that one piece of information may be tied or linked to another. An increase in our knowledge does not just mean an increase in the sheer amount of detail in our memory, but also in the richness of such connections.

Each time we think or use our cognitive capacities, some part of these networks is activated. Memory of former items or events can be retrieved from our knowledge base either when we encounter these same items or events again and the stored information is aroused from long-term memory (in *recognition*), or when there is no such reminder and we must somehow locate the information by tracking or 'searching' through the stored memories (by *recalling* the items). When we experience new items or events for the first time, there will probably be some activation of any part of our knowledge base that resembles or has some relationship with this new information, so that we constantly respond to our new experiences in the context of our past understanding of the world. (Refer to chapter 3 for further details on memory.)

The child in our circus example probably used all of these facets of memory during the clowns' performance. The representation of the performance would have been faithfully registered in sensory memory, with only the important or dominant details surviving into short-term memory and possibly then into long-term storage. It is also feasible that the child engaged in retrieval of information from past memories during the performance, if there was already some stored information about clowns in the child's knowledge base. This information could have been triggered by recognition (if some detail of the current clowns matched that of the stored information) or by recall (if the child made an effort to retrieve the prior information without any current reminder).

Research over the past few decades has firmly established that recognition memory operates from birth. The habituation procedure used in so many studies of infant cognition depends on this very fact. During this procedure, the infant is repeatedly exposed to the same stimulus or item and then re-presented with this item along with a new one. If the infant has no memory capacities, then there should be no storage or retrieval of information about the familiar or habituated item and hence no preference for the new item (since both items would seem equally 'new'). Even in the first moments after birth, babies will respond with a preference for the new item in such tests (Slater, Morison & Rose, 1983), indicating recognition of, or memory for, the familiar item. Indeed, studies have now confirmed infant memory for most significant features of the child's world, including the colour, shape, angle, size, number, smell, pitch, volume, tempo, texture and temperature of objects, as well as more complex stimuli such as human faces or toys (mobiles, etc.). Undoubtedly, even in the early months of life, infants are able to recognise objects in these terms after only brief exposure during the course of the testing procedure. Such recognition has even been shown in very young babies (two month olds) after delays of two weeks (Fagan, 1973).

Another procedure has also provided clear evidence of *long-term* recognition in 3- to 4-month-old babies. The 'conjugate reinforcement' method uses a natural response of babies to test memory (Rovee-Collier & Fagen, 1981). Babies show kicking behaviour when placed in a semi-reclining position in their cots. The natural 'rate' of kicking can be measured by counting the number of times the baby kicks in a given timespan. A 'mobile' with toy figures and shapes is then suspended above the baby's cot and a loose ribbon is tied to the mobile and, at the other end, to one of the baby's ankles. Babies soon learn that the faster they kick, the more the mobile moves, and their natural rate of kicking increases. In fact they will even show faster kicking to the training mobile (and *only* to that one) when they see it without the ankle ribbon attached. This suggests that babies can recognise the correct mobile. This response persists, without further training or exposure to the mobile, for up to two weeks, suggesting long-term recognition for the mobile. It would thus seem likely that for items, people or events experienced by infants on a daily basis, there would be strong recognition memory in early life. Indeed, recognition abilities appear to be equivalent or even superior in young children relative to adults (Siegler, 1991).

There is also evidence of long-term *recall* capacity in young children. This has been assessed within the context of natural routines or games. For example, in games which require children to recall the location of a hidden toy, even two year olds will readily achieve this after delays of an hour (De Loache & Brown, 1983). In another example, two year olds have shown they can recall an instruction (to remind their parents to do some task) after a delay of 24 hours, provided the information was of interest to them (such as buying cookies at the store) (Wellman & Somerville, 1980). Studies with older (kindergarten) children have shown a high percentage of retention for information about an excursion to a museum, with over 60 per cent of the details of the event being able to be recalled two months later (Jones, Swift & Johnson, 1988).

Although children's recall abilities are potentially equal to those of adults, in reality children often do not make full use of those abilities (Siegler, 1991). Part of the reason for this is that recall is easier when it involves a familiar area of knowledge or experience. Familiarity helps recall by providing a knowledge network for processing new information and retrieving stored information in that area. In general, adults have a knowledge advantage over children. However, in situations where the 'tables are turned' and children have more knowledge (of games, television shows, etc. (Chi, 1978; Lindberg, 1980)), then it is children who show better recall. In other words, children (and adults) show best use of their recall capacities for material of most interest and familiarity to them. Our child at the circus may well recall less about the price of the circus tickets than an adult companion, but may well recall more detail about the clowns' costumes and performance.

Another factor thought to influence age differences in recall is that young children may be less aware of their memory limitations and as a result may be less likely to use strategies to assist their recall. Even children younger than six or seven will use some strategies in this regard, such as repeating or rehearsing items that have to be remembered, but more effective strategies such as grouping related items together or creating some image or story that links items together are less likely to be employed. (See chapter 3 for details on these strategies.)

To sum up, memory capacities underlie all learning and appear to be in operation from early infancy. Children have excellent recognition abilities and show good recall abilities in areas which relate to their interests and prior knowledge. The ongoing development of recall abilities is at least partly due to growing knowledge and growing use of strategies for organising the material for memory.

Combining information: reasoning and problem solving in early childhood

Cognition does not consist only of storing and retrieving pieces of information in isolation from each other. It also often involves using the basic processes described so far in order to *combine* or *associate* information. This can be a fairly aimless activity (as perhaps occurs in our dreams and fantasies) or it can be directed towards the achievement of some goal or solution to a problem (as in logical deduction) and/or finding a 'novel' solution to a problem (as in 'creative' reasoning or thought). In any case, such activity probably consists of activating the selected information (either from the present environment or from long-term memory) and holding this in short-term memory until some link can be established. (Some association or combination of information may also occur in a less central way, almost away from our focus of attention — as perhaps occurs when we seem to 'suddenly' solve or understand some problem that has been 'in the back of our minds' (Martindale, 1991).) The child at the circus may engage in such activity as she or he tries to mentally solve the clowns' problem of having to share an undersized bicycle. The child may attend to and encode selected information regarding the size and shape of the bicycle and the size and shape of the clowns. Past memories of the child's own experiences of sharing bicycles with friends may be aroused. All of this information could then battle for attention via the child's short-term memory until the child arrives at some combination of this information (possibly by 'analogy'), such as a representation of one clown riding the bicycle and the other sitting on the handlebars.

Young children clearly engage in activities involving the combination of information to provide solutions to problems. Their fantasy play obviously requires the activation of stored memories and the combination or association of that information in often novel ways. Even young infants have long been described as avid 'problem solvers', engaged in testing out 'hypotheses' about the world (Piaget, 1953). However, it was once thought that there were marked differences between children and adults in regard to the cognitive processes used during such activity. The differences were seen as most apparent in logical problem solving or reasoning, in which information must be combined in systematic ways to reach one (and only one) correct solution. Adolescents and adults were thought to use such processes to solve problems, whereas children under six or seven were seen as capable only of dealing with such a narrow ('egocentric' or 'centred') band of information about a problem that correct solutions could not be obtained. In fact, the reality is that *all* age groups find such activities challenging and even adults are likely to use a rougher 'rule-of-thumb' (or 'heuristic') approach to problem solving, which relies more on past knowledge and experience than on logic per se. It seems that at all ages human cognition is best at 'fuzzy' problem solving. Adults may appear to think more logically than children, but often this is due to more experience or knowledge of the task at hand. Knowledge provides an advantage by allowing more selective or appropriate encoding and representation of the problem, easier processing of the information in short-term memory, and faster retrieval and combination of information from long-term memory (Siegler, 1991). Children are far more likely to show evidence of effective problem solving if they have prior experience of the problem area and the task thus has some connection to their knowledge base. Many of the tasks previously used to assess logical problem solving in young children did not take full account of such factors as prior experience and of the implications of this for children's understanding of task requirements and processing of task details into memory.

This was the case for the tasks assessing whether young children were 'egocentric' in their thinking. For example, in the 'three mountains' task (Piaget & Inhelder, 1956), children are placed before a model of three mountains and asked to select from a set of photographs of different views of the mountains the one which most closely matches that for a doll placed at a different location to that of the child. Children of preschool age or younger typically find this difficult and often choose the view that matches their own, rather than that of the doll — thus giving the impression of 'egocentric' thinking. Such evidence seems to fit with children's apparent social egocentrism in regard to unwillingness to share. However, the description of children's cognitive abilities in these terms has been shown to be oversimplified. Children who fail the mountains task are quite capable of showing non-egocentric behaviour on other tasks.

For example, in one study, 3-year-old children were seated next to a model of a country village and opposite was a duplicate model (Borke, 1975). The puppet Grover was then introduced and made to drive his car around the duplicate village. The car was stopped at various points and the child was asked to turn his or her model to match the view being seen by Grover. Children aged three who failed the mountains task were able to complete the Grover task successfully. In another example (Donaldson, 1978), children were seated at a table on which was placed a model of two intersecting 'walls' to form four quadrants or areas on the table surface. A police doll was placed at one end of one of the walls (in a different location to that of the child) and the child was asked to hide another doll in one of the quadrants where it would not be seen by the police doll. If children were egocentric, they should hide the doll where *they* couldn't see it. However, even three year olds were able to provide the correct (non-egocentric) answer (Donaldson, 1978).

Tasks such as these have dispelled the idea that young children are necessarily egocentric in their reasoning and problem solving. It seems possible that children revert to egocentric responses in tasks such as the mountains example because they are unfamiliar with requirements such as matching photographic images to real views of mountains. The other tasks described may be simpler because they more closely resemble prior experiences of children, such as playing hide-and-seek, or because they do not require the children to deal with abstract and unfamiliar materials. We know that young children can even solve verbal, logical reasoning tasks, provided the task is of interest and value to them and offers a basis for detecting similarities with prior knowledge. For instance, four year olds have been shown to use correct deductive reasoning in logical problems such as: 'Pogs wear blue boots. Tom is a pog. Does Tom wear blue boots?' (Hawkins, Pea, Glick & Scribner, 1984). It is possible that such items have sufficient resemblance or *analogy* to the children's own experience and knowledge, that even such hypothetical problems can be resolved logically.

It was previously believed that one of the biggest hurdles for young children's logical problem solving was the tendency to be distracted by the way things appeared. The classic demonstrations of this tendency involved the 'conservation' tasks in which children were asked to reason whether the number, mass, weight, or volume of objects had really changed when only the physical appearance of these objects had been altered (Inhelder & Piaget, 1958). For example, in the conservation of number task, two equal rows of objects (beads or buttons) are arranged side by side, with the items in one-to-one correspondence. When the child has indicated that the rows have the same quantities, the items in one row are moved closer together or further apart. Under these conditions, children younger than six are likely to say that the changed row has (respectively) less or more items than the other one, indicating that they have drawn an incorrect conclusion on the basis of the change in appearance of the rows. While there is no doubt that young children will indeed respond in this way on conservation tasks, more recent studies have made it clear that this does not mean that they are always incapable of correct reasoning or even that they fail the conservation tasks because they are restricted to reasoning on the basis of appearances.

In other studies, young children have been able to draw correct conclusions despite being faced with deceptive physical appearances (Gelman & Markman, 1986). For example, four year olds were taught information about the

properties of two different kinds of things (such as dinosaur and a rhinoceros) and were then asked to make a
judgement about the properties of a third new item that
looked like one of the former items, but had the same name
or label as the alternative former item (for example, another
dinosaur that looked more like a rhinoceros). The children
were able to reason correctly about the new item (assign it
the correct properties) and ignore the distracting physical
similarities to the incorrect item.

In addition, many studies have re-evaluated the conservation tasks and shown improved performance for young
children if the tasks are made more 'user-friendly' by
taking greater account of the restricted knowledge base
and experience of young children, and are made more
manageable in terms of the demands made on short-term
memory. For example, even three year olds can perform
on tasks requiring conservation of number or one-to-one
correspondence, if the task items have some 'meaning' in
terms of the child's experience (such as matching tea-
spoons to cups (Sophian, 1988)). It is even possible that
some young children misunderstand the language of the
conservation tasks, believing 'same' to mean 'looks the
same' (hence giving an incorrect answer on the basis of
the changed appearance of the items). It has also been
suggested that children give the answer they think the
adult tester wants (Rose & Blank, 1974) and will be more
likely to perform correctly if a 'naughty teddy' does the
testing rather than an adult (Donaldson, 1978).

The overall view of children's reasoning and problem-
solving abilities is a complex patchwork, with the same
capacities being easily used in some tasks but not in others.
It seems likely that young children will reason or problem
solve quite effectively in situations which have relevance to
their knowledge and experience (indeed this is also the
case for adults), but may have difficulty when the language
and materials are unfamiliar, when the demands on
memory are high and when the goal or purpose of the
task is not clear. This situation offers a challenge to early
childhood educators. It is no longer acceptable to simply
classify a child as belonging to a 'stage' in which problem-

solving abilities are described as limited. Children will show a varied pattern of performance across a range of situations. The aim should be to track down the particular situations which best elicit the problem-solving behaviour of individual children.

In conclusion: the message for early childhood professionals

What does this recent research mean for early childhood caregivers and educators wishing to monitor and facilitate the early cognitive competence of young children? There is *no simple link* between research findings and early childhood practice. The factors influencing children's cognitive development are too complex for any simple answers or 'prescriptions'. However, the following comments and suggestions may serve as a useful starting point for reflecting on these issues.

Evaluating children's cognitive capacities

For the reasons explained in this chapter, it is no longer appropriate to categorise young children's cognitive skills as belonging to one 'stage' or another. The picture is much more complex than that. Children may show superior cognitive skills in areas of experience and interest, but weaker skills in other areas. Of course this makes the task of attempting to characterise or describe a young child's cognitive abilities much more difficult, but it is by no means impossible. It simply means that any attempt to describe children's abilities must carefully outline the context and materials used for that evaluation.

The base line for any assessment of children's cognitive

capacities would thus seem to be the areas of knowledge or interest relevant to the child in question. These areas can serve as the tool or medium to evaluate almost any cognitive processes and would seem more likely to offer information on the child's potential or optimal capacities than areas which are unfamiliar or uninteresting to the child. This is not to imply that young children should necessarily be subjected to any formal appraisal of their knowledge in some area. On the contrary, simple informal observations during the course of routine activities or fantasy play can be highly informative. For instance, a simple 'running record' of a child engaging in some sort of adult role play may reveal not only the extent of detail in the child's knowledge base in a particular area, but may also reflect the exercise of essential cognitive processes (see figure 2.3).

The following sets of questions may serve as a *guide* for reflecting on the cognitive capacities of young children during the course of everyday activities or tasks:

Attention

- Does the child ever show sustained attention to any task or activity?

- What kinds of tasks or activities seem to engage the child's attention?

- Does the child show more sustained attention in some contexts than in others (e.g. in the company of some peers rather than others)?

Encoding, representation and knowledge networks

- In areas of interest to the child, what kinds of information are apparently incorporated in the child's encoding or representations (as evidenced through the child's own verbal dialogue, drawings, play behaviour, etc. or through the child's response to enquiries about these areas of interest)?

- Is there evidence of perceptual detail for items of interest (e.g. for a child interested in football, is there knowledge of the favoured team's guernsey colours)?

<u>Record of</u>: Jimmy Smith, age 4y. Im.,
12/1/93

Jimmy <u>looked at</u> the pile of papers on the *attention, encoding*
floor and and then suddenly he began
<u>sorting them</u> into two piles — one with *categorisation*
newspapers and one with magazines. He
turned to Sally and said 'There! Now we
can play newsagents! I'll be the <u>man who</u> *concepts*
<u>owns the shop</u> and you can be the <u>cus-</u>
<u>tomer</u>.' He ran to the cupboard and <u>took</u> *recall of location*
<u>out some pencils</u> and counters. He looked
up at the shelves and tried to get the toy
cash register which was out of reach. He
<u>pulled over some large</u> wooden blocks *problem solving*
and stood on those to reach it. 'Last
week, <u>Mummy bought me a comic</u> at the *long-term recall*
news store', he said. The teacher told
him to fetch some books from book cor-
ner and <u>he ran to do this</u>. He arranged all *short-term recall*
the items in <u>separate groups</u> on the big *categorisation*
blocks. 'This paper is <u>the same</u> as the one *connections*
my Mum and Dad buy. See <u>the big "C"</u> *long-term recognition,*
on top,' he said. Billy came and tried to *representation*
take one of the papers. Jimmy said, 'No.
You have to <u>pay money first</u>.' *script*

<u>Comment:</u>
Jimmy shows clear evidence of using the basic cognitive processes
of attention, encoding, representation, concept formation, short-
term and long-term memory, use of scripts and problem solving
by making cognitive links. He showed sustained attention to and
engagement with the task for 30 minutes. His knowledge base
and conceptual representation of the 'newsagent' context shows
a rich information network, including both symbolic and sensory
details. He was able to recall this information and apply it in a
coherent way.

**Figure 2.3: Example of a running record indicating
evidence of cognitive processing in a 4-year-old child.**

- Are there any signs of more general or categorical or even symbolic representation (e.g. does a child interested in dinosaurs show knowledge of the different types of dinosaurs)?
- Has the appropriate language been mapped onto the child's concepts and knowledge base in the area of interest?
- Does the child's knowledge structure in this area show rich connections (e.g. does a child with an interest in the latest super-hero figure refer to the television, movie *and* the comic book stories involving the figure in the same conversation)?

Memory

- Again, in areas of interest, does the child show effective use of short-term memory during tasks or activities (e.g. can a child with a fascination for 'Barbie' dolls follow a suggestion to 'pack a suitcase for Barbie's holiday with her swimsuit, hat, black shoes, blue blouse, red skirt, toothbrush and pyjamas')?
- Does the child show recognition of familiar items (stories, pictures, games, etc.) and people?
- Does the child show good use of recall abilities by such routine behaviours as relating the events of the weekend family excursion or describing the details of a birthday party?
- Is there any evidence of simple strategy use by the child (such as repeating a list of items or tasks given to them by someone else)?

Problem solving

- Does the child show any kind of problem-solving capacity, even in the most mundane situations (such as deciding which of two friends to sit with at lunchtime)?
- Does the child fully attend to and encode the information in problems of interest or is important information ignored?
- Does the child show effective use of short-term memory

during the solution of problems or is information often
lost or not retained in memory?

- Does the child draw on relevant information from long-
  term memory and apply this to reasoning tasks or
  problem-solving activities (e.g. can a child who has
  recently listened to a story involving a wise queen who
  dealt with some unpleasant gnomes on behalf of her
  subjects, also solve a problem for a wise king with similar difficulties with some nasty goblins?)?

This schedule of questions is only meant as a starting point
for early childhood educators for reflecting on the cognitive capacities of young children. The basis for answering
such questions must be careful and open observation of
children in contexts and activities of interest and value to
them.

Facilitating early cognitive development

The new evidence on early cognitive development leads to
the question of whether or how much these early capacities
should be stimulated or encouraged by adult intervention.
It is clear that many of these abilities will emerge naturally
in young children, but even innate capacities need supportive environments to be maintained (as was shown in studies of visual abilities in young kittens (Held & Hein, 1963)).
Deciding on the degree or type of support to offer young
children is no simple matter, however. At one extreme are
advocates of the idea that there should be little direction
of early cognitive activity, with as little 'content' as possible
introduced by adults. At the other extreme are advocates
of the position that children should be maximally stimulated by adults, with a veritable barrage of information
directed at them from the moment of birth. There are
dangers in both of these approaches. Avoiding any intervention in children's cognitive activities can lead to a relatively barren cognitive environment for the child. In the
past, many early childhood programs, in an effort to avoid

being too directive, have presented children with early learning contexts which stimulated fine or gross motor skills or sensory development, but provided little opportunity for the arousal of more complex cognitive capacities such as conceptual representation, use of recall, reasoning, or the development of rich connections in the knowledge base for some topic. On the other hand, the opposite approach of overdosing young children on adult-directed information has the inherent danger of weakening children's natural motivation to explore and learn under their own initiative. There is also the risk of forcing the pace and direction of learning inappropriately for a child's level of understanding. So where does this leave parents and early childhood professionals in regard to their role in the early cognitive development of children?

The answer is obviously to adopt a balanced approach that starts with children's own interests and concerns, thus preserving the natural motivation or incentive to learn or think, but allows space for adults to offer children opportunities to enrich or diversify their interests, and exercise their cognitive capacities to the full. This does not mean that adults must always play a reactive rather than a proactive role. Children's natural interest in learning is probably robust enough that it can survive suggestions from adults, even if these prove to be of little interest. The important message is that for many early learning activities the same cognitive ends can be achieved through many different means and adults needn't doggedly persist with some line of intervention with young children if there is clearly no response or interest from them.

For very young children in the first one or two years of life, caregivers can rest assured that many of the early cognitive competencies will emerge intact if a moderately stimulating physical and interpersonal environment is provided. The extremes of sterile, blank surroundings or alternately of an overwhelming array of gadgets, bells and whistles would seem equally undesirable. The most important aspect of early learning environments is that they should both invite and permit sensory exploration. For example, the visual environment around an infant's bed should offer variety in contour, pattern, shape, colour and so on, without being so complex that the child cannot select or deal with particular components at any one time. In addition, the physical environment should invite and permit 'problem solving' by the child in regard to basic properties of objects (and people). There should also be an opportunity for the child to employ more than one of the senses together, such as offering objects which provide both visual and auditory stimulation. There is no need to continually change the environment, since familiarity is important to learning, but simple changes should prevent undue boredom and 'habituation' from setting in. The best plan is to follow children's interests, since babies typically give very clear signs about the items that interest them and those that do not.

In addition, early stimulation should not be restricted solely to the sensory capacities of children. As discussed in this chapter, many 'abstract' or general aspects of understanding are forming in the first year of life and it is useful to expose children to different types of information at this time. Strategies such as keeping a child's stuffed animals in one toy box and the cars and trucks in another may facilitate an understanding of the categorical difference between these items. It is also particularly important that the caregiver engage in verbalisation about the items in which the child shows interest. This helps to forge the link between concepts and language that is so critical to subsequent classroom experience. In all such activities, however, the key concern is to retain a balance between the adult agenda and the child's interests and concerns, without sacrificing the child's natural motivation to learn.

One of the most important considerations in the early learning environment for young children may be the interpersonal qualities of that environment. Infants who display 'secure' attachment or relationships with their caregivers are believed to be more likely to initiate or engage in exploration of their environment than are infants who appear anxious or insecure (Ainsworth, 1979). This emphasises the close connection or interdependence between a child's social-emotional experience and the quality of early cognitive response.

In order to explore ways in which adults may be involved in the cognitive growth of older (and verbal) children, consider the circus example. The excursion to the circus provides ample material for encouraging further exercise of the cognitive capacities discussed in this chapter. If the child were to show an ongoing interest in the circus after the event, then the child's caregiver or teacher could capitalise on this by:

- Providing opportunities for the child to consolidate and define her or his representations of the experience through discussion, role play, drawings and so on (e.g. the colour and shape of the clowns' clothing or facial features could be targeted as could the emotions that the child experienced during the clowns' performance);

- Assisting the child to develop or clarify any conceptual representations arising from the experience through activities (stories, role play, etc.) which highlight or give information on these concepts (e.g. by getting the child to think about the features that are involved in basic concepts such as 'clowns' or broader and more abstract concepts such as 'entertainer');

- Encouraging the child to map the appropriate language onto any representations or concepts through a range of activities requiring verbal expression of the circus information (e.g. the child may be able to describe the performance of the trapeze artist, but may not be able to assign this name or label to the performer);

- Establishing links and 'networks' of information in the child's knowledge base through discussion, role play, stories and so on (e.g. by asking the child to think about all the circus acts that used animals or by bringing to the child's attention the links between the kinds of animals found at the circus and those found in zoos);

- Exercising the child's short-term memory capacities by games or activities that require the maintenance of circus items in short-term memory (e.g. simple games which show the child one at a time the pieces of a puzzle depicting a circus performer or animal, and requiring the child to retain the information in short-term memory long enough to guess the identity of the item);

- Encouraging the child to retrieve information from long-term memory by recalling details of the experience (e.g. by simply recounting information about the performances or by acting out aspects of the performances, etc.);

- Facilitating the use of strategies in recall by games using circus items (e.g. by giving children a pile of items to remember which could be connected in some story relating to a circus performance, such as 'clown, swing, bucket, water', and demonstrating how these could be linked in a humorous story or image with the clown riding the bicycle into a bucket of water, thereby aiding memory for the items);

- Providing opportunities for the child to solve problems or reason with circus materials, in tasks requiring logical solutions or tasks of a more open-ended nature, and in tasks requiring verbal or hypothetical reasoning as well as tasks with more concrete materials (e.g. in role play which requires children to address problems concerning the scheduling of the events in their 'circus program' or in guessing games which give clues to the identity of circus animals or performers).

Much of the focus for these activities consists in aiding the child to clarify or define fuzzy ideas and knowledge that may have been acquired by the circus experience, and to elaborate or extend that experience by encouraging the child to explore further connections and links with related areas of understanding or experience.

Conclusion

This chapter has presented contemporary information and perspectives on cognitive development in the early years of childhood. It is clear that during these years children actively use the same basic cognitive processes as those of adults in an effort to understand or deal with the world around them. In a short timespan, they are able to acquire a complex tapestry of information about their world, representing and storing not only sensory detail but also the basic elements of more abstract or general knowledge. Moreover, they are able to apply this knowledge to solve problems and reason about their experiences. However, children's knowledge base and experience of life will obviously for the most part be limited relative to that of adults, hence early cognitive activity must be seen in this context. In order to evaluate or facilitate the cognitive competence of young children, the most fruitful starting point will always be the areas of concern and interest to them. By considering children's abilities from this viewpoint, it will be possible to reveal the potential for those abilities rather than the limits.

References

Ainsworth, M. D. S. (1979) Infant-mother attachment. *American Psychologist, 34*, 932–7.

Baillargeon, R., Spelke, E. S. & Wasserman, S. (1985) Object permanence in five-month-old infants. *Cognition, 20*, 191–208.

Bauer, P. J. & Mandler, J. M. (1989) Taxonomies and triads: conceptual organization in one- to two-year-olds. *Cognitive Psychology, 21*, 156–84.

Bomba, P. C. & Siqueland, E. R. (1983) The nature and structure of infant form categories. *Journal of Experimental Child Psychology, 35*, 294–328.

Borke, H. (1975) Piaget's mountains revisited: changes in the egocentric landscape. *Developmental Psychology, 11*, 240–3.

Bremner, J. G. (1988) *Infancy*. Oxford: Basil Blackwell.

Broerse, J., Peltola, C. & Crassini, B. (1983) Infants' reactions to perceptual paradox during mother-infant interaction. *Developmental Psychology, 19*, 310–16.

Campbell, B. A., Hayne, H. & Richardson, R. (1992) *Attention and information processing in infants and adults: Perspectives from human and animal research.* Hillsdale, New Jersey: Lawrence Erlbaum Associates.

Carey, S. (1985) *Conceptual change in childhood.* Cambridge, MA: Bradford Books.

Chi, M. T. H. (1978) Knowledge structures and memory development. In R. S. Siegler (ed.), *Children's thinking: What develops?* (73–96) Hillsdale, New Jersey: Erlbaum.

Cohen, L. B. & Strauss, M. S. (1979) Concept acquisition in the human infant. *Child Development, 50*, 419–24.

Dannemiller, J. L. & Stephens, B. R. (1988) A critical test of infant pattern preference models. *Child Development, 59*, 210–16.

De Loache, J. S. & Brown, A. L. (1983) Very young children's memory for the location of objects in a large-scale environment. *Child Development, 54*, 888–97.

Donaldson, M. (1978) *Children's minds.* Glasgow: Fontana.

Dowling, W. J. & Harwood, D. L. (1986) *Music cognition.* New York: Academic Press.

Eimas, P. D. (1975) Speech perception in early infancy. In L. B. Cohen & P. Salapatek (eds.), *Infant perception: from sensation to cognition, vol. 2. Perception of space, speech and sound* (193–231). New York: Academic Press.

Fagan, J. F. (1973) Infants' delayed recognition memory and forgetting. *Journal of experimental child psychology, 16*, 424–50.

Fantz, R. L., Fagan, J. F. & Miranda, S. B. (1975) Early perceptual development as shown by visual discrimination, selectivity, and memory with varying stimulus and population parameters. In L. B. Cohen & P. Salapatek (eds.), *Infant perception: From sensation to cognition.* Vol. 1. Basic visual processes (249–345). New York: Academic Press.

Gelman, S. A. & Markman, E. M. (1986) Categories and induction in young children. *Cognition, 23*, 183–209.

Haith, M. M. (1990) Progress in the understanding of sensory and perceptual processes in early infancy. *Merrill-Palmer Quarterly, 36*, 1–26.

Harris, P. L. (1983) Infant cognition. In M. M. Haith & J. J. Campos (eds.), P. H. Mussen (series ed.), *Handbook of child psychology: vol. 2. Infancy and developmental psychology* (689–781). New York: Wiley.

Hawkins, J., Pea, R. D., Glick, J. & Scribner, S. (1984) 'Merds that laugh don't like mushrooms': evidence for deductive reasoning by preschoolers. *Developmental Psychology, 20,* 584–94.

Held, R. & Hein, A. (1963) Movement produced stimulation in the development of visually guided behaviour. *Journal of Comparative and Physiological Psychology, 56,* 872–6.

Inhelder, B. & Piaget, J. (1958) *The growth of logical thinking from childhood to adolescence.* New York: Basic Books.

Jones, D. C., Swift, D. J. & Johnson, M. A. (1988) Nondeliberate memory for a novel event among preschoolers. *Developmental Psychology, 24,* 641–5.

Kellman, P. J. & Spelke, E. S. (1983) Perception of partly-occluded objects in infancy. *Cognitive Psychology, 15,* 483–520.

Lindbergh, M. A. (1980) Is knowledge base development a necessary sufficient condition for memory development? *Journal of Experimental Child Psychology, 30,* 401–10.

Ludemann, P. M. & Nelson, C. A. (1988) Categorical representation of facial expression by 7-month-old infants. *Developmental Psychology, 24,* 492–501.

Macfarlane, A. (1975) Olfaction in the development of social preferences in the human neonate: In *Parent-Infant Interaction.* (CIBA Foundation Symposium No. 33). Amsterdam: Elsevier.

Martindale, C. (1991) *Cognitive psychology: a neural network approach.* Belmont: Brooks-Cole.

Myles-Worsley, M., Cromer, C. C. & Dodd, D. H. (1986) Children's preschool script reconstruction: reliance on general knowledge as memory fades. *Developmental Psychology, 22,* 22–30.

Nelson, K. (1978) How children represent knowledge of their world in and out of language: a preliminary report. In R. S. Siegler (ed.), *Children's thinking: what develops?* (253–73) Hillsdale, New Jersey: Lawrence Erlbaum Associates.

Piaget, J. (1929) *The child's conception of the world.* London: Routledge & Kegan Paul.

Piaget, J. (1953) *The origin of intelligence in the child.* London: Routledge & Kegan Paul.

Piaget, J. & Inhelder, B. (1956) *The child's conception of space.* London: Routledge & Kegan Paul.

Roberts, K. (1988) Retrieval of a basic-level category in prelinguistic infants. *Developmental Psychology, 24,* 21–7.

Rose, S. A. & Blank, M. (1974) The potency of context in children's cognition: An illustration through conservation. *Child Development, 45,* 499–502.

Rosner, J. & Rosner, J. (1990) *Pediatric optometry.* Boston: Butterworths.

Ross, G. S. (1980) Categorization in 1- to 2-year-olds, *Developmental Psychology, 16,* 391–6.

Rovee-Collier, C. K. & Fagen, J. W. (1981) The retrieval of memory in early infancy. In L. P. Lipsitt (ed.), *Advances in Infancy Research, vol. 1,* (225–54). Norwood, New Jersey: Ablex.

Ruff, H. A. (1984) Infants' manipulative exploration of objects: effects of age and object characteristics. *Developmental Psychology, 20,* 9–20.

Siegler, R. S. (1991) *Children's thinking.* Englewood Cliffs, New Jersey: Prentice Hall.

Slater, A., Morison, V. & Rose, D. (1983) Perception of shape by the new-born baby. *British Journal of Developmental Psychology, 1,* 135–42.

Slater, A. M. & Bremner, J. G. (1989) *Infant Development.* Hove, U.K.: Lawrence Erlbaum Associates.

Sophian C. (1988) Early developments in children's understanding of number: inferences about numerosity and one-to-one correspondence. *Child Development, 59,* 1397–414.

Spelke, E. S. (1979) Perceiving bimodally specified events in infancy. *Developmental Psychology, 15,* 626–36.

Teller, D. Y. (1979) The forced-choice preferential looking procedure: a psychophysical technique for use with human infants. *Infant Behaviour and Development, 2,* 135–53.

Teller, D. Y. & Bornstein, M. H. (1987) Infant colour vision and colour perception. In P. Salapatek & L. Cohen (eds.), *Handbook of Infant Perception.* Vol. 2, *From perception to cognition* (185–236). Orlando: Academic Press.

Wellman, H. M. & Somerville, S. C. (1980) Quasi-naturalistic tasks in the study of cognition: the memory-related skills of toddlers. In M. Perlmutter (ed.), *New Directions for Child Development: Children's Memory. No 10*. San Francisco: Jossey-Bass.

Werner, J. S. & Lipsitt, L. P. (1981) The infancy of human sensory systems. In E. Gollin (ed.), *Developmental plasticity: behavioural and biological aspects of variations in development* (35–68).

Younger, B. (1985) The segregation of items into categories by ten-month-old infants. *Child Development, 56*, 1574–83.

MEMORY, COGNITION, LEARNING AND TEACHING FROM THREE TO EIGHT YEARS

Gillian Boulton-Lewis

This chapter presents a constructivist view of the development of cognitive processes. This view rests on the belief that each child chooses, within cultural and social constraints, what aspects of knowledge to attend to and store, and therefore to remember and learn. When you finish studying this chapter you will know something of current research and thinking about cognitive development, learning and the implications for teaching from approximately three to eight years. You will also be encouraged to consider your own learning as an adult to gain insights into the learning process generally. The chapter begins with a brief discussion of how children process information and how aspects of memory develop. This is followed by an overview of recent theories that explain how cognition develops. The final section explores the implications of organising good learning environments for young children.

Cognition and information processing

Cognition can be described simply as mental activity that includes receiving, storing, retrieving and using knowledge. This process requires interest and often demands effort. Cognitive activity depends heavily on memory processes and usually leads to learning. That is why memory is discussed first. What do you know about your own memory processes? Do you think children's memory processes differ from your own?

When you want to remember an unfamiliar telephone number what do you do? When your telephone number is changed how do you try to remember it so that you can dial home? Talk to a few other people and find out if they try to remember in the same way. How long do you think a telephone number could be before you would find it hard to remember while you were dialling it? Are some strings of numbers easier to remember than others? Why?

Do you look for patterns when you try to remember? Keep these ideas in mind as you read about children's memory.

Miller (1956) proposed that adults can remember from five to nine pieces of unrelated information. There are more recent theories of how much information children and adults can remember but Miller's formula is still a good rough guide. The usual lengths of lists of unrelated numbers that children can remember are 2 at 2 years, 4 at 4 years, 5 at 7 years, 6 at 9 years, and 7 at 11 years, while the number of unrelated letters and words is generally a little lower (Dempster, 1981).

Do you remember differently if the information is in pictures rather than words? Look quickly at the cucumber man in figure 3.1. Now look away and tell someone else where the spots are. Do the same with the second clown. That was harder and so it should be. Case (1985) used these tests with both children and adults and found that at the following ages the average number of spots that they could remember using visual and spatial processes were 1.4 at $3\frac{1}{2}$ to 5 years, 2.2 at 5 to 7 years, 3.2 at 7 to 9 years, and 3.7 at 9 to 11 years.

Descriptions of how children process information

From the mid-1960s models of memory have been proposed in which a distinction has been made between holding information for a short time by repeating it and storing information for long periods by encoding and practising it (Waugh & Norman, 1965). The models have become progressively more detailed and provide a description, modelled partly on computer and computer programs, of the components of human information processing. Of course the major difference between computers and humans of all ages is that we can choose to a great extent what information we hold in any part of memory, whereas computers cannot.

Children and adults process information using the same structure but there are differences in the efficiency of the

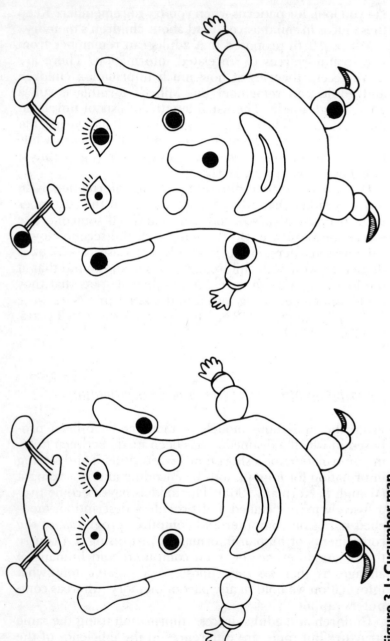

Figure 3.1: Cucumber man.

processes they use due to neurological development and world knowledge. The most popular model of memory has been that proposed by Atkinson and Shiffrin (1968, 1971). The structure they described included sensory registers, short-term memory, and long-term memory. This was a three-store model in which information was received through the senses, held in short-term memory where it was processed along with information from long-term memory, then stored in long-term memory which supposedly had an unlimited capacity. This model was criticised because it did not take into account the level to which an individual processed information or the procedures used to do that.

More recent structural models of memory and thinking include descriptions of processing and storage components as well as procedures that affect the level of information processing. A simplified version of such a model is shown in figure 3.2. Notice that a distinction is made between short-term memory and working memory.

The sensory register

Figure 3.2 shows that the sensory register is where we detect features and recognise patterns of objects or events in our environment. We do this through sight, sound, touch and so on. If we do not pay attention to and process this information then we hold it for less than a second. The sensory register does not change much with age. The ability to perceive information is present soon after birth for most senses, as was noted in the previous chapter. What does change with age is knowledge, based on experience, and this affects what children know about, are interested in and therefore choose to attend to.

Short-term memory

As the name implies, short-term memory is where, in the model but not in any particular part of the brain, we hold information for a short time. It is where you hold, for example, that telephone number while you dial it. Adults and children can only hold such information for a few

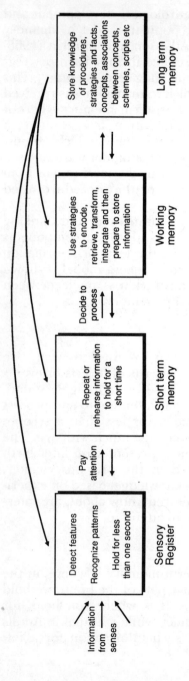

Figure 3.2: Information processing model of memory.

seconds unless a strategy is used to retain it. This is generally repetition or, to use the more technical term, rehearsal.
Before information-processing explanations of cognitive
development were proposed, much of intellectual development was explained in terms of increases in memory
capacity and studies were conducted to identify and
describe the development of memory span (e.g. Ebbing-
haus, 1885).

As memory span tests show (Dempster, 1981), the number of unrelated separate items of information that can be
held in short-term memory increase with age. From three
to eight years the memory span, as described earlier,
increases from approximately three to six items of unrelated numbers or words. There is no general agreement as
to why memory span increases with age. Schneider and
Pressley (1989) summarised the present position, concluding that there is no reason to belive that memory span
increases are due to some biologically determined growth
in capacity, or alternatively to use of strategies alone, which
was another popular hypothesis. They proposed that
increases in speed of processing information, due to more
efficient carrying out of operations, as suggested by Case
et al. (1982), might free more space for storage. Siegler
(1991) used the analogy of packing a car boot to explain
the workings of short-term memory:

> The capacity of a car's trunk does not change as the owner
> acquires experience in packing luggage into it. Nonetheless,
> the amount of luggage that can be packed into the trunk does
> change. Whereas the trunk at first might hold three or four
> suitcases, it might eventually come to hold four or five. With
> more-efficient packing, trunk space is freed for additional
> materials.

Working memory

In some descriptions of the information-processing system
short-term memory and working memory are taken to be
the same. Halford (in press) made a strong case for short-
term memory and working memory to be considered as
separate parts of the memory structure. Baddeley (1990)

proposed that there is evidence to distinguish short-term store (STS) in memory from long-term store and that there is probably a multi-component working memory system as opposed to STS. This multi-component system would contain a controlling executive system as well as subsidiary systems such as an articulatory or phonological loop. Figure 3.2 indicates that working memory is where we combine information from long-term memory and short-term memory and use strategies such as encoding, retrieving, transforming and integrating to process information so that it can be stored in, and later retrieved from, long-term memory. When you consciously decide to break your telephone number into parts or note the pattern of the numbers, you are using working memory.

Long-term memory

Long-term memory contains almost everything a person knows. This includes procedural and declarative knowledge (Anderson, 1990). Procedural knowledge is knowledge of how to do things, while declarative knowledge includes such things as facts, concepts, associations between concepts, and schemata and scripts. A script is a set of procedures something like a script for a play which guides our behaviour in familiar situations. For example, people develop scripts to represent such activities as eating in restaurants — they know not to order dessert before the main course unless they want to puzzle or annoy the waiter. Nelson found sets of common elements mentioned by young children when they described such events as eating at home or eating at a day-care centre. Over a period of three months spent eating at a day-care centre children progressively added more basic events to their scripts (Nelson, 1978).

As well as storing words as representations of facts and procedures we also store sensory information in the form of events, images, smells, tastes, movements and so on. Some of these we encode deliberately and some unconsciously enter long-term memory. Basically, the information is organised semantically, that is, according to meaning.

The association between concepts in memory is often represented in diagrams in the form of a semantic network, or a network of meanings. The length of the line joining the concepts is an indication of how close the association is between them. Collins and Loftus (1975), for example, developed a hypothetical example of a semantic network in an attempt to represent the way in which concepts are related in memory. In the figure the word red is joined by lines of more or less equal length to concepts such as orange and fire on the basis that these ideas would be prompted more or less equally by red. On the other hand the line from red to fire engine is longer because fire engine is more likely to cause one to think of other vehicles. I actually think of blood, wounds, first aid and so on when I hear red. Try it yourself and with a few other people. Did you all respond in the same way? As you can see, we all construct an individual knowledge base in long-term memory as a result of existing knowledge and interests from our own unique encounters with our environment.

Long-term memory is believed to be infinite and not to change in capacity with age. However, because children have had less experience than adults we would expect them, to the limits of their capacity as described below, to have quite well-developed knowledge of some things and limited knowledge of others. This makes it very important in early childhood to try to find out what a child already knows and to try to relate new to existing knowledge. What does develop from about five years of age is a range of strategies to encode, store and retrieve information in long-term memory. When we cannot retrieve information from long-term memory it is usually because we have not encoded and stored it effectively or there is interference from other memories.

Development of memory strategies

Most of the information that is stored in long-term memory must be encoded, and strategies must be used to commit the information to memory in a way that will allow us to retrieve it. A brief summary of the development of these strategies in children to about eight years is included here. If you find this aspect of development interesting you should read Schneider and Pressley (1989) and Siegler (1983, 1991) for further details. If you are interested in memory generally read Baddeley (1983 or 1990).

Most of the research indicates that strategies for memorising begin to develop from about five years of age. They may be present earlier but it is difficult to carry out studies with younger children because it is hard to get them to understand and do what you want (DeLoache, 1980).

Rehearsal

The earliest developing strategy seems to be rehearsal or repetition of information to fix it in memory. It is not the most effective strategy for learning large amounts of material because it requires a heavy investment of time and effort in order to remember a small amount of information. Children under five or six years are less likely to rehearse information to remember it than older children or adults; they just think they will remember. Five year olds rarely move their lips or say words aloud, instead they name, point or fix their eyes on objects when they attempt to remember. They can be taught to rehearse in specific situations and this improves their recall of information, but often they do not transfer the strategy to other situations. When children rehearse they do it differently from adults. Even nine year olds usually repeat single items in a string separately in order to remember the string, whereas adults usually repeat whole strings (Ornstein, Naus & Liberty, 1975).

Semantic organisation

Semantic organisation is the strategy of organising information to be remembered according to meaning, that is, grouping together words or ideas of a similar kind into categories. Even two year olds can recall two-word lists better if the words are related in meaning (Goldberg, Perlmutter & Myers, 1974). Use of semantic relations in

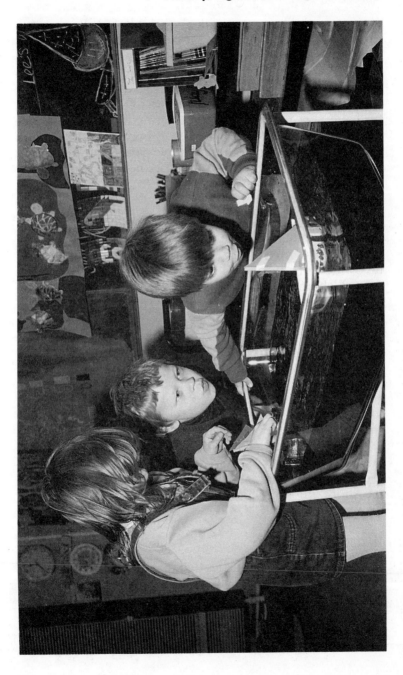

memory steadily increases during childhood. Young children often try or are encouraged to use phonemic features such as rhyming while older children and adults concentrate more on meaning. Young children also use associative strategies such as 'spoon and egg', whereas adults use taxonomic strategies such as 'spoon, knife, fork'. Primarily, probably because of limited knowledge, children use smaller and less stable categories to organise information. Children as young as four or five years can be taught organisational strategies, but this does not necessarily mean that they will transfer the strategies to other situations or use them effectively.

Elaboration

Elaboration is the strategy we use when we impose semantic connections between ideas where no obvious relations exist. Elaborations can be in the form of images or words. For example, a child who needs to remember to take his or her book, lunch and homework to school might construct an image of the homework in the book in a vegemite sandwich. There are some good examples of such strategies used in 'Sesame Street', like tying string around one finger, to remember that there is string on the next finger, and so on, until the last piece of string helps to recall something else. The process of tying string on each finger and explaining why it is there helps to fix the information in memory. Young children can benefit from elaborations made up by others, whereas older children and adults usually benefit more from their own elaborations which are more idiosyncratic and often amusing and slightly risqué.

Mnemonics

Mnemonics are the strategies that depend on a short rhyme or word. They are typically made up from the beginning letters of a list of words, or they summarise a rule that a person wants to remember. They are task- and domain-specific tricks. For example, the well-known mnemonic, 'i before e except after c', helps with an unusual spelling rule. No doubt you have learned or devised some more interesting mnemonics than this. Young children can be taught to use mnemonics devised by others but adults usually benefit more from constructing their own. If you want to know more about these tricks then read Slung (1985).

Metamemory

People of all ages choose whether or not to use strategies in certain situations, depending on how much they know about their memories. Such knowledge of memory is usually referred to as metamemory. Some examples of the development of metamemory are as follows.

Knowledge of remembering and forgetting

By three years of age most children know that they have a memory. Most children over six know that they can forget, whereas about a third of five year olds in one sample did not believe that they did (Kreutzer, Leonard & Flavell, 1975). When asked how many of ten pictures they could remember, more than half of a sample of nursery and kindergarten children thought that they could remember them all, while very few older children thought that they could (Flavell, Friedrichs & Hoyt, 1970). An early indication that four and five year olds are becoming aware of their capacity to remember is when they ask someone else to remember for them. Knowledge of one's own capacity to remember is probably learned mostly by experience and perhaps by guidance. Up to about five years of age most children make unrealistic estimates of their capacity to remember, although they are beginning to try to manipulate and monitor their memory.

Knowledge about strategies

Knowledge about strategies also increases with age. It is possible, however, that children know about strategies but do not choose to use them. Siegler (1983) cited the study by Kreutzer et al. (1975) in which children of various ages were asked what they would do to remember a telephone number. Forty per cent of kindergarteners compared with 95 per cent of third and fourth graders thought they should phone quickly before they got a drink of water. Almost all third and fifth graders said they would write it down, repeat it or take some other step to keep it in memory. Only 60 per cent of the kindergarten children thought they would need to take such a step. Flavell and Wellman (1977) considered factors that might lead a child who knew a strategy not to use it. They suggested the possibilities that a child might think some other strategy was better in the situation; might think the task simple enough not to require the use of the strategy; might know about the strategy but not be able to use it; or might decide it was not worth the bother. What influences you to use strategies?

Implications for learning and teaching in early childhood

What does the information about memory mean for those of us who are concerned about young children's learning? We know that young children can be hindered in their learning by the limit to the amount of information that they can hold in short-term memory, process in working memory, and by their limited knowledge in long-term memory. On the other hand, they find and can be taught ways of overcoming these constraints. They can learn to use rehearsal to keep information in short-term memory and can be taught other strategies to encode information in long-term memory. They can use books and writing as aids to reduce the load on working memory once they learn to read and write. And they do, and can be helped to, break problem-solving tasks into smaller parts. This last procedure however may not facilitate understanding, as discussed later, if it is wholly controlled by the teacher and if as a result the child does not consider the problem as a whole.

Overloading of their working memory can cause children to find a task very difficult or to make mistakes. Teachers need to consider this and analyse activities carefully for potential demand on memory so that they can help children reduce the load if necessary. Ways of doing this are discussed briefly in the third part of this chapter.

Finally, we should actively discuss with children, from the early school years onwards, their memory and the strategies that they can use to remember better. This is because some children seem to work out for themselves the basic memory processes, while even some adults have very limited knowledge of their own memory processes and their relation to learning.

Theories that explain how cognition develops

Piaget's theory of cognitive development

Piaget's theory of cognitive development (Inhelder & Piaget, 1958; Piaget & Inhelder, 1969) made significant contributions to our knowlege of young children's thinking and decades of teachers have been strongly influenced by the development of the stages of thinking that he described. Piaget was concerned with the development of generalised intellectual competence. In his view the child was a developing thinker who constructed increasingly more powerful interpretations of the world in terms of logico-mathematical operations that were based on internalised representations of actions. The important features of Piaget's theory were that the child was active in constructing her or his own knowledge and that each child's knowledge became progressively more organised. He, and others who replicated his work, also showed that many sequences of cognitive development were universal within and across cultures; that children were unable to solve a large number of logical problems until quite a late age; that it was difficult to train young children to solve such problems; and that a large number of these problems were then solved spontaneously in middle childhood by children in western technological cultures.

Piaget (1950) proposed four stages of cognitive development. The first was the sensorimotor stage from birth to two years. During that stage he believed there was an absence of symbolic representation in children's thinking. The second stage he described as preoperational, and this lasted approximately from two to about seven years. Piaget and Inhelder (1969) described children in that stage as preoperational because they believed that they were not able to reason on the basis of operations. During the preoperational period children were described as developing symbolic functions such as imitation, play, drawing, mental imagery, aspects of memory and language (Piaget & Inhelder, 1969). Much of Piaget's description of preoperational thought drew attention to the absence of concrete operational abilities such as classification, seriation, conservation and transitive reasoning and, in that sense, the picture he painted of the stage was one of deficits.

The third stage from about seven to 11 years was called the concrete operational stage. Piaget believed that proper thought did not begin until this stage, when children began to think in terms of internalised concrete operations. He believed that the thought of children in the concrete operational stage was different in quality from that of children in the preoperational stage. He demonstrated this with a variety of clinical tests. A typical test for conservation of number, for example, was to show the child two sets of objects, with numbers beyond their counting range, lined up and matched one-to-one as shown on the next page.

O O O O O O O O O O O
O O O O O O O O O O O

When the child had made and examined the two lines, and decided that there was the same number in both because they were 'lined up' or they 'had partners' or for some similar reason, one line was spread out or moved closer, as shown here.

O O O O O O O O O O O
O O O O O O O O O O O

Typically, the child who was concrete operational would say that there was still the same number of objects because they had just been moved, or they could be moved back, or nothing had been added or taken away. The child who was not concrete operational, that is who was still pre-operational, would say that the lines were different because one was longer or shorter. That child would not be able to reason beyond the perceptual changes.

The fourth stage, which is not of direct concern here, was that of formal operations. The formal operational stage began at about 11 years of age and did not change from adolescence through adulthood.

Applications of Piaget's theory to teaching young children

Piaget was not an educator. Other people drew a range of implications from his work for teaching, to the extent that an article entitled 'Will the real Jean Piaget please stand up?' was presented at an annual meeting of the American Educational Research Association (Kaufman, 1975). This paper described the way in which Piaget's contributions were interpreted and applied differently in three early childhood programs.

or wrongly, Piaget's theory was interpreted by
and curriculum makers to mean that children
who were not in the concrete operational stage could not
learn from activities that required concrete operational
thinking. They therefore focused on the need to develop
symbolic functions during the preoperational years and
believed that, for example, children did not know about
numbers and could not learn to add or subtract if they
could not conserve numbers on the test above. On the
basis of these interpretations, some teachers thought that
they should just wait until the child became concrete
operational before introducing operations and representing them with conventional written symbol systems. They
were led to believe that this readiness would 'just happen',
in most cultural contexts, at about six or seven years of age
if they provided appropriate learning environments. At
the same time, ignoring the contradiction, many began to
teach children to add and subtract in the first year of
school.

The view that children develop through stages and that
all their responses to cognitive tasks are typical of a particular stage is no longer acceptable. In particular the
theory did not satisfactorily explain exceptions to the general pattern of development. Tasks that Piaget proposed
as having the same structure were achieved at different
ages, for example by five or six years children could conserve number but they could not conserve weight until
about seven or eight years. Training studies produced
improvements on specific tasks (Gelman, 1969), but
although other tasks were supposedly at the same structural level, transfer to those other tasks did not necessarily
occur. In cross-cultural situations there was usually a time
lag in success with tasks and in some cultures, including
western cultures, on some tasks adults did not reach the
stage of formal operational thinking in some domains or
go beyond it.

Neo-Piagetian theories of cognitive development

Since the 1980s a number of theorists, who can be described
as neo-Piagetian, have proposed alternative theories of

cognitive development which have moved beyond the cognitive structural descriptions proposed by Piaget. Notable among these are the theories of Case (1985, 1988a, 1988b, 1991), Fischer (1980; Fischer & Farrar, 1988), Halford (1982, 1988, in press) and Biggs and Collis (1982, 1989). These theories are all complex, have their own empirical bases and jargon, and differ from each other (Case, 1988b). However, there are also commonalities which are described briefly here. If you want to understand more about a particular theory you should begin by reading some of the short descriptions in Demetriou (1988), some of the applications of the theories to education in Demetriou, Shayer and Efkliades (1992), then some of the actual theories in more detail.

All the theories propose four main levels of structure in cognitive development. Case, Fischer and Biggs and Collis also describe sub-levels within each of the four levels, with the highest sub-level of a lower level being the first sub-level of the next level. In all the theories higher level structures include lower ones and depend on their integration and coordination into more complex structures. Fischer and Biggs and Collis describe additional sub-levels well into adulthood. In all the theories, to a greater or lesser extent, learning is task specific and the structure in each content area is developed in context and depends on the child's previous experience in that context. There are differences between children, in the content areas in which they choose to develop conceptual structures and the rate at which they do this, which depend on cultural and biological factors. None of the theories propose that there are all-encompassing stages, as Piaget described them, that determine children's success on all tasks with the same structure. However, all the theories propose a shifting upper limit, until about 15 years of age, to the kinds of concepts that can be learned. This upper limit can give the impression of stage-like behaviour when experiential and individual differences are controlled (Case, 1985; Halford, 1988). The reasons for the upper limit are explained differently in each of the theories but all the explanations depend to an extent on increase in a child's capacity to process information which is related to aspects of short-term or working memory as described earlier.

Despite the differences in terminology and theoretical perspectives, the descriptions of ability from three to eight years are similar and can be summarised. Table 3.1 is a summary of the cognitive capacity of children as proposed by the four theories.

Table 3.1: Summary of neo-Piagetian theories of cognitive development in young children.

Age	Level/Theory	Kind of learning
3–5 years	Interrelational stage, substage 3 (Case)	Children can understand systems of relations such as counting without double tagging or errors.
	Ikonic mode of learning dominant from $1^{1}/_{2}$ until about 6 years (Biggs & Collis, Biggs & Moore)	Children form internal representations of actions, objects and feelings. This is generalised by language. Thought is usually unidimensional.
	Representational sets then mappings (Fischer & Farrar)	Children can control single physical or other representations, then combine two or more in a mapping.
	Relational mappings (Halford)	The relation between two elements is mapped from one structure to another. Children can understand, for example, the relation between small numbers represented by sets of objects.
5–8 years	Dimensional stage, substages 1 & 2 (Case)	Children can coordinate systems in two or three dimensions. For example, they can make predictions about a balance beam on the basis of numbers of weights, size and distance.

Table 3.1 (cont.)

Age	Level/Theory	Kind of learning
	Concrete symbolic mode until about 16 (Biggs & Collis, Biggs & Moore)	Children can learn and use symbols in reading, writing, mathematics, maps, music. They can apply symbols to real world situations and process them in disembedded contexts.
	Representational systems (Fischer & Farrar)	Two or more mappings are combined to form a system. For example, children can combine and demonstrate both mean and nice actions for each of two dolls simultaneously.
	System mappings (Halford)	Three elements with a set of relations between them are mapped from one structure to another. For example, children can perform binary operations such as addition.

At the risk of over simplifying these theories it is possible to extrapolate from them a general description of the cognitive capacity of children in these years.

From about three to five years

- Children first relate symbols singly to other symbols and to objects in their environment. For example, they relate a word or an action to an object or event. They begin to name things and to represent them in actions.

- They then describe relations between pairs of symbols, objects, events or classes. For example, they can describe differences in sizes between objects, they can classify objects by a single attribute such as colour, they can construct patterns in one dimension, and they can note (but not explain cause and effect) concurrent events such wind blowing and trees moving.

From about five years onwards, depending on maturation and enculturation

- Children combine representations and relations together in systems and they begin to succeed with tasks that require binary operations such as addition or subtraction, or information in two dimensions, such as Piaget's conservation tasks, as long they have the prerequisite knowledge.

Specific knowledge and its effect on learning and development

While changes in content knowledge have long been recognised as a factor in cognitive and memory development, Chi and Ceci (1987) noted that it was not until the mid-1970s that developmental psychologists gave serious consideration to the effects of knowledge on children's memory and cognition generally. The focus before then, from the Piagetian perspective, was on the development of logical structures that were presumed to affect performance in all areas of knowledge. As a result, improved content knowledge was usually attributed to changes in stage of development. We all know intuitively that it is easier to learn and remember new information if we already have some related knowledge. Chi and Ceci (1987) provided a detailed discussion of the role of content knowledge in memory development. They maintained that existing knowledge affects memory and learning in at least the following ways:

- It influences what and how much children and adults can recall and it allows a learner to go beyond the facts and use a constructive process to fill in the gaps of what he or she does not remember. Chi and Ceci cited results from research which showed that second grade snake experts could answer questions better after they had read a text on snakes than children who were not experts. Third, fourth and fifth grade soccer experts could answer questions about a soccer game better than novices and their expertise predicted their understanding better than age or ability.

- Age-related changes in performance, particularly after about five or six years, are partly attributable to increased content knowledge. For example, Chi and Ceci suggested that increase in digit span norms, used to measure short-term memory, could be due to greater speed of recognising and encoding the digits as a result of knowledge and recognition of numbers. They also pointed out that adults process unfamiliar lists of words or invented numbers more slowly than familiar ones.

- Some differences in content knowledge are more important in certain situations than age-related differences. Chi (1978) found that 10-year-old expert chess players, who had lower short-term memory spans than the adults, remembered meaningful chess moves better than the same adults. Chi and Koeske (1983) described a 5-year-old dinosaur enthusiast who could remember more dinosaurs on a list that had some link to those he already knew than those on an unrelated list.

Chi and Ceci also discussed the question of better memory for content knowledge when the motivation to remember is high. For example, Isotima (1975) showed that three year olds could remember twice as many items from a shopping list when they were playing shops than when they were asked to remember in a laboratory testing situation.

The studies described above, and others that Chi and Ceci cited, provide a convincing argument for the conclusion that knowledge gained from everyday experience is critical in allowing a child to learn to the best of her or his capacity. Even non-literate children and adults who cannot reason successfully with abstract concepts can succeed if the tasks are related to personal experience of real world contexts. On the other hand, we need to be aware that everyday incorrect knowledge can interfere with the learning of accurate scientific knowledge (Reeve, Palincsar & Brown, 1987).

It is possible that greater knowledge results from greater

interest, as well as greater experience, in a content area. Some studies show that children learn more when they are reading about things that interest them and others show that the use of strategies varies with the meaningfulness of the material to be learned. These are important considerations because in formal educational situations we often require children to learn information that is of no interest to them and that seems quite irrelevant to their everyday lives (Resnick, 1987). The question of learning in and out of school is discussed further later.

Case's middle ground position

Case (1991) described a possible compromise position between theories that characterise children's development as progressing through a sequence of general stages, such as Piaget's and to a certain extent the neo-Piagetian theories, and those that propose that children's development proceeds in many areas at once in a continuous and concept-specific manner (Carey, 1985; Gardner, 1983; Chi, 1988). On the basis of an extensive research program, concerned with the development of logico-mathematical, social and emotional and spatial thought by Case et al., and related research by others, he proposed from different theoretical perspectives the principles summarised below. These are described in detail in chapter 19 of Case (1991).

From contemporary modular theory we can conclude that:

- Children's thought develops in a set of basic domains of functioning much like those suggested by Gardner (1983) which would include logico-mathematical, social and emotional and spatial thought as well as, for example, motor and musical functioning;
- The development in these domains depends on the modular structure of the human nervous system (Fodor, 1982; Gardner, 1983);
- The conceptual systems that children construct reflect

this modular structure, although they are capable of developing conceptual systems that transcend the modular systems;

- In the course of development there are reworkings of children's conceptual systems in a major way at the age of five or six and in a minor way at seven to eight and nine to ten;
- There is a core set of elements in each of these conceptual systems that Case describes as a central conceptual structure. He proposes, for example, the system shown in figure 3.3 as the central conceptual structure for numerical understanding.

From domain specific theory we know that:

- Central conceptual structures are like semantic networks as suggested by Chi (1988). These are similar to the hypothetical structure proposed by Collins and Loftus (1975) or the one proposed above by Case for numerical understanding;
- Experience in specific domains is necessary for development of such semantic networks;
- The strength of the relationships in these networks is as important as the semantic content. That strength depends in part on practice;
- The cognitive strategies that children use at any age depend heavily on the development of their central conceptual structure.

From contemporary sociocultural or contextual theory it seems that:

- As children grow older specific cultural experience becomes more important in the development of conceptual structures because they are dependent on bodies of knowledge that are significant in or unique to a specific culture;
- With age schools and other social institutions play an increasingly important role in determining the development of specific conceptual structures.

From contemporary neo-Piagetian theory:

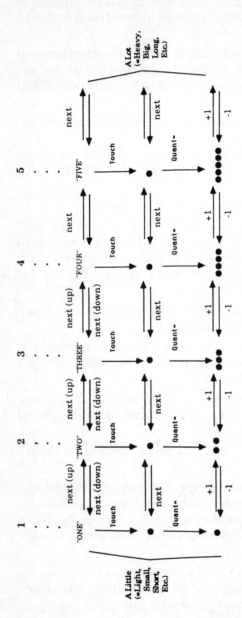

Figure 3.3: Cognitive structure underlying 6-year-old's numerical understanding (Dotted lines indicate 'Optional' i.e. non-universal).

- Children's central structures are subject to maturational age-related constraints as proposed by the neo-Piagetian theories;

- These constraints are closely related to the development of the system that attends to and stores information, which is something like the working memory described above;

- The constraints are likely to be biologically determined to a certain extent;

- The pattern of development that results from the above constraints occurs hierarchically across levels and results from the coordination of earlier conceptual structures.

From classic Piagetian theory:

- It is important that each child actively constructs each central conceptual structure if genuine understanding is to occur;

- New structures are formed by the differentiation and coordination of existing structures;

- When a reworking of conceptual structures takes place children become potentially capable of qualitatively different thought processes and they can perceive events in a different way;

- There is a general progression from sensorimotor to representational structures that become increasingly more complex, more abstract and more powerful.

Implications of theories of cognitive development for learning in early childhood

So what do these theoretical perspectives mean for the contemporary teacher of young children? Briefly, the implications that might guide the teaching and learning of children aged three to eight years are as follows.

First we need to take into account the shifting upper limit to thinking that places constraints on the kinds of conceptul structures that children can usually construct at a particular age. We should not let our understanding of these constraints influence us in the way that Piaget's stage theory did when it caused teachers to believe that they could only provide a rich and stimulating environment and then wait until children themselves demonstrated that they were ready. Rather, we should use this knowledge as a guide to challenge children to learn to the limit of their capacity. As Halford in Demetriou (1988) stated, 'most children are performing below their theoretical limit on some tasks and more refined task analysis can result in very substantial improvements'. We have in the past underestimated as well as overestimated young children's capacity to learn. Children are capable of understanding and learning a great deal if the content interests them and if it is available in a form that does not overload their working memory. Content and teaching strategies should be carefully analysed to determine whether what we have planned as teachers will help or hinder the learning process.

It is crucial to find out what each child knows and is interested in. Only in this way can we help a child to clarify his or her existing knowledge and relate new knowledge to what is already partly known. Early childhood teachers have always believed that this was necessary, but beyond the preschool years the procedure has not always been used effectively.

Despite children's natural curiosity we cannot always expect that they will be interested in what we are obliged to teach them, particularly when the work becomes more formal and symbolic and requires some effort. This is also the case when the content seems quite unrelated to their cultural or social experience of the world, as discussed below. It is then that real skill is required in teaching in order to present problems, activities and information that seem meaningful to children and will develop and foster new interests. Learning environments for children should ideally be organised to allow them to develop conceptual structures in all the domains suggested by Case (1991) and

Gardner (1983). It is also important to help children to realise that practice and other memory strategies will help them to remember and learn.

Learning and teaching

Learning in and out of school

Resnick (1987) identified four general differences between learning in school and learning out of school. First, cognition in school is usually individual, that is, students are judged and examined by what they can do themselves. She contrasted this with the need, outside school, for people in many situations to depend on the mental and physical performance of others to function effectively. She gave as one example the activity of piloting a large modern ship into harbour, which can involve up to six people collaborating on the basis of their expertise to succeed with the task.

Second, thinking in school often depends purely on a person's thought processes without the aid of tools such as calculators and computers. Outside school much activity is dependent on tools, from computers to gyrocompasses. Not only are tools a way for people with limited knowledge to participate in complex activities, they also enhance the capacity of knowledgeable people.

Third, school activities are often concerned with the apparently meaningless manipulation of symbols divorced from context, whereas outside school activities are closely connected with objects and events. Resnick provided the example of a weight watcher finding $2/3$ of $3/4$ of a cup of cottage cheese by dividing the actual cheese into parts rather than by arithmetical calculations. She also contrasted so-called problem solving in school with the way a child would decide what coins to use to buy an ice-cream by looking at what she or he has in her or his pocket rather than calculating the combination arithmetically. Finally, she

maintained that learning in school is generalised whereas outside school people develop situation-specific knowledge and competence.

Resnick then asked whether school prepares children effectively for the world outside of school or the world of work, and whether it equips people for learning outside of school or whether it actually inhibits them. She suggested ways in which school might teach thinking skills more effectively. These all involve shared intellectual work and collaboration on tasks, making thinking processes overt presumably by child and teacher discussion, and by organising activities around specific bodies of knowledge. Such procedures are often adopted in preschool, although the activities there sometimes appear to be artificial. Such activities tend to occur less and less frequently in the early years of school. This is probably due to the implicit belief of teachers that all learning in the compulsory years of schooling must be, as Resnick suggested, ultimately individual and assessed individually. The challenge for teachers is to make learning meaningful in terms of the real world, to use collaborative processes, and at the same time to make sure that each child still learns as an individual.

Procedures to maximise learning in early childhood

Child and adult learning

Early childhood educators, particularly in preschools and kindergartens, traditionally have been concerned with providing a stimulating environment in which each child will develop and learn at his or her own rate. Children have to a large extent been encouraged to follow their own interests and to engage in what is of immediate interest to them. In some respects this is like andragogy as Knowles (1990) described it. That is, he suggested that the organisation of environments for adult learning and teaching (andragogy) should be different from those for children (pedagogy). The distinguishing features of andragogy are that adults are motivated to learn something because they have decided that they need to know it or they are interested in it; genuine self-determined problems cause them to decide what is important to learn; adults often bring knowledge, experience and other success to new learning; adults usually prefer self-direction in learning; and individual differences in knowledge and skills increase with age so that adults are more different from each other than younger learners. More recently Knowles and associates (1990) and others have suggested that good learning environments at all levels should be more like those he proposed for adults. Teachers of three to five year olds have known this for many years and described it from the perspective of early childhood philosophy. However, in the early years of primary school and in subsequent years such beliefs have not typically influenced teaching behaviour. If, as recent research suggests, knowledge is important for subsequent learning then it is obviously necessary for teachers all through the early years to be more proactive about ascertaining children's existing knowledge and strategy use, as well as their interests, and to use this information as a basis for further learning. Some procedures that are compatible with cognitive descriptions of learning such as scaffolding and reciprocal teaching, a phenomenographic approach, assessing and controlling processing loads, situation-specific and context-dependent learning, and concept mapping, are briefly described below.

Scaffolded instruction and reciprocal teaching

Scaffolded instruction is a process that enables a child to carry out a task with assistance from an adult, that she or he normally would not succeed with unaided. Vygotsky (1978) believed that in order to facilitate cognitive development teachers need to know not only what a child knows and is capable of doing at a particular time, but also what the child is likely to be able to do next. He used the term 'zone of proximal development' to describe the distance between 'actual developmental level as determined by independent problem solving and the level of potential development as determined by problem solving under adult guidance or in collaboration with more capable peers'. By providing children with meaningful experiences in that zone teachers can help children to move from one level of learning to the next. To promote development it is not sufficient simply to help the child succeed with the task. The child must also be making sense of the process. Palincsar (1986) reviewed the attributes of scaffolded instruction as presented in the literature and concluded that dialogue was most important in the process. She then explored the process of instructing students in the acquisition and application of cognitive strategies in scaffolded instruction where the teacher and the child shared the responsibility for the learning. She provided a metascript for scaffolded instruction to teach reading comprehension strategies to first-grade students which she described as reciprocal teaching. The process consisted of the teacher modelling procedures for predicting, generating questions, summarising and clarifying and then gradually leading the children to do this for themselves. She also believed that this process could be used for early mathematical learning and gave an example of a possible procedure (in Reeve, Palincsar & Brown, 1987).

Computer-assisted learning

There is not the time or space in this chapter to do this question justice. However, a good computer program can also provide scaffolded instruction. You will no doubt be introduced to programs such as LOGO and Boxer which are the most recent developments in this area. If not, read about them for yourself.

A phenomenographic approach to teaching

Bowden (in Ramsden, 1988) maintained that 'in a sense phenomenographic research mirrors what good teachers do'. It tries to understand what students are doing in their learning. Ramsden (1988) argued that teaching should be directed towards helping students to change their conceptions of aspects of the world around them rather than just towards acquisition of facts and ability to reason quantitatively. He proposed that the solution lay in teachers recognising that teaching and curricula should take much more careful account of what students already know about subject matter and the educational conditions in which they learn best. He also reminds us that students often interpret what teachers present quite differently from the way the teacher intends. His book is mainly concerned with adult learning but no good early childhood teacher would disagree with the principles. However, in the early years of formal schooling the principles are often lost from sight and there is too much emphasis on the transmission of information. Ramsden cited an example of the worst kind of child-teacher interaction from Bennet et al. (1984). A small section, in abbreviated form, is as follows;

Fiona: Miss, I can't work out . . . 54 [divided by 2]

Teacher: Well, you ought to be able to, oughtn't you? And your pencil's thick and black for a start . . . You've forgotten how to do this? You'd better practise at home this weekend. How many twos in five?

Fiona: Two

Teacher: Where does the two go?

Fiona: In there

Teacher: Write it down at the top. How many left over?

Fiona: One

Teacher: Now what do we say? How many twos in . . .?

Fiona: Four

Teacher: . . . But that number isn't four

Fiona: One

Teacher: But you can't say how many twos in one can you . . . Yes now come on. You were busy talking and you're stopping other people from working as well . . .

I am sure you can work out for yourself what is wrong with this exchange. The teacher is making no effort to find out what the child does or does not know. Nor is any attempt being made to change the child's conception so that the child does not see it as a meaningless task. The teacher is merely leading the child, none too gently, through the process so that the right answer is obtained. In the meantime the child's self-concept and self-efficacy are taking a battering, as no doubt is her attitude towards mathematics. It is not scaffolding, as described above, because the child is led step by painful step to an answer, and is not helped to understand and perform the task so that she might then perform it on her own.

Assessing and controlling the processing demand of tasks

Teachers often introduce materials and strategies with the very best of intentions which actually increase the processing load of tasks and make them more difficult to understand and learn. In order to avoid this problem it is important to analyse the difficulty of content that a child is expected to learn both for the demand it will make on processing capacity and the extra demand that use of particular procedures and materials will make. Halford and Boulton-Lewis (1992) have done this for use of some concrete representations in teaching mathematics.

An example of the consequences of not considering such loads is provided in Boulton-Lewis (in press). Children's use of strategies and concrete materials for subtraction in years one to three were studied in three suburban schools in Brisbane. The teachers were following the Queensland State curriculum and expected the children by year 3 to be solving three-digit subtraction tasks with and without trading. Despite the fact that teachers were teaching the algorithms by year 3, when children were asked to choose solution procedures, they mostly gave mental explanations based on knowledge of place value and decomposition of tens and hundreds in preference to written algorithms. When they used written algorithms they were usually incorrect. The children were making little if any connection between their successful mental strategies and the formal written procedures that the teachers were introducing. This behaviour was explained in terms of the heavy processing load of the algorithm, combined with concrete materials, and the strategies that the teachers used in an attempt to reduce the load, such as teaching children to subtract to three digits without 'borrowing' before introducing subtraction that required decomposition.

Other neo-Piagetian theorists such as Fischer (Biddell & Fischer, 1992) and Case (Case & Sowder, 1990; Case & Griffin, 1990) have considered early learning from the perspective of their theories. Bidell and Fischer argued that because Fischer's skill theory is designed to capture the context-embedded aspects of cognitive development it can provide a useful lens through which to examine the role of cognition in education, that is, in assisting in the understanding of cognitive development in the educational setting. They maintain that cognitive skills must be predicted and measured in academic content areas rather than predicted from some general level of development. They illustrated the procedure with a recent study of arithmetic knowledge. They also describe the implications of the 'developmental range' which is similar in some ways to Vygotksy's zone of proximal development.

Case and Sowder (1990) applied Case's theory of intellectual development to predicting when children would be able to estimate the results of increasingly more complex addition tasks. The predicted performances were confirmed at 50 per cent level or greater for a range of tasks for a sample of children from six to 16 years. The pattern of success and failure were congruent with the theoretical analysis and with the assertion that the majority of children would be able to compute a simple two-digit sum by the age of six with the aid of a mental number line. Case and Griffin (1990) and colleagues predicted and measured children's cognitive development in a variety of cognitive domains including logico-mathematical thought about balance beams, projection of shadows, distribution of rewards, expected and actual receipt of a number of marbles, musical sight reading, time telling and money handling. They then postulated the central conceptual structures of 6-year-old logical-mathematical thought and constructed training activities to teach each component of the structure. Their findings indicated that 57 to 100 per cent of the treatment groups mastered transfer tasks compared with very few of the control groups. They then undertook similar studies with a postulated central conceptual structure for concepts in the social domain with similar results.

Situation-specific learning

Resnick, Bill and Lesgold (1992) argued that human mental functioning must be understood as fundamentally situation-specific and context-dependent. They assessed the early mathematical knowledge that children bring to school, designed a program that drew on that knowledge, developed children's trust in that knowledge, used correct formal notation from the start to link that knowledge to the formal language of mathematics, introduced key mathematical concepts as quickly as possible (including multi-digit subtraction in the first grade, allowing children to use manipulatives or expanded notation as they chose), encouraged everyday problem solving, and caused children to talk about mathematics rather than just do it. The grade 1 children in this program, who were not restricted to a limited range of numbers (e.g. within ten), performed significantly better on standardised tests than a similar group of children taught in a more conventional manner. The teaching involved a great deal of discussion guided by the teacher. In the process a kind of 'cognitive apprenticeship approach' assisted the children to use a range of strategies effectively.

Concept mapping

Novak and Gowin (1986) take a metacognitive approach to learning. That is, they believe that from an early age learners should understand the structure of knowledge and the process of acquiring that knowledge. They describe procedures that can be used to make concepts and their relationships explicit for children in their learning from grade 1 onwards and for teachers in their planning of the key concepts that a child should learn in a content area. These are concept mapping, vee diagrams and clinical interviews. Clinical interviews are valuable in finding out what each child knows and can be carried out while a child is working on a task in or out of the classroom. They provide a good description of how to conduct and draw conclusions from various kinds of interviews. Of the other two procedures I find concept maps the most useful. They can even be adapted for use in preschool where objects are used in place of words to denote concepts. Basically, a concept map is like a semantic network, as described earlier, except that along the lines joining the concepts to others, the nature of the relationship is represented by a word or two. Two examples of concept maps, taken from Novak and Gowin, are shown in figures 3.4a and 3.4b. They show (fig 3.4a) a concept map constructed with a first grade class to illustrate how to make concept maps and a map constructed a week later by a child who had a good knowledge of the concept meanings and the relationships for animals (fig 3.4b).

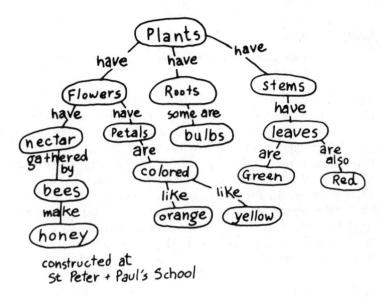

Figure 3.4a

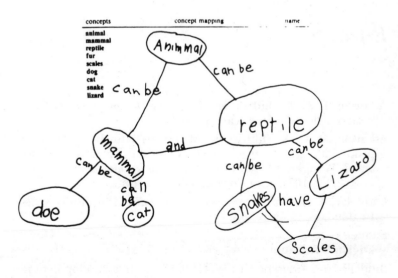

Figure 3.4b

Conclusion

This chapter has presented a view of learning in early childhood which emphasises the crucial role that children's own construction of knowledge plays in meaningful learning. It was also concerned with how children and adults learn and remember, with the developmental constraints and possibilities that exist in the early childhood years, and what these mean for teaching and learning. Finally, a few ways of making learning meaningful for young children have been discussed. These of necessity have been selective and limited. As a general rule if you devise or are introduced to methods and procedures for teaching young children examine them carefully to see whether they are in keeping with what you have learned about cognition, learning and teaching in this chapter. In other words, be metacognitive about your teaching and children's learning.

References

Atkinson, R. C. & Shiffrin, R. M. (1971) *The control of short-term memory*. Scientific American, 82–90.

Atkinson, R. C. & Shiffrin, R. M. (1968) Human memory. A proposed system and its control processes. In K. W. Spence and J. W. Spence (eds.) *The psychology of learning and motivation* (Vol. 2, 90–107). New York: Academic Press.

Baddeley, A. (1983) *Your memory: A user's guide*. Harmondsworth, England: Penguin Books.

Baddeley, A. (1990) *Human memory: Theory and practice*. Hove, England: Erlbaum.

Biddell, T. R. & Fischer, K. W. (1992) Cognitive development in context: applying skill theory to education. In A. Demetriou, A. Efkliades & M. Shayer (eds.) *Neo-Piagetian Theories of Cogni-*

tive Development: implications and applications for Education. London: Routledge and Kegan Paul.

Biggs, J. B. & Collis, K. F. (1982) *Evaluating the quality of learning: The SOLO Taxonomy.* New York: Academic Press.

Biggs, J. B. & Collis, K. F. (1989) Towards a model of school-based curriculum development and assessment: using the SOLO Taxonomy. *Australian Journal of Education, 33,* 149–61.

Biggs, J. & Moore, P. (in press) *The process of learning.* Ringwood, Victoria: Prentice-Hall.

Boulton-Lewis, G. M. (in press) Young children's representations and strategies for subtraction. *British Journal of Educational Psychology.*

Brown, A. L., Bransford, J. D., Ferrara, R. A. & Campione, J. C. (1983) Learning, remembering and understanding. In P. H. Mussen (ed.) *Handbook of child psychology* (4 ed.) Vol. 3. New York: Wiley.

Carey, S. (1985) *Conceptual change in childhood.* Cambridge: MA, MIT Press.

Case, R. & Sowder, J. T. (1990) The development of computational estimation: A neo-Piagetian analysis. *Cognition and Instruction,* 7(12), 79–104.

Case, R. & Griffin, S. (1990) Child cognitive development: The role of central conceptual structures in the development of scientific and social thought. In C. A. Hauert (ed.) *Developmental Psychology: Cognitive, perceptual-motor, and neuropsychological perspectives.* North Holland: Elsevier.

Case, R. (1985) *Intellectual development: Birth to adulthood.* Orlando, Florida: Academic Press.

Case, R. (1988a) The structure and process of intellectual development. In A. Demetriou (ed.) *The neo-Piagetian theories of cognitive development: toward and integration* (267–87). Amsterdam, North-Holland: Elsevier.

Case, R. (1988b) Neo-Piagetian theory: Retrospect and prospect. In A. Demetriou (ed.) *The neo-Piagetian theories of cognitive development: toward an integration* (267–85). Amsterdam, North-Holland: Elsevier.

Case, R. (1991) *The mind's staircase.* Hillsdale, New Jersey: Erlbaum.

Chi, M. T. H. (1978) Knowledge structures and memory

development. In R. Siegler (ed.) *Children's thinking: What develops?* (73–96) Hillsdale, New Jersey: Erlbaum.

Chi, M. T. H. & Koeske, R. (1983) Network representation of a child's dinosaur knowledge. *Developmental psychology, 19,* 29–39.

Chi, M. T. & Ceci, S. J. (1987) Content knowledge: its role, representation, and restructuring in memory development. *Advances in Child Development and Behaviour,* 20, 91–142.

Chi, M. T. H. (1988) Children's lack of access and knowledge reorganization: An example from the concept of animism. In M. Perlmutter & F. E. Weinert (eds.) *Memory development: Universal changes and individual differences.* (169–4). Hillsdale, New Jersey: Erlbaum.

DeLoache, J. S. (1980) Naturalistic studies of memory for object location in very young children. In M. Perlmutter (ed.) *New directions for child development: Children's memory* (17–32). San Francisco: Jossey Bass.

Demetriou, A. (ed.) (1988) *The neo-Piagetian theories of cognitive development: toward an integration.* Amsterdam, North-Holland: Elsevier.

Demetriou, A., Shayer, M. & Efkliades, A. (eds.) (1992) *Neo-Piagetian Theories of Cognitive Development: Implications and Applications for Education.* London: Routledge and Kegan Paul.

Dempster, F. N. (1981) Memory span: Sources of individual and developmental differences. *Psychological Bulletin, 89,* 63–100.

Fischer, K. W. (1980) A theory of cognitive development: the control and construction of hierarchies of skills. *Psychological Review, 87,* 477–531.

Fischer, K. W. & Farrar, M. J. (1988) Generalizations about generalization: how a theory of skill development explains both generality and specificity. In A. Demetriou (ed.) *The neo-Piagetian theories of cognitive development: Towards an integration* (137–71). Amsterdam, North-Holland: Elsevier.

Fodor, J. (1982) *The modularity of mind.* Cambridge: MA, MIT Press.

Flavell, J. H. & Wellman, H. M. (1977) Metamemory. In R. V. Kail and J. W. Hagen (eds.) *Perspectives on the development of memory and cognition* (3–33). Hillsdale, New Jersey: Erlbaum.

Flavell, J. H., Friedrichs, A. G. & Hoyt, J. D. (1970) Developmental changes in memorization processes. *Cognitive Psychology, 1,* 324–40.

Gardner, H. (1983) *Frames of mind: The theory of multiple intelligences.* New York: Basic Books.

Gelman, R. (1969) Conservation acquisition: A problem of learning to attend to relevant attributes. *Journal of Experimental Child Psychology, 7,* 167–87.

Goldberg, S., Perlmutter, M. & Myers, N. (1974) Recall of related and unrelated lists by two year olds. *Journal of Experimental Child Psychology, 18,* 1–8.

Halford, G. S. (1982) *The development of thought.* Hillsdale, New Jersey: Erlbaum.

Halford, G. S. (1988) A structure-mapping approach to cognitive development. In A. Demetriou (ed.) *The neo-Piagetian theories of cognitive development: toward an integration* (103–36). Amsterdam, North-Holland: Elsevier.

Halford, G. S. (in press) *Children's understanding: the development of mental models.* Hillsdale, New Jersey: Erlbaum.

Halford, G. S. & Boulton-Lewis, G. M. (1992). Value and limitations of analogues in teaching mathematics. In A. Demetriou, A. Efkliades & M. Shayer (eds.) *Neo-Piagetian Theories of Cognitive Development: Implications and Applications for Education.* London: Routledge and Kegan Paul.

Isotima, J. M. (1975) The development of voluntary memory in pre-school age children. *Soviet Psychology, 13,* 5–6.

Kaufman, B. A. (1975) Will the real Jean Piaget please stand up? Paper at the annual meeting of the American Educational Research Association.

Kreutzer, M. A., Leonard, C. & Flavell, J. H. (1975) An interview study of children's knowledge of memory. *Monographs of Society for Research in Child Development, 40* (1, Serial No. 159).

Knowles, M. (1990) *The adult learner: A neglected species.* Houston: Gulf Press.

Knowles, M. & Associates (1990) *Andragogy in action.* San Francisco: Jossey Bass.

Miller, C. A. (1956) The magical number seven, plus or minus two: Some limits on our capacity for processing information. *Psychological Review, 63,* 81–97.

Nelson, K. J. (1978) Semantic development and the development of semantic memory. In K. J. Nelson (ed.)*Children's language* (Vol. 1) New York: Gardner.

Novak, J. D. & Gowin, D. B. (1986) *Learning how to learn*. New York: Cambridge University Press.

Ornstein, P. A., Naus, M. J. & Liberty, C. (1975) Rehearsal and organizational processes in children's memory. *Child Development, 26,* 818–30.

Palincsar, A. M. (1986) The role of dialogue in providing scaffolded instruction. *Educational Psychologist, 21,* (1 & 2), 73–98.

Piaget, J. (1950) *The psychology of intelligence*. London: Routledge and Kegan Paul.

Piaget, J. & Inhelder, B. (1969) *The psychology of the child*. London: Routledge and Kegan Paul.

Raaijmakers, J. G. W. & Shiffrin, R. M. (1981) Search of associative memory. *Psychological Review, 88,* 92–134.

Ramsden, P. (ed.) (1988) *Improving Learning: New Perspectives*. London: Kogan Page.

Reeve, R. A., Palincsar, A. S. & Brown, A. L. (1987) Everyday and academic thinking: Implications for learning and problem-solving. *Journal of Curriculum Studies, 19*(2), 123–33.

Resnick, L. B. (1987) Learning in school and out. *Educational Researcher, 16*(9), 13–20.

Resnick, L. B., Bill, V. & Lesgold, S. (1992) Developing thinking abilities in arithmetic class. In A. Demetriou, M. Shayer and A. Efkliades (eds.) *Neo-Piagetian Theories of Cognitive Development: Implications and Applications for Education*. London: Routledge and Kegan Paul.

Schneider, W. & Pressley, M. (1989) *Memory development between 2 and 20*. New York: Springer-Verlag.

Siegler, R. S. (1991) *Children's Thinking* (2 ed.) Englewood Cliffs, New Jersey: Prentice-Hall.

Siegler, R. S. (1983) Information processing approaches to development. In P. H. Mussen (ed.) *Handbook of child psychology* (4 ed.) Vol. 1. New York: Wiley.

Slung, M. (1985) *The absent-minded professor's memory book*. New York: Ballantine Books.

Waugh, N. C. & Norman, D. A. (1965) Primary memory. *Psychological Review, 72,* 89–104.

LANGUAGE

ACQUISITION

Judith Bowey

For centuries philosphers have argued over the unique-ness of human language as a communication system. No other species has yet been discovered with a communication system that resembles human language, which permits the expression of any new idea in novel and creative ways. To understand what it means to acquire a language and how this is accomplished, we need to understand what it is that children must acquire and how human language differs from the communication systems of other species.

Communication versus language

In social interactions, almost all our actions communicate or reveal information about ourselves. Our choice of clothing, our posture, where we are looking, even our decision not to comment verbally — all provide information about our attitudes and emotions. Much of our social communication is non-verbal; much of it is even unintentional. We do not have the mental resources to continuously monitor our own posture, eye gaze, non-verbal gestures, and so on, and few people can control their non-verbal behaviour well enough to mislead other people. Thus, we give out a series of messages communicating who we are and what our attitudes to the current situation are. Many of these messages are unintentionally transmitted and many are not consciously attended to by other people. Living in a social world, it is impossible not to communicate in this way; to withhold messages itself communicates.

Human languages are not unique in being able to communicate more than emotional states. However, only human languages can refer to objects and events that are displaced in both time and space. Although animal communication systems are mainly confined to the here and now, signalling current emotional states, conveying alarm signals, eliciting the next step of a courting or sexual ritual, marking territory, and so on, there are exceptions. On returning to the hive, the worker honey bee performs a dance indicating to her co-workers the location of nectar supplies. The angle of the dance from the vertical signals the direction of a distant nectar source and the speed of the dance signals its distance. However, the honey bee is restricted to referring to nectar location (and new nest sites) in essentially two-dimensional space. When a nectar source is experimentally located directly above the hive, the bee cannot communicate this vertical location to her fellow workers.

Worker honey bees can refer to events distant in space, but only human languages allow reference to events distant in both time and place. Human languages are not only unique in the range of concepts to which they can refer, but also allow new words to be freely and easily coined. Think of all the words that we commonly use that did not exist 50 years ago — *cassette*, *VCR*, *microwave*, *silicon chip*, *pc*, *junk food*, *zit*, and so on. In this sense, human languages are open communication systems. Worker honey bees can communicate about displaced location but they cannot invent new meaning elements.

The inability of the worker bee to add new elements to her dance may reflect the fact that her communication system is genetically programmed. Human languages are obviously learned; a Chinese baby will learn English if reared in an English-speaking family, Chinese if reared in a Chinese-speaking family, and Swahili if reared in a Swahili-speaking family. Some birdsongs have elements of learned dialect. For instance, the mating song of male white-crowned sparrows has a learned component. If a white-crowned sparrow is reared in isolation, then in maturity males will sing a similar song, but without the trills characteristic of the local dialect, and females will not respond. Furthermore, a white-crowned sparrow that has not learned the local birdsong dialect as a young bird within a particular timespan, called the *sensitive period*, will never acquire that dialect.

Australian English comprises approximately 44 sound units, or phonemes. This means that we typically perceive speech in terms of the 44 non-overlapping sound units that we need to understand differences in meaning between similar sounding words, such as *bin*, *pin*, *tin* and *kin*. These 44 phonemes can be combined and recombined to symbolise different concepts. For instance, the three units /k, æ, t/ can be rearranged to form the words *cat*, *act*, and *tack*, all of which have completely different meanings. In constructing words from a limited number of discrete phonemes, language reveals a dual patterning feature, in which meaningless elements (phonemes) are combined in various sequences to form meaningful elements.

The choice of sound sequence as symbol for a concept is arbitrary, the only requirement being that the symbol is agreed upon by the language community. Thus, in English, the concept of dog is conveyed by the word *dog*; in German it is *Hund*, and in French it is *chien*. There is nothing dog-like about any of these words; they are merely sound patterns agreed upon by convention to refer to dogs. It is the key features of discreteness, dual patterning, and arbitrariness that permit new words to be freely coined, providing that the language group agrees on their meaning.

In addition to the two layers of sound and meaning elements, human languages have an additional level of patterning. Individual words can be arranged to form sentences whose construction and interpretation depends on the application of grammatical rules. Thus, *Hunt dogs* means something quite different to *Dogs hunt*, and *The dog chased the cat* means something quite different to *The cat chased the dog*. By using a finite number of grammatical rules concerning both word order and morphological affixes (word endings like the *-s* in *dogs* and the *-ing* in *singing*), human languages allow us to both say and understand an infinite number of entirely new sentences by combining and recombining words in novel, patterned, ways. Although unusual, you would understand the metaphorical sentence *Dreamy trains jump lazily* even though you have never heard it before. Moreover, because grammatical rules can be applied over and over again in the same sentence, they potentially allow us to construct an infinite number of different sentences. In this sense, too, human language is open.

In summary, by combining and recombining a discrete number of meaningless phonemes to form arbitrary words through dual patterning, human languages can freely coin new words to convey any meaning. Furthermore, through arranging and modifying these words in rule-governed ways, one can form a potentially infinite number of novel sentences that will be easily understood. A truly open communication system capable of expressing such a range of meaning is uniquely human.

The young infant is faced with the apparently formidable task of acquiring a very economical and abstract symbolic communication system which even linguists cannot yet completely describe. This is achieved with apparent ease in a few years. To understand this process, we must look carefully at how the child gets 'a foot in the door' of the language system.

The prerequisites of language acquisition

As noted, humans use both linguistic and non-linguistic communication. Hearing infants gain entry into the language system by superimposing vocalisation on gestural communication. Their developing cognitive ability allows them to gradually acquire their first words as verbal symbols. Although far from complete, by about 20 months most children have acquired a dual patterning system in which discrete, meaningless sound elements are combined to form arbitrary symbols which convey meaning. At this point they have mastered several prerequisite skills, including the ability to perceive and produce basic phonological contrasts, non-verbal communication skills, and the cognitive ability of mental representation.

Prelinguistic phonological abilities

Phonemes can be described according to how they are articulated. This field of study is called articulatory phonetics. One way consonantal phonemes can be described is the manner in which they are produced.

When produced by human speakers, the syllables /ba/ and /pa/ differ in the time between the opening of the lips, previously closed in the formation of the /b/ or /p/ sound, and the commencement of vocal cord vibration. This lag is known as *voice onset time* (VOT). Synthetic speech stimuli can be created that are identical in all but voice onset time. Adults perceive phonemes categorically. For instance, English-speaking adults perceive all syllables with VOT values under 25 milliseconds as /ba/ and syllables with VOT values over 25 milliseconds as /pa/.

In 1971, Eimas et al. demonstrated that 1- and 4-month-old infants raised in an English-speaking environment were able to discriminate between the synthetically produced syllables /ba/ and /pa/. By demonstrating this ability at such an early age, Eimas and his colleagues discredited simple theories of infant speech perception, according to which infants only gradually learned to perceive speech contrasts. This study suggested instead that infants possess an innate ability to perceive some basic phonological contrasts.

This was a very exciting finding which sparked off a large number of studies investigating infant speech discrimination capacities. Rather than simply mapping the infant's perception of phonological contrasts, research has examined whether the infant commences life with the innate ability to perceive all contrasts used by all languages, or whether early speech discrimination reflects the influence of maturation or of the language environment.

Eilers, Gavin and Wilson (1979) investigated 6- to 8-month-old English and Spanish infants' discrimination between synthetic speech stimuli varying only in the VOT of the word-initial consonant. In English, the /ba/–/pa/ distinction is made as VOT approximates 25 milliseconds but in Spanish this contrast is made at a much smaller

VOT value. Eilers and her colleagues found that only Spanish infants were sensitive to the difference between synthetic speech stimuli with VOT values of –20 and +10 milliseconds. This suggests that Spanish infants have 'tuned in' to the linguistic environment, and are becoming sensitive to speech contrasts used by Spanish speakers to signal meaning differences.

However, Eilers et al. found that both English and Spanish infants could discriminate between synthetic speech stimuli with VOT values of 10 and 40 milliseconds. Because Spanish infants could make a discrimination that is not relevant in Spanish, this finding suggested that the ability to discriminate between these stimuli is innate. Further research has shown that chinchillas, small south American rodents, are also sensitive to similar VOT differences in synthetic speech. The fact that this discrimination is not unique to humans suggests that human languages exploit innate properties of the mammalian auditory system. This suggestion is supported by findings that many languages use VOT contrasts similar to English (see Ingram, 1989).

These results indicate that some aspects of speech discrimination are innate and others develop through exposure to a particular linguistic environment. An infant is able to discriminate some speech contrasts virtually from birth, but other discriminations appear to be learned.

Infants' control over the articulation process also appears to reflect a combination of innate, maturational and environmental influences (Stark, 1986). Newborn infants are able to communicate vocally only by crying. By about eight weeks, they begin to make comfort noises, such as cooing and gooing sounds and laughter. By about 16 weeks, they begin to engage in vocal play, making a large variety of sounds and apparently repeating them for interest's sake. By six months, the nature of the babbling changes to become more structured, with babbling taking on a typical consonant-vowel-consonant-vowel (CVCV) patterning, with the same consonant and vowel being repeated. By nine months this CVCV babbling becomes more complex, with different consonants and vowels occurring within a CVCV sequence. Infants may now produce long patterns in which babbling carries the typical intonation patterns of the surrounding linguistic environment.

It has been reported that deaf infants begin to coo at the same time as hearing infants (but see Gilbert, 1982). If true, the fact that deaf infants begin to babble would suggest that the onset of babbling is maturationally determined. Parents can increase the frequency of babbling by attending and responding to infant babbling but they cannot alter the structure of the babbling.

Although 12-month-old infants are not able to produce the entire range of speech sounds used by their linguistic community, they have gained sufficient control of the articulation process to produce a small range of basic sounds which will later be used to produce their first word-like utterances (see table 4.1 for a guide to some key phonemic contrasts). Typically, consonant sounds now tend to be produced in the front of the mouth, and include the sounds /b, p, m, n/, together with neutral vowels such as /a/. It is no accident that many language communities have words like *mama* and *papa* for *mother* and *father* (Ingram, 1991). These words have presumably evolved from what infants find easiest to produce!

Table 4.1: An introduction to phonemic contrasts referred to in this chapter.

Voiced sounds contrast with their voiceless counterparts, in that the vocal cords begin to vibrate earlier in voiced sounds. If you produce the following pairs of sounds, differing only in voice onset time, you will find that the voiced ones sound louder.

Voiced	b	d	g	z
Voiceless	p	t	k	s

The following sounds differ only in terms of whether they are produced near the front or the back of the mouth. Note where your tongue is located when you produce the following pairs of sounds.

Front	p	b	t	d	n
Back	k	g			ŋ
					si*ng*

Fricatives are sounds in which the air flow through your mouth does not completely stop as the sounds are produced. However, your

Table 4.1 (cont.)

tongue interferes with the flow of air, producing the friction or turbulence that make these sounds relatively noisy. The following sound pairs differ only in terms of whether the air flow stops completely at some point as the sound is made or whether this air flow is only partly impeded. Affricates are similar sounds, produced by a complete closure, followed immediately by a slow release of the closure characteristic of a fricative.

Stops	t	d				
Fricatives	s	z	θ	∂	š	ʒ
					<u>sh</u>in	mea<u>s</u>ure
Affricates					tš	dʒ
					<u>ch</u>in	ju<u>dge</u>

Non-verbal communication

As indicated above, newborn infants' only vocal communication is crying. At this stage they are not communicating intentionally; they are simply responding to feelings of discomfort, such as cold, hunger, thirst, or pain. However, a child's parents will interpret his or her behaviour and will consistently act to relieve any discomfort. Thus, crying communicates the state of discomfort, and the consistent behaviour of her or his parents will teach the infant to anticipate some kind of parental response to crying. By six months of age, infants have developed a kind of signature cry, which is far from the full-throated cry produced when truly distressed. By then, anticipation of a parental response has modified the communication system.

Bates, Camaioni and Volterra (1975) published an investigation of the origins of symbolic speech. To obtain objects that are out of reach, very young infants stretch as far as they can toward the object. If a parent is holding the object, infants will stretch towards the object but will not yet attempt to engage the parent in eye contact. But we know that much younger infants understand that eye gaze is an indicator of attention. The infant does not engage the parent in eye contact because he or she is not yet able to conceive of the parent as a tool of assistance in the attempt to gain possession of the object. We know this because the infant's communicative behaviour in this type of situation changes fairly dramatically at the same time as she or he is able to use objects as tools in other contexts.

Until about 10 or 12 months, if a toy is placed out of his or her reach on a rug, an infant will simply stretch towards the toy. However, by 10 to 12 months, she or he will pull on the rug to bring the toy within reach. This reveals that the child has passed a cognitive milestone. Understanding that an object may be obtained via an indirect action, he or she is now able to use tools. Tool use implies a fairly advanced understanding of indirect causation and is relatively rare in the animal kingdom.

Tool use is soon extended to the communication system. The infant now uses objects in social sequences, perhaps by showing objects to people to obtain their attention, monitoring their eye gaze while doing so. The infant also uses people as tools to gain access to objects. If Dad is absent-mindedly holding her or his toy car out of reach, the infant may now intently watch his eyes to monitor his attention, meanwhile tugging on his trousers to obtain his attention. Once the child has obtained Dad's attention, he or she will reach toward the car. At this stage, the child has realised that adults can be used to assist in achieving goals. Her or his behaviour is now intentionally directed towards gaining Dad's attention, then non-verbally signalling objects that he or she wishes to possess or wishes Dad to attend to. Non-verbal communication has become intentional.

Behaviours intended to communicate can of course be modified, as long as they are still communicating effectively. A full-stretch reach toward a toy that is out of reach now becomes a half-hearted reach toward it. Parents will interpret this gesture as indicating the infant's desire to possess the toy and will react accordingly. If the object is one that the child is permitted, then the parent will either pass it to her or him or place it within reach. If it is one the child is not permitted, the object will be removed, preferably placed out of sight; the parent will often accompany these actions with a *No*. The infant is learning that adults can fairly accurately interpret his or her communicative behaviour.

Behaviour that is intended to communicate becomes increasingly stylised. Thus, a half-hearted reach eventually becomes a conventional point. Pointing is first used to direct others' attention; it is only later used as a request. On average, infants can understand a pointing gesture by nine months and can use pointing to direct adult attention by about 12 months.

There is no value in gesturing if no-one is paying attention. The infant has already learned to use vocal sounds to attract attention. This has been achieved with cries from birth and has been elaborated on by recruiting other vocalisations, such as raspberries, to attract adult attention. Now that the infant understands the notion of tool use, she or he will combine particular idiosyncratic sounds with non-verbal gestures to ensure that Mum is watching when more meaningful non-verbal gestures are produced. For instance, a child may combine an idiosyncratic *ha*, which attracts Mum's attention, with a pointing gesture towards a drink.

Although by about 15 months infants have become very competent communicators, they are still relatively limited in terms of what they can communicate. They can even use a series of gestures to direct an adult to an object located in another room, but they are nevertheless limited. If they do not know where the object is located, they are unable to communicate about it. There is much scope then, for improvement in the communication system.

Mental representation

Parrots can mimic human speech very well. They can even be taught to say a particular sound sequence (*Polly wants a cracker*) for a particular reward. But parrots will never move beyond this to language. They lack the cognitive capacity to understand that these sound sequences have a symbolic value, that they are referring to particular classes of objects. We recognise this when we accuse people of 'parroting' a speech; we mean that they can recite the speech but it has no meaning for them.

Between the ages of 11 and 14 months, most infants acquire about a dozen phonologically consistent forms used to communicate in particular situations. Infants may imitate a few animal sounds, so that the forms *wu-wu* for dog and *mau-mau* for cat are not unusual. They may have a few idiosyncratic sound patterns accompanying non-verbal gestures. One infant, Marta, used *ayi* when she wished to gain or direct adult attention and *mm* when she wanted something.

Such phonologically consistent forms are termed *vocables* rather than *words*, to indicate that their meaning is not yet symbolic but is tied to a particular situation. Vocables represent an important step towards words. The infant is now using particular and consistent sound patterns in particular communicative contexts. Some vocables are clearly based on adult models. Thus, a young infant will learn to say *ta-ta* or *bye-bye* as part of the family ritual of bidding visitors goodbye. Holding her young son to her, Mum may manipulate his hand to form a waving gesture and coach, *Say bye-bye; say bye-bye*, until her son obliges. Eventually he will learn to say *bye-bye* whenever he takes part in this ritual. However, at this point *bye-bye* has no symbolic meaning; it is merely part of the goodbye ritual. It is no more language than the waving gesture itself. *Bye-bye* will not at this time be used in any other situation.

Similarly, mother and son will play object exchange games. Mum will hand her son a toy. At first he keeps the toy, but eventually he learns to give it back to prolong this exchange game. As he gives it back, Mum will mark the exchange with a *ta*. The infant soon learns to mark the exchange by saying *ta* as he gives the toy back to Mum. With continued coaching, he will eventually learn to say *ta* only when he receives the toy. Each exchange is now marked by the recipient saying *ta*. However, again, the vocable *ta* is used only in this exchange game situation.

The child will not yet say *ta* when given a drink!

Forms like *bye-bye* and *ta* should be classed as vocables rather than words, as their meaning is ritualistic rather than symbolic, forming an integral part of a particular social interaction. However, they represent an important advance in that the infant is now basing his or her vocalisations on conventional adult models.

The infant will shift from vocables to words once she or he has understood that words are sound patterns that can be used to symbolise or signify particular objects and that these words refer not just to individual objects but to a whole class of objects. Thus, the word *dog* is a conventional (arbitrary) sound pattern used to refer to all dogs, whether they be the family pet, the dog next door, a soft dog-toy, dogs in a book, or dogs on television. The infant who can use words as symbols has achieved the naming insight and has made a giant step towards language. What lies behind this enormous cognitive leap?

It has been argued that at this stage infants are first able to mentally represent objects. In other aspects of their behaviour, they show that they can internally visualise absent objects and events; they will imitate complex behaviour sequences such as temper tantrums after a lengthy delay. This type of deferred imitation reveals infants' ability to mentally represent the event to be later copied. At about this time, they will engage in their first symbolic play, perhaps picking up a spoon and pretending it is a telephone by speaking into the bowl, with the handle facing towards the ear. To play with a spoon in this way, an infant must use the spoon to represent (or symbolise) a telephone.

The naming insight comes at about the same time as infants first show the capacity to mentally represent or symbolise absent objects and events (Bates et al., 1975). Words are conventional symbols that stand in the place of objects and events. With the naming insight the infant has gained a very powerful means of supplementing gestural communication. The first words tend to be used in conjunction with gestural communication. Thus, infants may point to and name the desired object at the same time.

This is much more effective than a vocable accompanying a point.

With the naming insight, infants can refer to objects even when they are out of sight or when their location is unknown. Naming objects also serves as a powerful controller of adult attention. The increased precision of infants' communication acts as a powerful incentive to rapid growth in naming, and vocabularly usually grows very quickly from this point. Most infants achieve the naming insight at about 18 to 20 months, although there is huge variation in the age at which this is achieved. Although the 'average' infant reaches the 50-word milestone at about 20 months, the age at which this milestone is achieved ranges from 15 to over 24 months in normally developing children (Nelson, 1973).

A 20-month-old infant has not acquired a language, but he or she is well on the way. By this time, the use of words as symbols shows the important design features of discreteness, arbitrariness, duality of patterning, and displacement. Nevertheless, we cannot speak of an infant acquiring language until she or he has acquired a generative form of grammar that allows him or her to combine word symbols in a rule-governed and creative way. However, before turning to grammatical development, let us look at the infant's early use of words.

The one-word stage

It should be noted in passing that children's early words are often far removed from the adult forms. For instance, *dog* may be said as *do'*. Other words may be far more distorted. For the purposes of the present discussion, we will assume adult-like pronunciation. Phonological development will be explored in the next section. Here we will discuss the structure of children's early vocabularies and how words are used in the one-word stage of language acquisition.

Children's early vocabularies are highly functional (Nelson, 1973). At this stage, children are generally either naming desired objects or directing others' attention toward particular objects. Slightly over half of their first words are names of objects and their favourite people. They rapidly acquire the names of foods (*juice, milk, bikkie, water*), favourite people (*Dada*), family pets (*Dizzie* the dog), security blanket (*blanket*), and favourite toys (*ball, blocks, boat, truck, book, doll*). Children also learn the names of objects they can manipulate. Items like *shoes* are fairly common in early vocabularies. Although children cannot yet put them on, shoes are small articles of clothing which they enjoy manipulating. They are certainly good at taking them off! In contrast, larger items of clothing, like pants, coats and jumpers, are less easily manipulated, and their names rarely make their way into children's early vocabularies. Likewise, names of household items that can be manipulated (*keys*) tend to be learned in preference to names of items that are simply there (*sofa, table, window*). Items that change or move in interesting ways are often those that children wish to point out to others, and so words like *clock, light, car, dog, cat* and *bird* are fairly common. The rest of children's early vocabularies comprise words describing or requesting actions (*go, up*) and regulating social interactions (*hi, bye-bye, look, want, more, no, yes, please, ouch*). They also have a few descriptive words (*hot, dirty, allgone*).

Already it is clear that parental influences are at work. Within these early vocabularies are animal names (*duck, horse, bear, cow*) which parents have labelled for children from books. Some children also have names for quite a few body parts (*nose, eyes, ear, knee*), learned from naming routines as they are being bathed and dressed. From such naming routines, some children learn that words are used to label things. This style of vocabulary is more common in children whose parents are well educated and in first-born children. Where there is only one child, parents are somewhat more likely to engage in book-reading and picture-naming activities and the child may have a greater amount of undivided adult attention. Other children have a higher proportion of words that can be used in social interactions. This type of expressive vocabulary is more common in later-born children and in children whose parents have lower levels of education. These children are learning from their family that language can be used to express needs and desires and to control social interactions.

These differences in the structure of early vocabularies are minor stylistic variations; all children learn that language can be used both to name objects and to express social needs. Neither style is superior and neither predicts later language proficiency. However, the fact that differences can be observed at such an early stage shows that children are learning about language from the way it is used in their immediate social environment.

Although by around 20 months children may have acquired about 50 words, many are seldom used. The core group of commonly used words is much less than this, at around eight to ten words. Children now understand that words are a powerful communicative device but are equipped with only a very limited repertoire. How are these words used?

Parents will notice that the first words are typically used with meanings corresponding to adult usage. Thus, a child will first use *dog* for dogs, *ball* for balls, and *juice* for juice. Close monitoring of word use may even reveal that a child at first uses *dog* only in relation to the family pet, or perhaps to live dogs, and uses *blanket* only in relation to her or his own security blanket. This over-restricted usage of a word is termed *underextension*, in that the child under-uses a word to refer to only a subclass of its referents (objects to which a word refers). Underextension is relatively hard to detect as the child never actually makes an error in word choice; he or she simply under-uses it. Not all words are underextended, and most words are extended to a range of referents within a month of their first appearance.

Underextension is rapidly followed by *overextension*. This is far more obvious because the child is now over-using a word, by extending its usage to cover a wider range of referents than adult usage permits. A child may now use *dog* to refer not just to dogs, but also to cats, horses, goats and indeed any animal with fur. *Ball* may now be used to refer not just to balls, but to any round object, and even the letter *O*. Not all words are overextended (Rescorla, 1980). In the process of acquiring their first 75 words, children overextend only about one-third. Most overextensions occur in relation to names of things, but other types of overextension are also apparent. For example, a child will learn that *hot* is used when parents are holding cups of hot tea and coffee, when an adult is cooking at the stove, and when her or his food is too hot to be eaten straight away. The child may eventually overextend *hot* to refer to any object that should not be touched, such as forbidden glassware.

Children overextend their early words for several reasons. Their conceptual development is still quite immature, and objects may not be categorised in the same way as adults. Children may call weeds *flowers* or goats *dogs* because they do not yet know that these are different categories. They may call wristwatches *clocks* because they do not yet realise that these objects have different names. Many overextensions then, reflect conceptual immaturity.

Other overextensions, however, represent a communication strategy. Children may use a word in a way that differs from adult usage patterns simply because they either lack the appropriate vocabulary or they cannot recall it at the time. Although originally correctly used, children overextend early words more than later-acquired words (Rescorla, 1980). This may reflect the fact that the later-acquired words cannot be remembered as well. Children who label a picture of an orange *apple* will nevertheless tend to point to a picture of an apple in preference to a picture of an orange when asked to point to *apple* (Thompson & Chapman, 1976). The fact that overextensions are more common in production than in comprehension suggests that overextensions partly reflect children's desire to communicate despite vocabulary limitations. This view is also supported by the fact that overextensions are most common in the period of 18 to 30 months. With the acquisition of routines such as *What's that?* to elicit unknown object names, overextensions decrease quite rapidly, and vocabulary size increases markedly.

As well as this type of categorical overextension, children may use a particular word in a variety of contexts, where the meaning conveyed by the word appears situational in nature. For instance, a child may say *comb* when he or she sees a centipede to comment on its many legs. Similarly, she or he may say *Nonno* when approaching Grandpa's house with her or his parents. Here the child is clearly not overextending the meaning of *Nonno*, but is apparently recognising Grandpa's house. These one-word utterances have a relational meaning that is tied to the situation. The child seems to be commenting on a whole situation, but appears to be restricted to the production of only one word at a time.

In this type of relational one-word utterance, the child uses a single word to comment on a topic implied by the situation as a whole. For this reason, the one-word stage of language development is termed *holophrastic speech*, with the implication that the meaning intended by the child's one-word utterance is more than the single-word, corresponding loosely to what would be expressed in a phrase or a sentence in adult language. Thus, *Nonno* in the context above probably means something closer to *Nonno's house*.

This analysis of children's intended meanings late in the single-word stage implies that what they know about language (their linguistic competence) may be ahead of their production capacity or performance. If this is true, then we would expect children to be able to comprehend multi-word sentences before they can produce them. What does research have to say on this question?

Sachs and Truswell (1978) investigated the comprehension of two-word sentences in 12 children aged from 16 to 24 months who were still at the one-word stage. The children were first presented with sensible word combinations such as *throw ball* and *pat teddy* to check that they understood that their task was to enact the researcher's instructions. All children managed these plausible commands. They were then asked to carry out some unusual actions, like *tickle bottle* and *smell truck*. These unusual instructions can be enacted correctly only if it is understood that two-word combinations have relational meaning. Despite the unusualness of these instructions, all but one of the children correctly enacted at least some of them. Although we cannot really tell whether these children understood the importance of word order, this study shows that children at the one-word stage know that word combinations have relational meaning.

If holophrastic children are using their one-word sentences to convey relational meaning and if they can comprehend two-word sentences, what is stopping them from producing word combinations? Research suggests that children at the one-word stage are limited by their capacity to produce an articulation program for a sequence more than one word long. Until now, we have not discussed children's phonological development, other than to briefly comment on speech perception and babbling within the prelinguistic phase before they even produce vocables. Given that speech therapists are most often approached about concerns with children's phonological development, it is appropriate that we should digress to examine its basic features at this point. This will show us why children initially find it so difficult to combine words.

Phonological development

We have seen that prelinguistic infants are able to discriminate basic contrasts between syllables. At this stage we cannot claim that children have acquired phonemic discrimination. Phonemes are the minimal units of sound used by a language to contrast words differing in meaning. Thus the /p/–/b/ contrast is used to signal meaning differences in English in words like *pin* vs *bin*, and *nip* vs *nib*. By definition, prelinguistic infants are not using sound contrasts to differentiate the meanings of similar-sounding words (Ingram, 1989).

Children differentiate newly learned names for objects on the basis of phonemic differences in their second year. Not all phonemic differences are yet perceived, and sometimes basic contrasts discriminated by very young infants are not yet perceived in relation to meaningful speech (Ingram, 1989). For instance, Russian infants perceive contrasts between phonemes differing in voice onset time later than a range of other contrasts (Shvachkin, 1973).

One factor affecting the ease of phonemic contrast perception is the perceptual salience of a particular contrast. For instance, in Russian, vowels are louder and much more frequent than consonants. Thus, vowel distinctions are phonologically more obvious, or salient, and so contrasts between vowels are perceived before contrasts between consonants. The linguistic importance of a given contrast also determines the relative ordering of particular contrasts. English uses non-palatised consonants. The /k/ in *cute* is pronounced differently to the /k/ in *cool*; the former is somewhat palatised in this phonological context, but this difference is never used in English to signal a meaning contrast. Russian relies heavily on palatisation differences to signal meaning differences, and many consonants have palatised counterparts. In fact, in Russian palatised consonants are twice as frequent as non-palatised consonants. Palatisation contrasts are therefore much more important to Russian than to English speakers and it comes as no surprise to discover that Russian infants perceive palatisation contrasts very early (Shvachkin, 1973).

Phonemic contrasts are perceived before they are produced (Ingram, 1989). However, articulation difficulty also affects perceptual difficulty; easily produced phonemic contrasts also tend to be perceived early. Furthermore, articulation errors do not simply reflect perceptual errors; some contrasts that are accurately perceived cannot be produced. Thus, the distinctions between *den* and *then*, *shoe* and *zoo*, and *ray* and *way* are perceived accurately before they are produced. Older children will sometimes comment on the fact that they cannot pronounce a particular word: 'Only Daddy can say *dup* [jump]' (Smith, 1973).

Of the other factors influencing articulation accuracy, ease of articulation is clearly critical. All English speech sounds are produced by modifying the flow of air from the lungs through the oral and nasal cavities. Some of these sounds require more complex control of the tongue than others. There are striking similarities in the relative frequency with which basic contrasts are used across languages and the order in which children first master these contrasts. Children at the end of the babbling stage are predominantly producing sounds like /b, p, m, d, t, n/ that are formed in the front of the mouth. Contrasts among these sounds are produced before contrasts among sounds produced at the back of the mouth /g, k, ŋ/. These types of sound are also produced before noisier sounds, called *fricatives* /f, s, ʒ, š, θ, and ∂/. The parallels between the frequency of particular classes of sounds across language groups and the order in which particular sounds are produced by young children suggest that languages have tended to capitalise on sound contrasts that are readily mastered.

Nevertheless, not all languages use the same phonemic contrasts. Between-language differences observed in the order in which particular phonemes are produced toward the end of the holophrastic stage reflect the influence of a child's linguistic environment. Here, the absolute frequency of phonemes within a language is not especially important. Rather, it is the functional importance of the phoneme within the target language that is critical (Ingram, 1989). For instance, the phoneme /∂/ (*th* in *the* and *this*) is the second most frequent phoneme in English but is acquired quite late. Despite its high frequency, /∂/does not carry a high functional load. It occurs in relatively few words and these do not contrast minimally with other pairs. When children pronounce *this* as *dis* and *that* as *dat*, they are therefore able to be understood.

Children's first vocabularies are frequently made up of a series of very similar sounding words, with mastery of only a few phonemic contrasts. With the spurt in vocabulary development that occurs after children have acquired the naming insight, the phonological repertoire becomes greatly enlarged, although some sequences are not fully mastered for many years.

One of the most well-known studies examining the order of emergence of English phonemes is that of Templin (1957; see also Ingram, 1989). She asked groups of children varying in age to produce target words. Although by four years the majority of children can produce most consonants, it should be realised that some common speech sounds, like /θ, ð, z, ʒ, v/ have not yet been mastered by all five year olds. Some consonant clusters, like /sl-/, /fr-/, and /-lf/, also cause difficulty and three-phoneme clusters like /spl-/ and /spr-/ are only reliably produced by about six years.

More recent studies of phonological production have focused on understanding the consistency of children's mispronunciations of adult forms (Ingram, 1986). These studies show that these mispronunciations do not simply reflect 'errors' but systematic attempts to simplify the articulation process. In addition to other phonemic substitutions, complex syllabic structure will be simplified in several ways. Children's first words tend to reproduce the CV or CVCV structure of late babbling. Thus, *dog* may become *do'* or *doggie*. Consonant clusters may be reduced, with the most difficult sound tending to be dropped; so *play* becomes *pay*. Unstressed syllables may be omitted, so *banana* becomes *nana*.

In addition to the simplification of syllabic structure, children's substitutions are often quite systematic. Easy sounds tend to be substituted for more difficult ones. For instance, *sing* may be said as *tin*, and *shoe* as *zoo*. Some substitutions reflect word-level processes. For example, it is quite common for children to use voiced sounds before vowels and voiceless sounds after them — *pig* becomes *bick*, *bed* becomes *bet*. Often both consonants in a word are pronounced in the same place in the mouth, so that *tub* becomes *bub* and *doggie* becomes *doddie*. Within a word, unstressed vowels are sometimes pronounced the same as the stressed vowel.

Several of these processes may operate at the same time.

Thus, a word like *sky* becomes *guy*, with the consonant cluster being reduced and the voiced sound /g/ substituted for the unvoiced sound /k/ before the vowel. Or *paper* becomes *baybay*, with voiced sounds being produced before the vowels, and the unstressed /ə/ vowel being replaced by the stressed /e/. These processes may apply to the whole utterance in early word combinations. For instance, one child who forced consonant-initial single-word utterances into a strict CVCV pattern at first reduced CVCV single words like *baby* to *bay* when they appeared in two-word combinations so that the word combinations maintained a CVCV structure (Matthei, 1989).

These phonological processes have been illustrated in some detail because they demonstrate the patterned nature of many apparent articulation errors. Because these substitutions are lawful and consistent, parents learn to interpret the child's speech. With some consideration of these types of common phonological simplification processes, teachers can also learn to understand individual children's non-adult pronunciation patterns.

Children vary considerably in the accuracy of their early pronunciation. Some achieve a fairly high degree of accuracy by actively avoiding words with sounds they cannot yet accurately produce. One child achieved great accuracy in initial consonants of words by avoiding forms not already in her inventory (Matthei, 1989). This same child was quite unconcerned about the consistency of vowels! She pronounced the same words in different ways at different times. This variability is quite common in children's first words. In addition, it is possible in very young children to observe perfect pronunciation of a phonologically complex word such as *pretty*, particularly one acquired early on, among a sea of immature forms. Sometimes the pronunciation of these words deteriorates over time, as they are gradually assimilated into the child's still immature, but nonetheless patterned, phonological system.

The large individual differences in the accuracy of pronunciation of early words are reflected in the fact that articulation accuracy is sometimes fairly weakly related to other aspects of language development such as vocabulary and grammar (Newcomer & Hammill, 1988). This can make it difficult to know when a child needs remedial help. Although it is best to err on the safe side by referring children to speech therapists when doubts exist concerning their language progress, it is not unusual for children to be quite difficult for strangers to understand. If the child's phonological substitutions tend to be patterned, as illustrated above, then the child may be best considered just as somewhat slow in the development of her or his phonological system. When a child commonly mispronounces adult words in a way that is relatively unpredictable, there is more cause for concern.

Grammatical development

Most English-speaking children begin to combine words when they have acquired a vocabulary of about 50 words. Most of their first word combinations encode one of the following eight semantic relations: Agent-Action (*boy kick*); Action-Object (*pull train*); Agent-Object (*Daddy ball*); Action-Location (*sit chair*); Entity-Location (*cup table*); Possessor-Possession (*Mummy scarf*); Entity-Attribute (*ball red*); Demonstrative-Entity (*there car*). Longer utterances tend to combine these basic types of relations, with utterances such as *Boy kick ball* or *Sit Daddy chair*.

These types of multi-word utterances show that children have acquired the beginnings of word-order rules. Word-order rules tell how individual words should be combined and interpreted. We use word-order rules to understand *Kendall read* as an utterance informing us that Kendall is reading. Children learn word-order rules very quickly but errors can be detected in some of their early combinations. For instance, both *Kendall pick up* and *Kimmy kick* were among the word-order errors made by one child in her very first word combinations. We recognize such errors when we know about the situation in which they were spoken. *Kimmy kick* was said as Kendall kicked Kimmy!

Children appear to learn word-order rules through semantic bootstrapping procedures (Braine, 1976). For example, over half of Kendall's first Agent-Action combinations featured only three agents, *Kendall*, *Mummy* and *Daddy*. Kendall may have learned first to place *Kendall* before an action word to indicate that she performed the action. This permits combinations like *Kendall sit*, *Kendall read*, *Kendall walk*, *Kendall bounce*, and so on. Kendall now has a procedure for generating two-word utterances featuring herself as the agent. She may later place *Mummy* before action words, giving her the combinations *Mummy read*, *Kendall Mummy walk*, *Mummy tie-it* and *Mummy oops*. Later still she may add *Daddy* to the category of words placed before action words. At this point she may have a limited semantic rule which allows her to place a person's name before an action word to indicate that the action is being performed by the person named. At a later point, she may expand that rule to cover both unknown people and non-human entities (*spider move*). Here she has acquired a semantically based word-order rule of the form Agent-Action. Later, the Agent role may be expanded to include abstract nouns (*governments*) and much more elaborate grammatical subjects (*The thing that really gets on my nerves*). Once action words are reliably placed after agents and before the objects they act on, they begin to acquire the distributional properties characterising them as verbs.

Once a child has become fully proficient in the word-order rules, he or she can potentially construct sentences of considerable semantic complexity. After being found at the age of 13 years, Genie, a child deprived of most language input from about 20 months, eventually mastered telegraphic speech of this type, and was finally able to convey complex and abstract (displaced) ideas in utterances such as *Teacher said Genie have temper tantrum outside* and *Father hit Genie cry longtime ago* (Curtiss, 1981). This type of speech is termed *telegraphic* because it contains the content words necessary to convey information, and they are sequenced in the correct order to be unambiguously understood. However, Genie's sentences are clearly ungrammatical in that grammatical function words and morphological inflections are missing.

Children's telegraphic speech is not nearly as complex as Genie's when morphological rules are learned. Indeed, the chief characteristic of Genie's speech is that the concepts conveyed are extraordinarily advanced relative to the primitive linguistic means used for expression. Her language development is clearly incomplete. Although it is true that the use of a wider variety of structures such as questions and negatives (*Are you coming with me? What are you making? I don't want any salad*) requires the use of both grammatical function words and inflections, Genie's ability to communicate complex concepts with telegraphic speech demonstrates that the primary motivation for progress beyond telegraphic speech may not be communicative efficiency.

Children's acquisition of basic grammatical morphemes, be they function words such as *the*, *a*, *am*, *is*, *are* and *does* or inflections such as *-ing*, *-s*, *-ed* and *'s*, is accomplished fairly quickly. The frequency of particular morphemes in adult speech directed to children does not determine the order in which they are acquired (Brown, 1973). Rather, it is the complexity of the underlying concepts encoded within the morphemes and the complexity of the grammatical rules governing the appropriate use of the morphemes that primarily determine when particular morphemes are learned.

Children acquire morphological rules by abstracting grammatical patterns from the speech they hear and comprehend. We know this from the types of errors they make. For instance, in English the most frequent verbs are irregular, meaning that there is no rule for converting present tense forms to past tense forms. There is no pattern transforming *go* to *went*, *see* to *saw*, *break* to *broke*, *fall* to *fell*. When children first use different forms of a verb to denote a past action, they tend to use irregular forms simply because they are more common in the speech that they hear. At this stage, they use different forms such as *see* and *saw*, *go* and *went*, *break* and *broke*, and *fall* and *fell*, depending on whether or not they are talking about a past action. Eventually, they also learn some regular past tense forms like *carried*, *hugged* and *played*. In these regular forms, a past action is signified by adding some variant of the phoneme /d/ to the present tense form of the verb. At first, this pattern is difficult to perceive, being obscured by the presence of irregular forms for which there is no pattern. However, children eventually acquire enough regular forms to filter out a rule that is useful in determining how to convey past action. We know that children have acquired a rule because, having discovered it, they over-use it and treat irregular forms as regular. The child now makes a series of *over-regularisation* errors, such as *goed*, *seed*, *breaked*, *falled*, and so on. These errors persist for several years and are still quite common in children in the early years of primary school. Gradually children will relearn the irregular forms.

Over-regularisation errors tell us a great deal about language acquisition. They tell us that children do not acquire grammatical rules through imitation, as they are exposed to relatively few mistakes of this type. (Even if children were raised only with their parents, and had no contact with children of their own age who made similar errors, these errors would still be observed.) Since children are not reinforced for these, over-regularisation errors also indicate that they do not acquire grammatical rules through reinforcement. Correction of such forms is futile. These characteristics of over-regularisation errors suggest instead that children are essentially rediscovering the language system for themselves. To acquire language, children need exposure to large amounts of language that they can understand. If they understand the language around them, they discover the regularities themselves (see below).

Over-regularisation errors are not restricted to past tense -*ed*. English-speaking children over-regularise plural -*s* forms, creating words like *childs*, *sheeps*, *mans*, *peoples*, and so on (Brown, 1973). This is also observed in other languages. More to the point, over-regularisation errors are observed in the acquisition of syntactic rules as well.

For example, children who are just starting to combine words will do fairly poorly in games requiring them to use toys to act out sentences spoken by a tester. By four, children have truly understood that English predominantly uses word order to signal the Agent-Action-Object sequence and are fairly good at enacting implausible sentences like *The dog pats the mother*, as well as semantically reversible active sentences like *The tiger chases the alligator*. These children do very poorly on tasks assessing their comprehension of semantically reversible passive sentences like *The tiger was chased by the alligator*. In such a sentence, both the tiger and the alligator can be the chaser. Normal word-order rules would indicate that the tiger did the chasing. However, in the passive sentence the grammatical function words *was* and *by* indicate that the normal word-order rules are reversed. In this sentence, it is the alligator that chased the tiger. Four-year-old children generally enact these sentences as though they were active versions, unaware of the processing implications of the additional function words (Bever, 1970). Sometimes children of this age will produce passives, but typically they will use them with the meaning reversed (*The dog was chased by the ball*). Most children reliably comprehend semantically reversible passive sentences only by about five years of age, and produce them only by about 11. Semantically non-reversible forms (*The cup was broken by the boy*) will be understood earlier because in these sentences only one of the nouns can plausibly act as the agent (Cups cannot break boys). Children interpret non-reversible passives by assuming the most plausible meaning.

Passive sentences are difficult for several reasons. They are very rare in adult speech, generally being used when the speaker wishes to emphasise the object of the action. But they are also difficult because they violate the normal word-order interpretation rule, in which Noun-Verb-Noun sequences are interpreted as Agent-Action-Object sequences (Bever, 1970). The types of errors that young children make in both comprehending and producing full passive sentences suggest that they are over-regularising the word-order rules used in active sentences.

Passives are not the only sentences in which over-regularisation can be observed. Children also tend to misinterpret other types of sentences by over-using a comprehension rule, according to which the noun preceding the verb is the agent of the verb. In relation to complement structures (e.g., *Tom asked Mary to feed the dog*), this rule has been called the *Minimal Distance Principle*. Note that this principle is completely consistent with children's general understanding of word-order rules. The Minimal Distance Principle allows children to correctly interpret sentences such as *Bob tells Foster to do a somersault*, *Bob asks Foster to do a somersault*, *Bob wants Foster to do a somersault*, *Bob hopes Foster will do a somersault*, *Bob thinks Foster will do a somersault* and *Bob wishes Foster would do a somersault*. However, the Minimal Distance Principle fails with certain structures such as *Ask Joe what time it is* and with certain verbs such as *promise*, with children misunderstanding sentences such as *Bob promises Foster to do a somersault*. The more difficult complement structures are not fully comprehended until late childhood (Chomsky, 1969).

Children's difficulty with the comprehension of semantically reversible passives and some forms of complementation reveal the child's discovery (and over-application) of linguistic rules. These instances do vary slightly from the over-regularisation observed with morphology, in that here children gradually learn exceptions, whereas in the over-regularisation of past tense *-ed* and plural *-s*, children make errors on forms that were originally correct. Parallels to the latter phenomenon do exist in syntax, but they are rarer.

By three or four years of age, most children have become skilled in a wide range of sentence structures. Furthermore, they are now able to combine sentences fairly easily using conjunctions like *and*, *before*, *because*, and so on. They can also produce linguistically complex forms, although these frequently contain errors, such as *I don't know what is it* or *I wonder how old is he*, which suggest that their grammatical understanding of these structures may be incomplete. The acquisition of these types of sentences is, theoretically, a very significant achievement. When children acquire complex sentences, they have acquired a truly open language in that, because the rules combining simple sentences can in principle be applied over and over again, they can theoretically produce an infinite number of sentences.

Close observation of children's use of less common sentence structures suggests that although four and five year olds are very competent communicators, whose control of language most second-language learners would envy, there are still notable gaps in their grammatical knowledge. In particular, children's grasp of complex sentence structures is incomplete. Most children enter primary school having mastered the basics of grammar and able to use common-sense to interpret sentences that they have not fully grasped. As children are exposed to more complex sentences in which their earlier comprehension strategies sometimes let them down, they continue to refine their grammatical system as they first comprehend and later acquire productive control over the complex grammatical rules that will allow them to qualify sentence meaning and convey different topical emphases to express finer shades of meaning and abstract ideas more precisely. As they acquire the grammatical rules required to produce complex sentences structures, they attain full control over the displacement and openness features that most strongly differentiate human language from animal communication systems.

Theoretical issues

As noted earlier, language, in the sense of being an open communication system that potentially allows any concept to be expressed through an infinite number of rule-governed combinations, is uniquely human. When children have mastered the grammatical rules governing complex sentence formation, they have achieved the final stage of competence in this system.

The uniqueness of human language raises another issue:

Does human language have an innate component? In other words, have we as a species evolved in a manner that specifically favours language acquisition? At this stage of the debate, the answer to these questions appears to be 'yes', although it is also noteworthy that human languages capitalise on our abilities. Let us consider the arguments for innateness. Some of these have been raised in passing in earlier sections.

First, human infants appear sensitive to a range of basic speech contrasts, being able to discriminate minimally contrasting syllables of synthetic speech from an early age. It appears that the contrasts which are innate reflect properties of the mammalian auditory system, as discrimination of some contrasts can be observed in chinchillas. Languages that use these types of phonetic contrasts take advantage of the human auditory system. However, human infants rapidly 'tune in' to the language system that surrounds them, thus learning from a very early age to discriminate other contrasts used in their linguistic environment.

Vocalisations at first support the gestural communication system, but as a child attains the cognitive capacity to symbolise objects and events, vocalisations are used to symbolise their referents, and the child utters her or his first words. The use of words provides a powerful communication system which can now refer to absent objects and events. However, at this stage, language is not yet fully productive; the holophrastic child does not use grammatical rules to sequence words. It appears that chimpanzees can be taught to use and combine signs, although they do not master word-order rules (Terrace et al., 1979). Some deaf children not exposed to signs will spontaneously create 'home signs'. Although these signs are often combined, consistent sign order rules are not reliably used (Feldman, Goldin-Meadow & Gleitman, 1978).

When children learn to use word-order rules to sequence words in a structured way, the power of the communication system is greatly enhanced. It appears that this aspect of language is very resilient. Genie, the child who was almost completely deprived of language input from 20 months to 13 years, nevertheless developed telegraphic language, although she never gained control of the morphological system (Curtiss, 1977).

In interpreting case studies like Genie, it is important to note that she was not intellectually disabled. On some spatial tasks, Genie had abilities superior to most adults (Curtiss, 1977). Furthermore, there is evidence that deprivation of language input for lesser periods appears not to produce permanent language impairment. For instance, after being discovered at the age of six, a child called Isabelle had acquired normal language by the time she was eight (Davis, 1947). Isabelle had been raised in virtual isolation with her deaf-mute mother and when first found it was thought she was deaf too.

The case of Genie can be directly contrasted with the case of developmentally delayed individuals such as Laura, who showed great proficiency in grammatical forms despite functioning at a preschool cognitive level at the age of 16 (Yamada, 1990). Laura produced sentences as complex as *The cook who does it, um, sometimes gives us these good enchilada an' oh, they're so good!* or *That's where my sister JB lives!* Other examples of linguistic proficiency despite severe developmental delay have been noted. Thus, Antony, a child with a mental age estimated at less than three years when he was six-and-a-half years old, produced sentences such as *I want to see who's in that class* (Curtiss, 1981).

The contrast between such cases suggests that there is a period, termed by biologists the *sensitive period*, in which children must be exposed to comprehensible and well-structured language input if they are to abstract the regularities forming the grammatical rule sytem. This type of sensitive period can be directly compared to the sensitive period observed for the learning of birdsong dialects. Further evidence for the sensitive period is provided by studies of congenitally and prelingually deaf adults who were first exposed to American Sign Language (ASL) after the age of 12. These adults showed morphological deficits in ASL despite relying on it for many years (Newport, 1990).

Studies showing dissociations between cognitive and grammatical development and implying the existence of a

sensitive period for language acquisition do imply an innate predisposition towards language in humans. However, language is learned. Exposure to well-formed language that is comprehensible in context is critical for language development.

In our culture, adults systematically modify their language when interacting with young children. First, adjustments are made to intonation patterns. Pitch is higher and more varied. Young infants generally prefer high-pitched and modulated speech, and this type of pitch patterning can signal to a child that the utterance is directed towards him or her. Speech is slower and clearer, with distinct pauses between utterances. These adjustments obviously assist children in analysing the speech stream and marking utterance boundaries. Syllable structure is also simplified, in accordance with the structure of late babbling and children's first words, with adult words like *dog* modified to *doggie* and *horse* modified to *horsie* to conform to a CVCV structure. Consonant clusters are reduced, with *stomach* becoming *tummy*. These modifications provide simpler target words for children.

Language directed to young children is also generally well formed grammatically, with few grammatical errors and few disfluencies. Verb structures are simplified and there are fewer complex sentences, although there are more directives (*Look at the flower*) and more questions (*What are you doing now? Can you put the block in the truck?*) in speech directed to children than in speech directed to adults. However, auxiliary verbs and subject nouns and pronouns are often dropped from questions (*Want a biscuit?*). Few modifiers, pronouns and grammatical function words are produced, relative to speech directed to adults. Adults speaking to a child often repeat their own utterances or recast the child's utterance, and provide feedback concerning missing grammatical morphemes, so that a child's *Sit truck* may be echoed in *Yes, you're sitting on the truck*. In addition, many words and phrases are produced in isolation. A mother directing her daughter to put a red block into a truck may say *Put the red block in the truck. The red block. In the truck. The truck.* This type of patterned speech informs the child how her sentence was constructed from several component phrases.

The social function of speech directed to children is often different from that directed to adults. As noted above, there are more directives and questions directed to children. Some directives focus children's attention on a particular object (*Look at the flower*), assisting their conceptual and vocabulary development. Others accompany a child's play, so that a mother may time her *Put another block on the tower* to accompany her son's actions, thus providing a running commentary that informs him how his actions are encoded linguistically. Questions are often intended to elicit a response. *What have you got there?* should elicit an object name.

Semantically, adult speech to young children is invariably focused on the here and now, with few references to the past. Mothers of very young children will tend to use the same limited semantic relations as are observed in children's first word combinations. The vocabulary used is more limited than in adult conversations. The same name will consistently be used for an object, which will be named at a level that is behaviourally useful for children. Thus, coins of different denominations and notes are all labelled *money* and various types of flowers (roses, dahlias, daisies) are all labelled *flower* for young children, whereas the label chosen for an object in adult speech depends much more on situational context, with more specific names (*rose, dahlia*) frequently being used. The almost exclusive reference to the here and now makes speech easy to interpret, and the changed patterns of word use make it easier for children to acquire a useful functional vocabulary.

Adults rarely make these adjustments deliberately. However, if they wish to maintain conversation with very young children, adjustments are needed. If children cannot understand what is being said, they do not attend. To maintain conversation, it is important to ensure that the meaning of what is being said is simple. Conversation therefore tends to be about the here and now and simple vocabulary is used. The attempt to ensure that meaning is simple in turn produces grammatical simplifications. For instance, pronouns like *I* and *you* are difficult for young children to understand and so they are often avoided (*Daddy will get Robbie a drink*). Finally, if an adult's aim is to keep the conversation going, she or he must ask many questions (*What are you doing now?*), which provides a turn in the conversation for the child. Many of an adult's repetitions are triggered by a child's failure to respond when it is his or her conversational turn.

It is clear that many adults' modifications represent attempts to keep conversation alive and this explains in part the large number of directives, questions, and repetitions in child-directed speech. This suggestion is supported by findings that mothers who believed their prelingual infant could understand most of what they heard modified their child-directed speech more than mothers who had lower opinions of their infant's ability to comprehend them.

By modifying their language, adults appear to be giving children ideally constructed language lessons. From this, it has sometimes been argued that such modifications are necessary for language acquisition. This claim was originally tested by asking whether there was any relationship between the extent to which parents modified their speech when talking to their children and children's linguistic proficiency. However, apart from the finding that more adult language input is associated with better child language, the results from these studies are not clear-cut (Bates et al., 1982). This type of study is rather difficult to interpret. Most importantly, the logic of these correlational studies assumes that the language acquisition process is adult-driven. However, child-directed language modifications tend to be produced when children's behaviour indicates comprehension difficulties. In other words, children indirectly elicit modifications from adults. Thus, more modified language input is elicited by children with less advanced linguistic skills. Even if child-directed language modifications facilitate language development, their effects may be disguised by the fact that linguistically immature children elicit more modifications. Moreover, it can be argued that most parents provide a threshold level of simplification that enables their children to acquire language easily and that minor variations over that threshold are not critical.

Given these types of difficulties, the best way of evaluating the effects of various child-directed speech modifications is to experimentally vary the levels of these modifications. Nelson (1977) investigated the effects of a common technique called recasting, in which an adult takes up a child's comment and elaborates on it. For example, a child may say *The donkey ran* and an adult may use her or his conversational turn to recast this as *The donkey did run, didn't it?*, thereby providing grammatical information concerning tags, pronouns, and the auxiliary verb *do*. Nelson divided a group of 28-month-old children into two groups, equated in terms of gender and level of grammatical development. One group received a series of experimental sessions in which researchers frequently used recasts that illustrated complicated question forms, while the other group received a series of sessions in which researchers focused on recasting complicated verb forms. Nelson's study showed that children selectively acquired the specific structures that the recasting sessions had focused on. In other aspects of grammatical development the two groups were still equivalent. These clear and selective effects of recasting indicated that some child-directed speech modifications are capable of enhancing language development.

Obviously, such studies do not demonstrate that child-directed modifications are necessary for language development. Furthermore, it is notable that Nelson trained children on what were for them difficult grammatical structures. Thus, Nelson's finding, while indicating the potential importance of child-directed speech, indicates the importance of comprehensible input, rather than simplified input.

The claims for the importance of child-directed speech modifications were originally based on arguments concerning the effects of language simplification. It was assumed that children learn best from simplified data. However, it has been strongly argued that simple sentences alone do not provide sufficient grammatical information.

For instance, the frequency of relatively complicated grammatical structures like yes/no questions (*Are you ready?*; *Are you putting that block on top?*) in maternal speech addressed to 24- to 27-month-old children predicts growth in children's auxiliary verb systems (Gleitman, Newport & Gleitman, 1984). By bringing the auxiliary verb (*are*) to the beginning of the utterance, these questions make perceptually salient what are normally unstressed and often contracted grammatical function words buried in the middle of utterances. In the more complicated yes/no question structure, auxiliary verbs are both stressed and uncontracted. Gleitman et al. argued that specific child-directed language modifications affect a relatively small class of grammatical structures, most notably grammatical function words, by providing information in ways that children find easy to process. A similar argument has been made for the effectiveness of the expansion technique, in which a child's utterance is repeated by an adult, but with the inclusion of function words and inflections that the child has omitted. For instance, an adult may expand the child utterance *Truck drop* by replying *Yes, the truck dropped* or *Yes, the truck did drop*.

Arguments against child-directed speech as a *necessary* component of the child's linguistic environment are bolstered by several cross-cultural studies showing that child-directed speech modifications are not universal. Heath (1983) carried out an ethnographic study of a small African-American community in which infants were continuously surrounded by a rich stream of language input. However, until children were linguistically mature enough to be readily understood within the ongoing conversation, their contributions were ignored. Thus, *mu mu* screamed by a 12 month old at the sight of a bottle of milk was not interpreted as *milk*. The adult, already getting milk for the child, responded *Okay, I'm lookin', hush yo' mouth all that fuss. Ain't no use hollerin'* (Heath, 1983). Adults do not interpret children's first attempts at speech; they simply regard them as 'noise'. They believe that a baby 'comes up' as a talker: 'When a baby's got sump'n to say, he'll say it'. Consistent with these attitudes, this community did not modify child-directed speech and mocked the baby talk they overheard in other communities. Similarly, adults in Western Samoa regard infants' first vocalisations as natural responses to physiological states rather than as intentional acts. If the child's utterance is not intelligible, the caregiver will not usually attempt an interpretation (Ochs, 1982). In accordance with social beliefs about status, adults in this culture do not modify their language for young children, even when the children have begun to talk. Pye (1986) studied the language addressed to several children ranging from 12 to 37 months of age in an Indian village in Guatemala. In this community, there is no concept of talking with children to stimulate their language developnent and there is minimal vocal interaction between infants and parents. Parents wait for a child's first words before conversing with him or her. The young child is most often ignored by the caretakers and conversation is oriented towards the interests of older children or adults. Pye observed no modification of intonation in the speech addressed to children, although there was some phonological simplification. With very few exceptions, the grammatical modifications in the language addressed to children were not simplifications. All three studies show that the type of language directed to children depends on cultural concepts about children and conventions for interacting with them; the child-directed speech modifications so widespread in western cultures are not universal.

Mere exposure to language is not sufficient to ensure that it is acquired; children will not acquire language just from watching television. The critical ingredient for language acquisition is exposure to a sufficient quantity of well-formed speech in situations in which meaning is comprehensible. Children are not thrown by linguistic difficulty per se. For instance, we have seen that some complicated structures provide children with critical information concerning function words. Furthermore, it has been experimentally demonstrated that increased levels of exposure to complicated grammatical structures may enhance their development. Finally, not all cultures provide modified input for young children and yet children in all cultures acquire language.

Such a conclusion suggests that we can assist children's language development very easily, simply by talking to them. If we genuinely wish to engage children in active conversation, then our attempts to communicate with them at their own level will produce modifications of our language that provide them with comprehensible and well-structured input. We can rely on children to do the rest of the work. They will analyse the grammatical information that we provide, focusing on the information relevant to the structures they are currently working on, and abstracting linguistic regularities from these. Our key role is to ensure that children are actively engaged in the conversation and that we are genuinely trying to communicate. This is often very difficult in situations where other children are clamouring for attention. It is our task to make the time and effort to ensure that each child in our care receives conversational attention.

References

Bates, E., Bretherton, I., Beeghly-Smith, M. & McNew, S. (1982) Social bases of language development: A reassessment. In H. W. Reese (ed.), *Advances in child development and behavior*. (Vol. 16, 7–75). New York: Academic Press.

Bates, E., Camaioni, L. & Volterra, V. (1975) The acquisition of performatives prior to speech. *Merrill-Palmer Quarterly, 21*, 205–36.

Bever, T. (1970) The cognitive basis for linguistic structures. In J. R. Hayes (ed.), *Cognition and the development of language*. (274–353). New York: Wiley.

Braine, M. D. S. (1976) Children's first word combinations. *Monographs of the Society for Research in Child Development*. Vol. 41, Serial No. 164.

Brown, R. W. (1973) *A first language*. Harvard, MA: Harvard University Press.

Chomsky, C. (1969) *The acquisition of syntax in children from 5 to 10*. Cambridge, MA: MIT Press.

Curtiss, S. (1977) *Genie: A psycholinguistic study of a modern-day 'wild child'*. New York: Academic Press.

Curtiss, S. (1981) Dissociations between language and cognition: Cases and implications. *Journal of Autism and Developmental Disorders, 11*, 15–30.

Davis, K. (1947) Final note on a case of extreme isolation. *American Journal of Sociology, 52*, 432–7.

Eilers, R., Gavin, W. & Wilson, W. (1979) Linguistic experience and phonemic perception in infancy: A cross-linguistic study. *Child Development, 50*, 14–18.

Eimas, P., Siqueland, E., Jusczyk, P. & Vigorito, J. (1971) Speech perception in infants. *Science, 171*, 303–18.

Feldman, H., Goldin-Meadow, S. & Gleitman, L. (1978) Beyond Herodotus: The creation of language by linguistically deprived deaf children. In A. Lock (ed.), *Action, gesture and symbol: The emergence of language* (351–414). London: Academic Press.

Gilbert, J. H. V. (1982) Babbling and the deaf child: A commentary on Lenneberg et al. (1965) and Lenneberg (1967). *Journal of Child Language, 9*, 511–15.

Gleitman, L. R., Newport, E. L. & Gleitman, H. (1984) The current status of the motherese hypothesis. *Journal of Child Language, 11*, 43–79.

Heath, S. B. (1983) *Ways with words*. Cambridge: Cambridge University Press.

Ingram, D. (1986) Phonological development: Production. In P. Fletcher & M. Garman (eds.), *Language acquisition*. (2 ed.) (233–9). Cambridge: Cambridge University Press.

Ingram, D. (1989) *First language acquisition: Method, description and explanation*. Cambridge: Cambridge University Press.

Ingram, D. (1991) An historical observation on 'Why "Mama" and "Papa"?' *Journal of Child Language, 18*, 711–13.

Matthei, E. H. (1989) Crossing boundaries: More evidence for phonological constraints on early multi-word utterances. *Journal of Child Language, 16*, 41–54.

Nelson, K. (1973) Structure and strategy in learning to talk.

Monographs of the Society for Research in Child Development. Vol. 38, Serial No. 149.

Nelson, K. E. (1977) Facilitating children's syntax acquisition. *Developmental Psychology, 13*, 101–7.

Newcomer, P. L. & Hammill, D. D. (1988) *Test of Language Development — Primary.* (2 ed.). Austin, TX: Pro-Ed.

Newport, E. L. (1990) Maturational constraints on language learning. *Cognitive Science, 14*, 11–28.

Ochs, E. (1982) Talking to children in Western Samoa. *Language in Society. 11*, 77–104.

Pye, C. (1986) Quiche Mayan speech to children. *Journal of Child Language, 13*, 85–100.

Rescorla, L. (1980) Overextensions in early language development. *Journal of Child Language,* 7, 321–35.

Sachs, J. & Truswell, L. (1978) Comprehension of two-word instructions by children in the one-word stage. *Journal of Child Language,* 5, 17–24.

Shvachkin, N. (1973) The development of phonemic speech perception in children. In C. A. Ferguson & D. Slobin (eds.), *Studies of child language development* (91–127). New York: Holt, Rinehart & Winston.

Stark, R. E. (1986) Prespeech segmental feature development. In P. Fletcher & M. Garman (eds.), *Language acquisition.* (2 ed.) (149–73). Cambridge: Cambridge University Press.

Templin, M. (1957) Certain language skills in children. *University of Minnesota Institute of Child Welfare Monograph Series 26.* Minneapolis: University of Minnesota Press.

Terrace, H. S., Pettito, L. A., Sanders, R. J. & Bever, T. G. (1979) Can an ape create a sentence? *Science, 206*, 891–902.

Thomson, J. R. & Chapman, R. S. (1976) Who is 'Daddy' revisited: The status of two-year-olds' overextended words in use and comprehension. *Journal of Child Language, 4*, 359–75.

Yamada, J. E. (1990) *Laura.* Cambridge, MA: MIT Press.

MOTOR DEVELOPMENT AND LEARNING IN CHILDREN

Carolyn O'Brien

Overview of motor development

I find the study of motor development an exciting process as some of the most obvious changes in behaviour in the early years are seen in the development of motor skills in infancy. At first the baby is relatively helpless and uses the few movement patterns that it has at birth, or develops soon after birth to survive. Yet within 12 to 18 months children can walk, manipulate objects and explore their environment (Gesell, 1973).

Have you ever wondered how babies develop motor skills or why they sit before they walk, or why they often fall over, or why they cannot grasp or let go of toys? In this chapter I will trace the changes in motor development after some of the processes that influence this progression have been identified. I will argue that attaining competence in motor skills is very important to the overall development of children. In the final section of the chapter I will discuss how to assist motor skill development in children and list some suitable activities.

Phases of motor control

Changes in movement behaviour can be thought of as progressing through three phases, each with distinct underlying processes. These phases are the sensory-motor, the perceptual-motor and the cognitive-motor phase.

Sensory-motor phase

The sensory-motor phase is an important phase in all animals. A kitten, for example, will play with its tail. It watches its tail and then catches and bites it. But, suddenly, this delightful play behaviour stops. I have often wondered why the behaviour occurs in the first place and what purpose it serves. My answer is that a kitten can move its tail almost automatically but is not receiving much sensory information about this movement, that is, it has low body/tail awareness. Because a kitten apparently cannot feel its tail, when it watches it moving it pounces on this 'object' and bites it. After repeating this behaviour for some weeks and receiving painful sensory information each time, a kitten becomes aware that its tail is part of its own body. Once this occurs, the behaviour is no longer repeated.

Children need sensory feedback from their bodies and their environment to acquire basic control of their bodies. Sensory-motor information is used and enhanced by children when they learn to sit, crawl and to control their balance. These skills represent basic control of movement and form the building blocks for locomotor and manipulative sequences of movement. To achieve these skills children rely on early reflex behaviour, internal and external sensory information and early movement patterns.

Perceptual-motor phase

Children and animals reach the perceptual-motor phase of development when they are able to consciously (cognitively) control their limbs, their balance and hand/eye or hand/paw coordination. Puppies seem to have a problem going down stairs and if they do, they certainly cannot control the speed of their descent so they often end up on some part of their body other than their paws. Such behaviour demonstrates that they have not achieved good perceptual-motor control over their movements.

Children in this perpetual-motor phase acquire sufficient knowledge and experience in movement situations to have developed body awareness, including the conscious (cognitive) internal awareness that the body has two sides (left and right) and that it can be moved in different

directions such as up, down, sideways, forwards and backwards. Children also develop spatial awareness in relation to their own bodies and to external objects. Moreover, they become more competent at visual-spatial awareness, thus enabling judgements to be made about speed and direction of moving objects and accurate manipulation of tools. Changes in the fundamental movement patterns also occur in this second phase because there is greater control of the limbs and postural stability as well as early control of the visual-spatial parameters of movement.

Cognitive-motor phase

When a cat can leap effortlessly onto the kitchen bench, a dog can go downstairs at a constant speed, or a young child learns how to play tennis, all of them are demonstrating that they have relatively advanced control over their movements. This third phase of motor development is demonstrated behaviourally by the acquisition of more complex movement skills. These involve the processing of relevant external environmental information, as well as controlling the spatial and temporal aspects of the response. Cognitive processes are used increasingly by children in their sport and recreational activities. For example, in order to intercept a moving ball children need to process complex visual information while at the same time achieving precise body control.

These three levels of motor control enable us to conceptualise that some different underlying processes are more important than others as we learn movement skills. The assumption is that there is a hierarchical progression from very elementary control over the body and its movements. Then children are able to combine many sources of sensory information and perform movement skills such as the fundamental movement patterns of walking, running, jumping, throwing and catching. Finally, they achieve advanced cognitive control over limb movements, and the spatial-temporal aspects of complex movements and sports skills.

Before the fundamental patterns are discussed, the next section will trace the sequence of motor development of normal babies and children before these patterns occur.

Progress of motor development

The foetus begins to move when it is only about 2 centimetres in length and only a few weeks old. These movements usually consist of the limbs being bent and moved in towards the body and the trunk curling forward (this is know as flexion). Some foetal movements involve stretching and straightening of the limbs and trunk (this is known as extension). After birth babies' movements are mainly directed towards survival, such as sucking when the side of the mouth is rubbed, grasping when the palm of the hand is touched, and blinking when something appears to be moving towards the face.

Reflexes

The early movements of newborns are known as reflexes because a fixed movement response (which babies cannot control) occurs to a stimulus, such as touch, sound or movement of the head. Although many reflex movements of the limbs are not used to achieve a specific goal, they do develop muscular strength and form neurological links which will be used later in more complex movements.

Some of the earliest reflexes enable newborns to suck, swallow, sneeze, turn their heads, support their own weight by hanging onto a rod, grasp objects and make alternate stepping and swimming movements. Reflex movements related to the position of the head also result in changes occurring in muscle tension in different parts of the body and so affect the position of the limbs and body. When the head is tipped forward, for example, the limbs bend and are moved in towards the body (flexion), but when the head is tipped backwards the limbs are straightened and moved out, away from the body (extension).

Older babies and toddlers spend a large amount of time trying to counteract the effect of gravity. One of the early signs of success in this is when babies can lift their heads up when lying face down. Babies progressively develop a series of reflexes which help them maintain postural stability and many of these need to develop before they can sit or stand.

In addition, reflexes such as the early grasp and release reflexes of newborn babies cause automatic patterns of finger movements which are incorporated into many more advanced skills. Some of these skills include the ability to grasp, manipulate and release objects, as well as the more advanced fine motor skills such as handwriting, typing and sewing (Pretchl, 1986; Twitchell, 1970).

What happens to these reflex movements as we grow older? It appears that many of the reflexes that control large and small body movements are incorporated into units of movement in some of our early walking patterns and hand and finger movements, while others assist in maintaining balance. The walking reflex is a good example of how these reflex movements are incorporated into movement skills. It has been shown, for example, that by regularly playing with babies in a specific manner, parents or caregivers can accelerate the appearance of walking. This type of play involves holding the baby under the armpits so that she or he is in a standing position, with feet flat on a supporting surface but not fully weight bearing. In this position the baby automatically performs alternate stepping actions (i.e. the walking reflex).

If the walking reflex is practised once a day between four and 12 weeks of age, then the reflex movement will continue rather than supposedly disappear at 12 weeks. As a result, in babies who received constant practice of this reflex the cyclic stepping action will become part of their movement repertoire, so that they walk at an earlier age than babies who have not had regular practice of this reflex (Zelazo, 1983). Similarly it has been shown that if visually attractive objects are placed within reach, visually guided reaching for objects will occur at about four and a half months of age. Again, this reaching behaviour is earlier in babies who are provided with an enriched visual environment (White, 1970).

It appears then, that if some reflex patterns and early motor responses are practised regularly, they are directly incorporated into early movement patterns and then into more complex movements as automated units of movement (Wolf, 1986). These automated units of movement form the basic building blocks of our complex and skilled movements.

You may also be interested in how babies use their movement patterns so that they can move around. Early movements based on reflexes can be used to achieve a sequence of movement, each one starting in a specific position such as sitting or crawling. An example here is the behaviour that leads to walking. At first children start in the sitting position, then proceed to crawling. This is followened by mastering a semi-upright stance with both hands and feet on the floor, to holding onto and cruising around furniture, to a tentative stance on the feet and finally to the first unsteady walking steps (Shirley, 1971). Although these movements are based on reflex movements once they are acquired, they appear to be used by infants to achieve specific goals.

We could argue, therefore, that early movement patterns form a link between an inability to control movement and the conscious control of skilled movements. Additionally, in many instances they are the source of the basic movement patterns used as automatic units of movements in more complex fundamental movement patterns like walking, running, jumping, catching and throwing.

Fundamental movement patterns mark the next level of developmental gross motor milestones. Children need to achieve and refine these movements so they can play and learn games and movement skills they will use everyday.

In learning these movement skills they also are learning more about their bodies and so how to control their movements better.

Fundamental movement patterns

The sequence of changes within each of the fundamental movement skills of walking, running, jumping, catching and throwing are called within task (intratask) movement sequences. These changes, which are partly due to increased maturation and experience, have been shown to be similar in the majority of children in regard to the refinement of limb and body movements (Rarick, 1982). The next section will describe some of the changes that occur in each of the fundamental movement patterns. (For a more detailed description of these movement patterns and extra references, see O'Brien, 1991).

Walking

How would you describe the walking pattern? A typical definition is that it is forward movement achieved by the legs in which one foot is in continuous contact with the ground. The age at which children begin to walk depends on the maturation of the nervous system and balance mechanisms and strength of the muscles, especially in the lower limbs and back. Children who have more developed neuro-muscular coordination acquire the motor development milestones of sitting, crawling and cruising and can walk before children who were less advanced at the same age. Other factors such as physique and weight influence the age at which children first start walking, which ranges from nine months to 18 months. Being able to walk shows that a child has begun to control his or her body and limbs while moving.

At the initial level of walking poor balance causes infants to be unsteady and to fall easily. To compensate for this infants usually walk with their legs wide apart and hold their arms out sideways, a little like a tightrope walker. They also appear to be very rigid, their movements are jerky and irregular, they sway sideways, have heavy flat foot contact with the ground and they bend their knees up high as they step. Look at the diagrams of the characteristic walking pattern at this level of development.

Progression to the next level, at about 19 months to two years (level 2 walking), is characterised by a less rigid body and limbs, and an overall smoother action. The feet are usually placed apart at about shoulder width. The heel of the front foot contacts the ground first and the weight is transferred to the toes before that leg is lifted off the ground. This results in a smoother transfer of body weight, so that the movement is now less jerky. The arms are dropped down by the side, the upper limbs now not being needed to assist the action of walking.

The next level of walking (level 3) appears between four and five years of age. It is characterised by a smooth transfer of weight from heel-to-toe contact, the arms are used in the walking action, although one arm is generally swung more than the other. The child rarely stumbles and there is consistent stride length with each step.

In the mature phase from seven years of age (level 4), walking is characterised by a smooth rhythmical action. There is consistent movement of the lower limbs with each step. Both the arms and legs move in opposition to each other, which assists in maintaining stability. The feet are placed at less than a shoulder width apart.

Now that you have read the description and studied the diagrams of the characteristic changes in the walking pattern, try to observe how children of different ages walk and identify the different levels of the walking pattern.

Figure 5.1: Developmental levels of walking.

Running

How do we distinguish between the movement patterns of running and walking, since running is similar to walking in terms of the limb pattern and the transfer of weight from one foot to the other? One distinct characteristic of running is that there is an airborne period during the leg cycle when both feet are off the ground. This is why running can be thought of as a series of jumps.

Although the limb coordination for running and walking is similar, greater strength is needed in the legs for running as the limbs have to be moved at increased speed so the body is propelled forward and remains airborne. In addition, the balance mechanisms must be developed to a point where a person can maintain balance during the airborne phase of the cycle, then transfer weight smoothly to.the forward leg.

When an action similar to running first occurs, usually between 18 months and two years, the infant holds the body upright with the arms sideways or held straight beside the body. The limbs move faster than in walking but there is no airborne phase. The feet contact the ground in a heavy flat foot action, the body sways sideways and there is a very wide base of support. Children stumble and fall frequently in the early phases of running.

At two to three years of age (level 2), there is more consistency in the action of the legs, with a strong push off from the back leg and greater knee bend in the forward leg. This results in a faster and longer stride length with a brief airborne or non-support phase. The arms are held at about waist height, with some elbow bend and some swing forward with each leg. In this and the next level of running children have difficulty in stopping, turning and dodging.

The next level (level 3), appears between three to five years and is characterised by a more efficient bent knee action and heel-to-toe transfer of weight when each foot contacts the ground. Both arms are swung backwards and forwards in the opposite direction to the leg on the same side of the body. This action counteracts the action of the

Level 1

Level 2

Level 3

Level 4

Figure 5.2: Developmental levels of running.

legs. There is also some forward lean of the trunk as well as a longer airborne phase, all of which show that the child can control balance better than at the earlier levels.

In the mature level of running from seven years of age, the body has a slight forward lean and the back leg is straight and at an angle of 45 degrees before it pushes off. This is followed by a high knee raise on the forward leg. The arms counteract the leg action and are swung backwards and forwards with a bent elbow.

Jumping (from a stationary position)

Jumping differs from walking and running because in the mature phase both upper and lower limbs move together to counterbalance the body's forward and backward movements. Additionally, the body is airborne for a much longer period than for running. Greater demand is placed on the balance mechanisms because the body must first be maintained in a balanced position while airborne, then balance must be maintained while the body position is changed in preparation for, and on, landing.

At about 30 to 36 months of age children begin to experiment with variations of jumping. They may jump up and down, along the ground, or over low obstacles. The initial movement pattern which develops into the recognised long jump pattern occurs when a child, for example, steps off a box with one foot and places it on a lower surface, while still keeping the other foot on the box. In other words, the child is stepping down off something. This early pattern is followed by coordinating a two-foot take-off, followed by a very brief airborne period and an unpredictable and often uncomfortable landing. The arms are not used to assist the action or for balance.

In the next level (level 2) between 30 to 36 months the child assumes a squat position, with some lean forward of the upper body, and when jumping off a box the body is projected relatively straight up in the air rather than outwards. A characteristic movement pattern of the arms

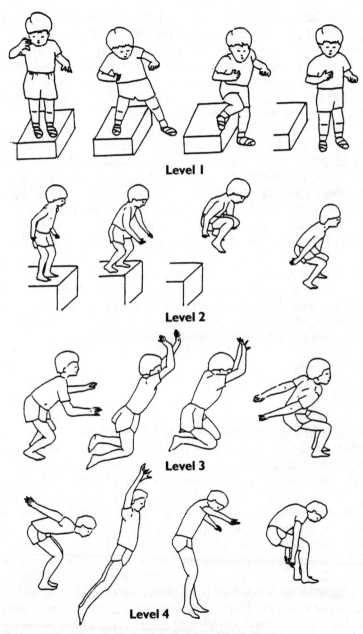

Figure 5.3: Developmental levels of jumping.

occurs at this level. In most children once the body is projected by the legs into the air, the head is tossed back, the arms are bent and held back behind the body in what is known as a 'birdwing' pattern. Some children land without falling. Note too, that even though both feet are used in the take-off phase, each leg position may differ in mid-air. Children may land on one or two feet.

In level 3 jumping (four to six years), the arms and legs are controlled better as a total movement. Both arms and head position are varied to help maintain balance. The child usually jumps from two feet and lands on two feet. In most children the arms are swung forward first, then up above the head and backwards during the landing.

The mature jump which usually appears from seven years is characterised by coordination between the actions of the arms, legs and head. Before take-off the trunk is inclined forward at about 45 degrees to the legs, which are in a deep squat position. After take-off the legs are held out straight at about 45 degrees to the ground during the airborne phase, then they are bent and kicked backwards to obtain the greatest distance before landing.

Catching

When did you learn to catch a ball? Although children can reach for and grasp objects by about the end of their first year, they usually cannot catch a large moving object until they are about three years old. Catching can be defined as an action of the hands and upper body to stop an object that is travelling through the air. The catching pattern in young children varies depending on the speed, direction and size of the ball. Young children are able to catch a large, light ball thrown slowly more easily than a smaller faster ball.

Children between two to three years generally make no response to a ball thrown at them, unless they are told how to hold their arms. If the ball lands somewhere on their arms it is immediately trapped against the body by a scooping action. This is why this first phase of catching is known as the robot phase, since the catching action only occurs if the ball touches the child's arms. At this level there is little or no visual tracking of the ball. The stance adopted is wide and throughout the catch the feet and legs are not moved.

In the next level of catching (level 2), children aged between three and a half and five years make a distinctive clapping action when the ball comes near them. The feet are still held in a stationary position and the catching pattern consists of a clapping action with the arms. There may be some knee bend, the eyes are shut and the head is often turned sideways before the ball reaches the hands. The turning of the head and the closed eyes is known as the avoidance response which usually is no longer present after about five years. However, I have found from personal experience as a doubles player in tennis, that it is worthwhile hitting a hard, fast ball at shoulder height, or above, at your opponent on the other side of the net. This shot often produces the avoidance response and you will usually win the point. Children who have attained this second level of catching can catch a medium size ball thrown about chest height and at moderate speed.

The first anticipatory responses to the ball are seen in the next level (level 3). The hands and fingers form a cup before the ball reaches the hands. Children at this level, who are usually aged between five and seven, now move their legs as part of the catching action so they may move sideways, forwards or backwards to catch a ball.

In the mature form of catching, which occurs from about seven years, children move with outstretched arms and hands ready to intercept the ball. As the ball is caught there is a backwards or sideways movement of the arms and shoulders in line with the flight of the ball which absorbs the impact force on catching.

Throwing

Children start to practise movements used in throwing whenever they hold some projectile material. For instance, much to the despair of most parents, they start dropping, then projecting unwanted food, cups and plates from their high chair. Parents who want their children to earn a fortune in later life as professional tennis players should allow this behaviour to continue, as they are practising a very complex skill which is vital to their sporting success!

Children develop the ability to voluntarily release objects towards the end of their first year. Subsequent development of more mature patterns is partly dependent on maturation and practice. The research literature shows that boys have a more mature throw than girls and can throw further and faster at all ages. The reason for this finding is controversial. It has been proposed that our culture encourages practice of these skills in males, and it has been claimed that males are biologically superior in strength of the upper limbs. What is your opinion? (This may make a good research topic and class discussion.)

The first true throw is based on the pattern infants use to release objects. The arm and wrist must be fully extended so that the fingers can straighten to release the ball. This pattern may occur in either the underarm or the overarm position. In the initial overarm throwing pattern children aged about two to three years face the target, with feet together. The arm is lifted at the elbow so that the forearm is at rightangles to the upper arm and from this position the arm is extended and the ball released.

The pattern of the next level of throwing (level 2) is similar to the earlier level, in that the throwing arm is the main part of the action. The throwing pattern of children aged between three and a half and five is more efficient than at the previous level as the trunk rotates on the backswing and the ball is swung through at head height (or above) before it is released. Like the earlier pattern, the feet and legs are not used to assist the throw except for some knee bend during the trunk rotation and arm swing.

The most characteristic action in the next level (level 3) is a stepping action by the leg on the same side as the throwing arm. Children aged between five and seven use variations on the previously described upper arm patterns.

In the mature level (from seven years), children face

Level 1

Level 2

Level 3

Level 4

Figure 5.4: Developmental levels of catching.

side on to the target. At the start of the throw the weight is rocked onto the back foot, the throwing arm is swung backward with marked trunk rotation, while the elbow is bent at rightangles. The throw forward starts with a step forward on the front foot (opposite foot to the throwing arm), the trunk is rotated towards the front foot and the arm is swung forward at rightangles and straightened prior to the release of the object.

Now that you have read about the fundamental movement patterns of walking, running, jumping, catching and throwing, try to observe some young children and see what other types of movement patterns they use in everyday life and play. See if you can place these movement patterns into a developmental sequence. Have you ever wondered why these movements change? I will attempt to identify why some of these changes occur in the following section.

Changes in the fundamental movement patterns

Changes in the movement patterns for locomotion and manipulation are due to children's increased body awareness and cognitive control over their bodies. This in turn allows them greater control to meet environmental demands. The developmental status of children, as well as early aspects of cognitive control of movement, can be traced by a close examination of the progression of the fundamental movement patterns. Between toddlers' movement patterns and the advanced levels of walking, running, jumping, catching and throwing, many changes take place. Some of these changes can be explained in terms of increased development of postural stability, increased control over use of the limbs and in the ability to control and learn new movements. Each of these processes will be discussed.

Postural stability

Postural stability refers to the ability to maintain balance in sitting, or standing (static balance), or when the body is moving (dynamic balance). In each of the higher levels of the movement patterns of walking, running and jumping, there is evidence of increased postural stability. In walking, for example, children start with a wide base of support which progressively decreases in width. Dynamic postural stability is well demonstrated in running, when the characteristic movement changes from one foot in continuous contact with the ground to an increasingly longer airborne phase. Similarly, in jumping the pattern changes from a 'step jump' to a longer airborne phase during which there is differing alignment of the body together with head adjustments in order to maintain stability.

Limb control

Another important change in movement behaviour is seen in the way the limbs are controlled. In running, walking and jumping the lower limb movements are more controlled than the upper limb movements, whereas in throwing and catching there is greater control over the upper limbs than the lower limbs. In each case the other limbs are hardly used, for example, there is very little arm movement in the early levels of walking and running and there is a lack of lower limb movement in the early levels of throwing and catching. Greater control of the limbs down one side of the body (unilateral) is evident in the one-foot take off in jumps; the leg and arm moved on the same side of the body in the third level of throwing; and the marked swing of one arm more than the other in the level three walking and running patterns. Contralateral limb control, in which the arm is swung on the opposite side to the forward foot, is present in the mature walking and running patterns.

Motor learning and control

There are two approaches to how we learn and control movements. One is known as motor learning, which stresses the importance of sensory information and central representation in memory of movement. The other is motor control which attempts to identify the processes other than sensory representation of movement which result in holistic control of movements. We will look at each of these major cognitive-motor theories.

Motor learning

Motor learning theorists are of the opinion that sensory information is very important to our ability to learn and control movement, because it provides the information for central representation of movement in motor memory which in turn results in more effective movements. When a person is learning a new skill, for example, her or his primary concern is acquiring the units of movement needed to perform it. Practice leads to refinement of the skill. In these early stages of acquiring motor skills attention can only be paid to a small aspect of the task, which makes it impossible to monitor all aspects of the skill. A good example here is when you learnt to drive a car. It took so much of your attention to change gears that you were usually unaware of other motorists and pedestrians! Your driving instructor, however, was very aware of your inadequacies and corrected your errors by using the dual control system. This is why parents often refuse to teach their children to drive, or if they do most lessons finish in an unfriendly manner. The child may think he or she is doing very well, but it is only the parent's concern for the child's safety that stops her or him from leaping out of the car!

Because performing newly learnt skills requires quite a lot of attention, there is a tendency to reduce the complexity of movements by reducing the number of components that make them up and even the amount of flexion or rotation of the joints involved. Well learnt skills, in contrast, can be performed with low attentional demand because it is feasible that some aspects can be performed virtually automatically, which means that far more complex movements can be performed and still not take up all a person's attention.

Some aspects of a motor skill, like driving or handwriting, always need ongoing monitoring, so they will always require some attention. In running, for instance, once a child is competent in the basic movements, the ongoing sequence only requires a moderate amount of attention to scan the environment. A great deal of attention need only be paid when the running surface changes, or the action has to be modified. How a movement such as running is stored in motor memory and how the action is formulated and performed has been explained by motor learning theorists under the concept of a generalised motor program (see Schmidt, 1986).

Generalised motor programs are assumed to contain prestructured commands for many movements, with specifications to vary them. The parameters that Schmidt (1988) identified, which are used to vary a particular class of movement skill, are the overall duration parameter, overall force parameter, muscle selection parameter and a spatial parameter. Some of these parameters he considered were invariant (i.e., they determined the unchanging features of a movement skill), while others he classified as variant (i.e., they are used when changes need to be made to a movement skill).

Walking, for example, has both invariant and variant

Level 1

Level 2

Level 3

Level 4

Figure 5.5: Developmental levels of throwing.

features. In walking there is 50 per cent phasing between the alternate actions of the lower limbs (Clark & Whitall, 1989), which is an invariant feature of this movement skill. Yet by changing the overall duration parameter, the entire action can be sped up or slowed down, while still maintaining the 50 per cent overall phasing between the lower limbs. In handwriting the shape of the letters form the invariant feature of the movement but if the overall force parameter is increased the letters will be larger and if it is decreased they will be smaller. If the muscle selection parameter were varied then letters with similar shape to those written by hand could be produced by muscles in the foot, or the mouth. The spatial parameter is used when throwing a ball at a target, for while the muscular pattern of the throwing movement remains the same, the direction of the ball can be changed by differing the angle of the shoulder, wrist and elbow joints (Schmidt, 1988).

The theory of generalised motor programs helps to explain how new movements can be performed and how well-learnt movements can be changed. It is also necesssary, however, to try to explain how we actually learn movements. Once again we will turn to Schmidt (1988) and to his motor schema theory for a hypothetical explanation. According to schema theory when a movement (generated by a generalised motor program) is performed, four aspects of that movement are temporarily stored in memory. These aspects are (a) body position and environmental aspects relevant to performing the movement; (b) storage of the parameters that were used to perform the movement; (c) the outcome of performing the movement stored as knowledge of results; and (d) the sensory feel of the movement while it was being performed. Once relationships between the stored information are formed these are stored in memory as recall and recognition schemas. In recall schema the relationships between the outcomes of the movement and the parameters used to perform the movement are stored in memory. In recognition schema the relationships between the initial conditions and the sensory feel of the movement are stored. According to Schmidt's motor schema theory, 'we learn skills by learning rules about the functioning of our bodies, forming relationships between how our muscles are activated, what they actively do and how these actions feel' (Schmidt, 1988, p. 488).

Not all aspects of a movement skill are best explained by generalised motor programs and motor schemas. This is because performance of a complex movement sequence would take up too much attentional space in memory. Some aspects of this type of movement then, are best explained by the action theory of motor control, which will be discussed in a later section. We must first identify differences between adults and children in motor learning.

Motor learning in children

It has been suggested that as children mature they become better at processing sensory information, and it is this factor which causes some of the age-related changes in motor development (Thomas & Gallagher, 1986). The reason why children appear slower at performing many movement tasks is because they have memory deficits in comparison with adults. There is evidence that children's memory systems operate more slowly in the perceptual mechanism, in which sensory information is translated into internal representations of a movement and where children have been shown to have less ability to discriminate between various levels of input of sensory information (Thomas, 1984).

Evidence also exists that encoding, rehearsal and organisation of all motor memory functions is less effective in children under seven than in 11 year olds, who are in turn less effective than adults. It has been shown, however, that children can be helped to learn a specific skill more effectively if they are provided with the strategy to help them remember the components which make it up (Thomas, 1984). In addition, because information in memory is derived from experience, in order to improve children's movement skills it is very important to provide a wide base of movement experiences for young children. This implies that it is better to provide general movement experiences for children than to only teach them specific skills.

Deficits in memory have important implications for the speed with which children can process movement-related information and for the number of components of a task which they can combine into a smooth sequence. One of the logical consequences of improved information processing ability in older children is that they become better at learning and controlling ongoing movement sequences and so are able to perform and learn more complex sequences of skilled movements.

Motor control

Motor control processes which are of particular importance to the understanding of skilled movement behaviour in adults have been identified as motor constancy, uniqueness and modifiability of action, and the stability and consistency of action. (See Schmidt, 1988, for more details.)

Motor constancy is the term used for achievement of a movement goal using different combinations of muscles and units of actions. For instance, you can sign your name with your dominant hand, with your non-dominant hand, with the pen in your mouth or with your feet and toes like some disabled people. Your signature will probably be most legible when you use your dominant hand but the important thing is that once you have learnt a movement pattern it can be achieved using many different combinations of muscles.

Uniqueness of action refers to the ability to initiate many types of movements to solve a movement problem. For example, try to imagine that you and a group of friends are out bushwalking and you have suddenly come round a bend in the track to find that the only way across a deep creek is via a narrow log. Try to work out how many ways you could get across the creek. Depending on the width of the log, I would treat it like a balance beam and walk across, or I would crawl across. Alternatively, I would straddle the log and grip it with my hands and legs and move slowly across like that. If I did not feel that any of these positions were safe, I would search up and down the creek for an easier way to walk or maybe swim across it. Remember that the movement goal is to cross the creek. It does not matter how this goal is achieved. Indeed, if there were a few creeks to cross on the bushwalk a different way may be chosen to cross each one of them.

Despite being able to generate novel movements to achieve a movement goal in highly learnt movement skills, such as a serve in tennis or letters in handwriting, the more skilled a person becomes the greater the consistency of the muscle contractions and the units of movements that are used each time he or she performs a specific skill. Some examples of the effect of these motor control processes can be seen as children gain greater contol of the walking, running, jumping, catching and throwing movements. Uniqueness of action is well demonstrated when a young child attempts to throw a tennis ball at a target on the wall. The child may hit the target by throwing the ball using an underarm action, or various levels of maturity of the overarm throw. Another concept, that of adaptability of action, is demonstrated when a child is able to run successfully over different ground surfaces without stumbling or falling over. Adaptability is also demonstrated by children when they can catch balls thrown at different speeds and heights.

Finally, greater consistency in controlling the force and timing of movement is evident in the progression of the early walking or running patterns. At first these movement patterns are characterised by jerky and irregular limb movements, which progressively become smoother and more regular.

We have examined progression of large body movement patterns so far in this chapter. It is now time to look at changes in the small movement patterns that we make with our hands and wrists as these contribute to the fine motor manual skills that we use every day.

Fine motor development in children

At the same time as all the changes are occurring in young children's large muscle movements, their fine motor manual skills (movements of the hands and fingers) are also undergoing marked changes. Children at about 15 months of age, for example, will have the basic motor patterns of reach, grasp, release and manipulation of objects that they can hold in their hands. These movement patterns are not yet fully developed, but they do form the building blocks for all later fine motor manual skills.

Fine wrist and finger movement patterns are the forerunners of all adult manual skills, many of which involve the use of tools and implements. This is why it is so important for young children to be provided with an environment which encourages them to practise by exploring different textures, shapes and sizes of objects and to experiment with various age-appropriate objects and tools. But before a child can be provided with developmentally appropriate activities, one needs to know her or his developmental level. For this purpose, the early development of finger and hand movements is outlined in the following section. (See O'Brien & Ziviani, 1991, for greater detail.)

Early reflex movements of the arms and fingers

Infants' earliest movement patterns include a reflex response to the arm being tugged upwards which causes the fingers, wrist and elbow of that arm to bend and create a downward pull of the arm. Other responses include the fingers bending when the palm of the hand is touched near the thumb and index finger. About a month later children will grasp objects firmly but will not be able to release them. All these early hand and finger reflexes occur in response to touch and are not controlled by infants. The effect of these hand reflexes can be readily observed in young babies.

At about five months infants are able to control their hand and finger movements, usually at first to reach out and grasp some visually attractive object. These early voluntarily controlled movements are often inefficient arm swipes followed by a total grasp with all the fingers to trap the object against the palm, but without thumb opposition. Such actions are followed by the ability to grasp objects in the hand with the thumb pressing in the opposite direction to the fingers (this is 'thumb opposition'). Next infants are able to grasp objects and hold them in the palm or fingers by pressing the thumb in the opposite direction to the fingers (thumb opposition), so that the object is trapped in the palm (palmar grasp). The palmar grasp allows children to hold heavy objects for the first time. A progression from this type of grasp is when the fingers can be used independently from the hand (hand grasp), then three or four fingers can be used. Progressive maturity of the grasp pattern sees the appearance of the superior palm grasp, forefinger grasp and finally the pincer grasp, in which the index finger and the thumb are used when grasping.

Grasp, release and manipulation actions

As adults we have variations of power grasps in which heavy and large objects are held using a modification of the toddler grasp, which traps objects against mainly the palm by using thumb opposition and gripping the object with all or most of the fingers.

Babies develop the ability to voluntarily grasp objects at about five months of age (primitive squeeze grasp), but they find it very difficult to voluntarily let go of an object until they are about ten months old. Before this they release objects by putting them from one hand to the other, then by pressing the hand hard against some surface which makes it easier for them to stretch their fingers and so release the object. When children can voluntarily

Superior palm grasp
Superior palm or inferior scissor grasp approximately 32 weeks.

Hand grasp
Hand or radial palmar grasp approximately 28–32 weeks.

Palmar grasp
Palmar or squeeze grasp approximately 24–8 weeks.

Superior forefinger grasp
Forefinger or neat pincer grasp approximately 44–60 weeks.

Primitive squeeze grasp
Primitive squeeze/grasp approximately 20–4 weeks.

Forefinger grasp
Inferior forefinger or radial digital grasp approximately 36 weeks.

Figure 5.6: Developmental levels of grasping, five to twelve months.

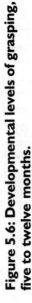

let go (release objects) they appear to enjoy experimenting with dropping and throwing their food, toys and just about anything they can reach.

Once children become proficient at grasping and releasing objects they are able to manipulate them. Early manipulation of food, toys and implements usually consists of mouthing, later shaking and banging and then shifting from hand to hand. These three basic manual patterns of grasp, release and manipulation are the building blocks for all adult tool use and fine motor manual skills.

Development is so rapid once children have acquired these basic grasp, release and manipulation movements that somewhere between three and five years they are able to do such things as build with blocks, and manipulate eating utensils, crayons and paint brushes. They also learn how to cut, paste, hammer and thread objects with some proficiency. When children start school they are taught handwriting, which is an important fine motor manual skill.

Handwriting

Handwriting is one manual skill that children in their early school years spend a great deal of time on mastering. It is a very complex skill requiring not only fine motor manual control, but also cognitive input in letter recognition and good hand-eye coordination. In the following description I will concentrate on the physical process that children undergo when learning to write.

The first process is not really handwriting, in fact, it is what we often call scribbling. Scribbling enables infants to learn how to make basic shapes such as circles, crosses and rectangles which they will use when they learn letters. Children also need to be able to see and recognise letters. Once they start copying letters they begin to store these shapes in memory and to compare what they have as a model of a letter with what they are writing. This is why it is very important to provide a correct model of the letters

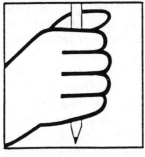

Palmar grasp

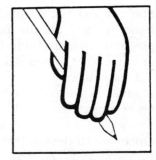

Incomplete tripod

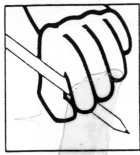

Tripod posture

Figure 5.7: Developmental levels of holding a pencil.

and the desired style in these early phases of learning. Children also need practice in controlling the force and timing of the movements they make.

Part of being able to control the force and timing of writing movements is learning to control the pencil. Young children hold the crayon or pencil against their palm in a fisted type grasp at the top of the writing implement (palmar grasp). Such a grasp only allows them to make large, forceful movements. Next they assume a grasp on the lower part of the writing implement, holding it with fairly stiff thumb, middle and index fingers (incomplete tripod). This grasp allows them to make wrist movements, but they still cannot make highly coordinated finger movements and so are unable to produce small letters. Finally, children should be able to hold the pencil in a relaxed manner with the thumb, middle and index fingers and the hand resting on the page (tripod grasp). This type of position enables children to make highly coordinated finger and wrist movements.

I have briefly described the progression of fine motor manual skills and an advanced skill, handwriting. Start observing children while they play and see what level of development they have reached. Note what interests them. Once you understand the normal developmental progression you will have the knowledge to devise developmentally appropriate activities to help improve children's fine motor manual skills. Similarly, you will have the background knowledge and understanding to improve their gross motor skills.

Activity ideas

In this section I will outline some activities designed to help young children become more competent in both gross and fine motor skills. You will also have your own ideas derived from what you did and liked as a child, what you have observed in young children, and what you have read.

Activities for gross motor development

It is advisable for people working with young children to provide wide experience in the early developmental milestones such as sitting, crawling and standing. Games such as 'What's the Time Mr Wolf?', hopscotch and handball, enable children to practise more advanced movement patterns. These types of activities should be followed by teaching them games and sports skills, as this helps them to develop more advanced levels of these skills. While providing these experiences activities which improve children's balance control and movement awareness should be incorporated, because these contribute to improved body awareness. I have included ideas to improve both balance and movement awareness, first by increasing sensory input with movement and then activities which will help children to learn and control their movements. The basic activities are suitable for toddlers and older more immature children, while the advanced activities are suitable for older and more mature children.

Children's ability to control their movements depends on their balance, first in relatively static situations, like sitting, and then in dynamic situations like running or jumping. They also need to improve their body awareness by increasing sensory input to joints and muscles as well as practising general body and limb coordination.

Balance activities

The sensory awareness of good balance relies on information from vision, from the muscles and joints (proprioception) and from the inner ear (vestibular). Many activities that you and even your parents did as children provided these sources of sensory information. Some common sensory type activities are listed below.

Basic balance activities

- swinging on swings or tyres
- sliding down slippery slides
- rolling down a slope
- swinging on monkey bars
- riding tricycles and scooters.

More advanced balance activities

- walking on a swinging bridge
- jumping on jouncing boards

- walking along lines on the ground
- walking on stilts made of cans (e.g. large coffee cans)
- walking forward, sideways and backwards on a balance beam
- walking up and down an inclined board
- stepping over obstacles placed on a balance beam.

Body awareness

To improve body awareness (proprioception) children should be encouraged to participate in activities which increase the load on the joints, particularly in the upper and lower limbs. They should also learn many different games to develop their movement skills and body awareness. The reason for this is that games often incorporate basic movement patterns in interesting ways, in addition to improving general coordination. In addition, many games encourage practice of the fundamental movement patterns of throwing, catching and hitting.

Upper limb activities

- hanging by the arms from bars or horizontal ladders
- performing wheelbarrows and animal walks
- children pulling themselves along a board or a slippery surface
- climbing or swinging on ladders, ropes or monkey bars.

Lower limb activities

- jumping on tyre tubes, or over low obstacles or ladders
- running around a large area
- hopping, skipping or galloping through an obstacle course
- moving to music.

General coordination activities

- solving foot and hand puzzles marked on the ground

- following the leader
- playing games such as 'statues' and 'What's the time Mr Wolf?'
- moving like an animal e.g. duck walks, kangaroo hops
- playing 'Simon Says'
- copying another person's movements.

Hand-eye coordination activities

- throwing bean bags at a rebounder (i.e. a mini trampoline)
- throwing bean bags or sock balls into large receptacles
- rolling and chasing hoops down a slope
- dodging soft balls
- playing with a ball in a stocking which is attached to a ceiling or support.

Fine motor manual activities

For success in fine motor manual activities children must be skilled in both power and precision grasps. These are based on the early finger and wrist movements of babies and toddlers. Children need to build on these early movements, but they cannot do this until they develop strong finger and thumb opposition. Any other changes in hand and finger patterns are due to learning new skills which depend on the acquisition of new movement patterns. The activity ideas listed below are grouped into four levels according to the difficulty of the movement to be performed.

Level 1 — for children aged to about 18 months

Children try to grasp objects that attract them from four to five months of age. It is important that as soon as children show an interest in the outside world they are encouraged to play with objects that stimulate the sensory areas of touch, vision, hearing and movement. They should also be provided with toys and taught simple games that help them to use a wide range of hand and finger movements. Suitable toys and activities include:

- mobiles placed above their cot that have a variety of shapes and colours
- game 'this little piggy went to market'
- feeling different materials such as satin, towelling and wool
- feeling opposites such as soft/hard and warm/cold
- water play
- sand play
- squeezing foam rubber filled with water
- squeezing foil, paper or plastic (always under supervision)
- dough play
- throwing or dropping a pom pom which has a bell in it or soft toys.

Level 2 — about 18 months to three and a half years

Children by this age should have developed basic grasp, release and manipulation patterns, so activities at this level aim at making them proficient in the elementary use of tools. Toys and experiences which will encourage them in this include:

- finger painting
- scribbling and drawing with crayons of various thicknesses
- tearing and pasting paper to make collages
- finger puppets
- screwing and unscrewing lids on jars

- picking up objects with tongs, tweezers and scissors
- squeezing activities using pegs and eye droppers
- threading objects such as macaroni
- building using wooden blocks
- doing puzzles.

Level 3 — three and a half to five years

Children by about this age should have acquired basic manipulation of objects and tools. They should now be encouraged to develop fine motor manual skills by experimenting with many types of implements including musical instruments, commercial construction sets, puppets, crayons, pencils and paint brushes. They should also continue to do some of the activities listed in the previous level.

Level 4 — five to eight years

By this age children should be competent in using a number of tools and implements. They should therefore have the basic movement patterns they need for learning crafts, art and handwriting. It is important that children have good control over the implement they are presently using before they are expected to learn more precise and complex fine motor manual skills. The following discussion will be limited to the steps required to learn handwriting.

At first children should be encouraged to experiment with scribbling, drawing and painting. When they are ready to write letters, models of what they are trying to produce need to be provided. Children can try forming letters in finger paint, on blackboards and in sand, as well as on paper. It is a good idea for children to decide themselves how to improve their early efforts by comparing these against desired work and discussing them with the teacher or caregiver. From a motor learning point of view it is also better that they produce the letters from the memory of a model, rather than trace them. Children need a lot of practice in order to control the force they use when writing and to form legible letters, and they need to be able to do both these things before they are encouraged to write more quickly. When teaching writing you should also make sure that children maintain a good sitting posture and hold their pen or pencil properly.

Conclusion

The development of motor skill competency is important because it enables children to perform everyday tasks such as feeding and dressing themselves as well as to acquire more advanced skills which they need as they grow older for school, general living, work, sport, recreation and leisure.

References

Gesell, A. (1973) *The First Five Years of Life*. London: Methuen.

Halverson, H. M. (1931) An experimental study of prehension in infants by means of systematic cinema records. *Genetic Psychology Monographs*, 107–285.

O'Brien, C. C. (1991) *Motor Development and the Preschool Child*. Brisbane: Department of Education.

O'Brien, C. C. & Ziviani, J. (1991) *Movement and the Young Child*. Brisbane: Department of Education.

Prechtl, H. F. R. (1986) Prenatal motor development. In M. G. Wade and H. T. A. Whiting (eds.), *Motor Development in Chil-*

dren: Aspects of Coordination and Control (53–64). Dordrecht: Martinus Nijhoff Publishing.

Schmidt, R. A. (1988) *Motor Control and Learning*. Illinois: Human Kinetics.

Shirley, M. M. (1971) *The first two years*. Minneapolis: University of Minnesota Press.

Touwen, B. C. L. (1976) *Neurological Development in Infancy*. London: William Heinemann.

Twitchell, T. E. (1970) Reflex mechanisms and the development of prehension. In K. J. Connolly (ed.), *Mechanisms of Motor Skill Development* (25–45). London: Academic Press.

White, B. L. (1970) Experience and the development of motor mechanisms in infancy. In K. J. Connolly (ed.), *Mechanisms of Motor Skill Development* (95–133). London: Academic Press.

Zelazo, P. R. (1983) The development of walking: New findings on old assumptions. *Journal of Motor Behavior*, 2, 99–137.

ARTISTIC DEVELOPMENT AND LEARNING: AN INTEGRATION OF PROCESSES FOR YOUNG CHILDREN

Susan Wright

I t would be very difficult to imagine a society without the arts. Since humans first gathered in groups to live, life has been defined, celebrated, preserved and rejuvenated through artistic expression. The rock and cave paintings throughout Australia and Norway, as well as the paintings in the caves of Lascaux in Southern France, bear witness to the importance of visual artistic expression in handing down cultural traditions from one generation to the next. People from many cultures have also shared knowledge, understanding and mutual concerns through storytelling, dance and song. For all groups throughout history, the arts have been and remain essential for cultural identity and continuity.

Artistic expression in a modest or grand way communicates and shapes our thoughts, perceptions and feelings. It helps us to represent our life experiences and to develop, strengthen and transform our beliefs and values. The arts provide a way for society to record and preserve its finest achievements — its visions, aspirations, attitudes and values. They not only reveal cultural heritage, but are a means by which a culture is defined and evaluated. Through the study of art forms, we can even reconstruct long-forgotten aspects of life and culture in societies where there was no written language or whose history has been lost.

The arts enhance the quality of life of all people. Most people voluntarily experience them because they provide pleasure, entertainment, meaning and satisfaction. The importance of the arts in Australia is evident in the extent to which art forms are supported through attendance at performances, galleries, cinemas and community events. In fact, the arts are a major factor in our economic growth and stability. As Boughton (1992) noted:

> recent estimates place the value to the Australian economy of arts related goods and services at $6,165 million for 1990–91, an increase from 1987 of 43 per cent. This represents a value to the total Australian economy of more than twice that of pharmaceutical products and about a third more than beer and alcoholic beverages. By these measures, the arts industry is clearly one of the most robust in the country.

But the arts are valued for more than their cultural and economic merit. They are also worthy of participation and learning because they encompass a unique body of knowledge, skills and ways of thinking. What is understood and communicated through the arts often is not available through other means.

In this chapter I will discuss how the arts involve different thinking skills and provide a unique form of language and way of knowing about the world. This will be illustrated by a discussion of the symbols through which we develop and communicate meaning. Such forms of communication are important aspects of early childhood education. The processes that children use when they are involved in artistic experiences are described in relation to their development and learning. The ways in which early childhood educators can foster learning in young children through the arts is discussed in terms of learning processes, particularly in relation to play. Finally, the value of play is viewed in the context of schools and society.

An alternative way of knowing and representing the world

While we can enjoy and appreciate artistic experiences, it is often difficult to explain in words precisely what it is that we have come to know or understand as a result of such experiences. This is because the arts can mean different things to different people, at different times, and in varying contexts. In essence, artistic expression communicates at least three forms of knowledge: information (for example, this is a picture of a lily pond); aesthetic appreciation (it is visually pleasing); and a personal implication that relates solely to our own life experiences (it makes me feel calm and relaxed because it reminds me of my childhood). In these ways art forms have suggestive qualities to which we attach special meaning, and they communicate these qualities through symbolic languages.

It is important to bear in mind that language is more than just audible, articulate, meaningful sounds. More generally, it is a systematic way of communicating using conventionalised signs, sounds, gestures or words. Hence, the languages of the arts can express and externalise ideas, feelings and beliefs and convey meanings and messages that evoke responses in ourselves and others and, like all areas of learning, the arts involve cognition, or knowing that involves the processing of information.

Because the arts involve the senses, cognitive processes such as perception, awareness, judgement and the expression of ideas are manipulated in ways other than purely linguistic or mathematical as in reading, writing, science and studies in technology (Eisner, 1978; Gardner, 1983). Some writers, like Vygotsky (1962), have linked the term cognition with a kind of inner speech — thinking ideas in your head through the use of words. However, people process information and become aware of themselves and their environment in ways that do not always involve words. Information may be taken in and understood through sight, sound, touch, taste and movement. These processes may be more obvious in young children who may not always be able to express themselves clearly through words.

The Scottish psychologist Allan Leslie and his colleagues believe that infants have their own 'language of thought' and use a kind of 'mentalese' through which they understand their world (cited in Gardner, 1991). For example, infants are able to experience the aural and physical sensations of gentle music, know when they are feeling ill, and identify objects long before this information can be expressed in words. Through the senses, young children can understand a number of concepts — ideas, images, impressions and thoughts — without requiring words. Indeed, some of these sensations or concepts, such as freedom or love, may not easily be expressed even by adults, but are understood through sensations or other non-verbal means. In early childhood, much of this knowledge is understood and communicated through gesture and through learning experiences associated with drawing, blocks, clay, dancing and music.

Just as knowing or understanding may not necessarily involve words, the meaning that is contained within an art work such as a musical composition, ballet, play or poem cannot be shared entirely through language. Language can only go so far — it cannot fully explain or replace the work of art (Simpson, 1988). This is because much of what we understand from a work of art is not literally there but, as mentioned earlier, is interpreted subjectively. A piece of music is a series of sounds (a structured form of knowledge), but it also has the power to communicate ideas or feelings through likeness, representation or analogy (that is, non-verbal metaphor). In other words, the music expresses or stands for other concepts, such as liveliness, patriotism, tranquillity, fear.

Most of us understand and express metaphor through physical associations. As Swanwick (1988) stated:

> We all know what is meant when someone says that they were made to feel 'small', or were weighed down with care, stiff with fright, 'heavy' with apprehension, 'light as air', 'depressed', and so on . . . such expressions [are not] unique to the English language.

Metaphor is used extensively in all art forms. For example, music can capture and communicate impressions similar to those mentioned by Swanwick, and an art work can give the impression of being stark, cold or full of energy. Clearly music cannot really be alive or the art work icy to touch. The properties of liveliness and coldness are associated with our personal experiences which have been re-created and implied by the composer or painter. This re-creation is achieved through the use of selected musical instruments, speed and volume or colour and brush stroke.

All artists — painters, writers, composers, dancers, actors — whether they are publicly acclaimed geniuses or pre-school aged children, work with artistic materials or actions and turn them into representations. This is done through the process of imitation; through representing the world through expressive gestures, textures, shapes, sounds, images or movements. What is important to the observer is that these symbols are universally recognisable. For instance, children as young as seven are able to describe music in terms of weight, size, stiffness, outward or inward direction and degree of activity (Swanwick, 1988).

While many art forms use essentially non-verbal languages, we should not assume that they necessarily have a low level of cognitive content. When discussing the contributions of Piaget to cognitive development, Gardner (1982) commented:

> We learn from his [Piaget's] writings about children's conceptions of water, but little about their fear of floods, their love of splashing, their desire to be minnows, mermaids, or mariners.

The arts, then, enhance our understanding of the world and have the capacity to link the cognitive and emotional domains. Because of this, it is false to make distinctions between the areas traditionally associated with literacy and the arts, for example, between head and heart, thoughts and feelings, knowledge and intuition, or scientific and humanistic realms. Why do we refer to the realms of language and logic as intelligence and the realms of music, movement and spatial ability as talent?

Gardner's (1983, 1988) theory of multiple-intelligences has provided a valuable alternative to the traditional notion of intelligence (p. 34). Gardner described seven domains of intelligence — musical, spatial, bodily kinaesthetic, interpersonal and intrapersonal intelligence, as well as linguistic and logical-mathematical intelligence. He stated that intelligence cannot be defined only by ability in verbal communication or number, or that children can be classified as 'smart' or 'dumb' based only on their capability in these two areas. A person can be considered intelligent because of competency in one or more of the seven more broadly defined areas.

Gardner has tested his theory of multiple intelligences through research using children who were guided in the development of all seven domains. His results revealed that even 4-year-old children showed distinctive styles of cognition. Some approached the world predominantly through the use of language; others through spatial or visual means; and others through social relationships (Gardner, 1991). Many preschool teachers have informally confirmed Gardner's 'discovery', noting that some children steer away from certain visually oriented activities such as block building or painting, yet spend a great deal of time climbing or digging in the sand. Others enjoy creating musical compositions or prefer to play in 'home corner' (the area of the centre that usually contains a miniature kitchen, bedroom and other home-related resources) but may not be very good at telling stories.

Gardner's views have particular appeal to early childhood educators because many young children interact with their environment through non-linguistic forms of knowing. Perception rather than logic governs their view of reality and they learn through sensory experiences and through interacting with objects and people. Many of these experiences occur as forms of play and involve turning materials or actions into representations. For example, when playing in home corner, children may imitate their parents and the daily activities that occur in their homes.

Knowing and the use of symbols

Between the ages of about two and seven, all children learn to use symbols and symbol systems. During this period — which Gardner (1991) called the symbolic period — children learn to use and understand language, to ask for things and information, and to tell others what they want. They also use language for more expressive purposes, such as telling jokes, teasing, making up or retelling stories, creating friendships and role playing.

In addition to verbal language, children also learn to communicate through symbols associated with drawing, imaginative play and dance. For instance, they draw a circle with four protruding lines to represent a human, place a tea towel on their head to represent a veil, or make up a dance called 'The Monster Romp'.

Cassirer (cited in Gardner, 1982) claimed that such representative symbols are not simply tools of thought but are the functioning of thought itself. In other words, symbols provide a way of representing reality and integrating ideas we have about our world. Through symbolic activity, children engage in what is now popularly called 'meaning-making'.

Much of young children's meaning-making occurs through playful experiences that alternate between reality and fantasy and that develop symbols to depict meaning. Often these symbols take the form of gestures, or movements that express or emphasise an idea or attitude. Usually gestures involve movement of the hands, arms and shoulders, such as the commonly used 'thumbs up' gesture to communicate the notion, 'well done'. Gestures can also include facial expressions, such as a wink or frown, or involve other parts of the body. While playing in home corner of a childcare centre, for example, the types of symbolic gestures that children might use would be: Mummy placing her fists on her hips with her elbows outright because she is annoyed that the baby has spilt milk; or pouring imaginary tea and eating imaginary biscuits while pretending to talk on the phone.

Two important thinking skills seem to influence the way in which children establish meaning in their play-based day-to-day interactions: learning to mentally cluster objects that are similar, and recognising familiar events or sequences that occur on a regular basis. Categorising objects and events helps children understand themselves in relation to their world, and this understanding can be seen clearly in their artistic processes and products.

Categorising objects

When children categorise objects, like adults they base their categories on a representational example. In other words, they think of a good version of something, create a prototype category, then see if other objects are like or unlike that version (Rosch, 1976). For example, children recognise a dog as a four-legged, hairy pet with a tail, with ears that are located on top of the head. When they encounter other dogs that are not exactly like their original mental image, they must decide whether the features are sufficiently similar to place it in the category dog or into a different category, say cat. Sometimes it is difficult to place an object into an existing category, thereby leading to the development of other categories, as in the case of the platypus.

We can see many examples of children applying this mental ability. Often, in the process of learning new categories, children make delightful errors, such as mistaking a horse for a cow. With time, they learn that there are larger or superordinate categories that can contain say cows and horses, dogs and cats; in this case the superordinate category is 'animal'. There are also smaller, subordinate categories that help us refine categories of cow by aspects such as sex (bull), age (calf), or type (Jersey).

While categorisation is often considered part of language development, it is also evident in children's artistic and creative activities. Even during infancy, children appear to categorise, although they often use senses other than sight (for example, recognising mummy by her perfume, or by her footsteps). Similarly, three year olds draw pictures that demonstrate their ability to use prototypes in a graphic way. The commonly drawn circle-and-stick-legs human is thought to be from a 'mid-level' category (for example, 'a lady') rather than from a superordinate category (for example, 'a human') or a subordinate category (for example, 'mummy').

A 3-year-old child, for instance, may draw a picture of a house, lady or tree. Yet the objects in the picture generally do not stand for subordinate categories (for example, Grandma's house, the neighbour's tree). Rather, they simply represent the categories of house or tree. This is because the child is representing general events in a symbolic way. Adults sometimes mistakenly believe that a child is drawing

a particular object or event and may ask who the lady in the drawing is, or where the house and tree are located. While the child may give a response, such as 'This is me standing outside the preschool' or 'This is my mummy and my house', these descriptors may be supplied because the adult's prompt causes the child to think 'This is what it could be called if you are supposed to call it something'. The objects or events described by the child could easily change five minutes later, depending on who is asking the question.

The graphic prototypes used in children's drawings often look very similar. Let us consider the drawings of two children, who we will call Tommy and Mary, who had both just turned three years old at the time the art works were created (see Wright, 1987). Tommy's human usually had a straight vertical stroke for a nose, a belly button, and hands with numerous fingers that radiated from a central dot, regardless of the subject of the drawing. Mary, in contrast, usually drew her humans with a squiggly line representing the hair and a triangular body (like a skirt) with legs that come off the points of the triangle. Even when Mary depicted a number of different people, such as 'This is me, my mummy, my daddy and my brother in the garden', each person had the same triangular body and squiggly hair.

Over time, however, Tommy's and Mary's prototypes, or graphic representations of people, began to show more variation in size, sex and shape and include more details such as eyelashes, teeth, dimples, changing hair styles, or new clothing styles. Mary discovered on her own that the lady in her drawing could not possibly stand with her legs so far apart and still have them be attached to her hips. Even if someone had told her that her original drawings were unrealistic, Mary more than likely would have preferred to stick with her standard prototype until she was ready to change. When she eventually discovered her repeated 'error', she shunned many of her earlier drawings as immature and stupid until a caring adult convinced her that they were part of growing up.

Again, with time, the houses or trees that had once suited a number of drawings also begin to have more details and variation. Tommy, for example, started to drawn 'Queenslander' homes on stumps, and the trees that once looked like lollypops began to include branches, sometimes laden with red fruit. Mary began to spend a great deal of time and care representing special events like 'A Day at the Beach' and takes particular interest in including dogs and cats in her drawings. At first Mary's drawings of animals included several legs, just as Tommy's hands on his drawings of people had included several fingers and toes. Eventually Mary's dogs and cats had four legs and Tommy's hands and feet had five fingers and toes.

At around the age of four, children seem to take an interest in capturing number and numerical relations, not only in their drawings, but also in music, play and storytelling. This tendency is what Gardner and Wolf (1982) called digital mapping and can be found in all arts areas. In music, for instance, children become more sensitive to the number of tones in a melody and can sing it more accurately. In their play they can get a general or specific impression of which pirate has the most jewels, or which string of blocks reaches the furthest. In their storytelling, children can establish and maintain a number of characters. This aspect of play and storytelling brings us to the second form of categorisation.

Categorising events

This form of categorising is related to familiar sequences of events, and is what Katherine Nelson (cited in Gardner, 1991) refers to as the use of scripts. Scripts involve identifying and ordering aspects that children (and adults) come to associate with events that occur on a regular basis. For example, children learn to recognise the event, or script, of going to the movies as involving a building that is recognisable from the outside because of its billboard displaying the film's title, and sometimes an associated picture. The script also includes the purchase of a ticket (and possibly junk food), sitting in a tiered theatre facing a large screen, the lowering of the lights when the film begins, and the rolling of credits at the end.

Like category labels, scripts help children compare familiar sequences of events with those that are newly encountered. To use a Piagetian term, children learn to assimilate going to the movies as different from going to, say, the art gallery, based on features such as the appearance of the building, whether you can or cannot eat food there, whether you stand quietly, walk around or sit and how you know when it is time to go home.

We commonly see children role playing the scripts of life through socio-dramatic, or pretend play. At times it is surprising just how set young children's scripts of life are. In *Frogs and Snails and Feminist Tales* (1988), Bronwyn

Davies described how some preschool children's scripts associated with male-female roles were so strong that, after having been read feminist fairytales, their play behaviour and values showed they could not accept reversals of traditional roles (for example, a female hero, or a boy who preferred to dance rather than play football).

Throughout our lives, scripts continue to help us assimilate new experiences into new sets of scripts (for example, the script of attending preschool, then school and possibly tertiary education, then employment, then old age). Scripts also play an important part in our emotional and interpersonal lives (see for example, Corey, 1991). Sometimes, as in senility, the rehearsal of familiar scripts continues out of context. My 88-year-old mother-in-law, who suffers from Alzheimer's disease, daily insists that she is visiting for the Christmas holidays even though she has lived with me for five years, and even though it might be a cold afternoon in July and there are no signs of a Christmas tree, presents or decorations.

Scripts, like category labels, can be found in all areas of young children's artistic development. An infant who has learned the script of a song while being bounced on an adult's knee (called a dandling song), such as 'This is the way the ladies ride', will show through facial expression and body language that she or he knows the very point in the rhyme when grandpa is about to 'drop' her or him off his knee. Preschool children experiment with behaviours that they have observed in real life or the media, such as being Batman or a shop attendant, and can imagine and play as if they are flying or being the wind.

The use of objects and scripts in young children's artistic experience

Infants

Infants use art materials in a way that often combines creating marks on paper with creating sound and making gestures (Tarr, 1987; Winner, 1986). They derive pleasure from making marks that seem to represent paths on a page, somewhat like footprints. Many parents and teachers have watched an infant use a crayon to draw a squiggly line on a piece of paper while making 'vrooom vrooom' sounds. Through such experiences, the infant is symbolising the pathway of a truck, similar to the way in which he or she would play trucks in an imaginative play experience. The final, visual result — which the child might even call truck — looks simply like a squiggly line on a piece of paper. To an adult who has not seen the child in the process of drawing and creating sound effects, the title will make little sense.

Similarly, infants begin to learn how to 'read' pictures in books, on the walls of the childcare centre, at the supermarket, and through the media. When listening to an adult reading a story, young children often become engrossed with the pictures and point to them and name them as enthusiastically as if they were real objects. For example, an infant might point to a picture of a bottle, grasp an imaginary bottle and pretend to suck.

The symbolic play of infants, like language, is often related to specific events and includes statements such as 'go swimming' or 'want ice-cream'. They will use dramatic props such as bottles, blankets and tea sets to play with their teddy bear or with other infants.

Three to five year olds

Three to 5-year-old children do not always require realistic, dramatic props to stimulate imaginative play. They often pretend that something is other than it actually is. For example, a block of wood may represent or substitute for an iron, and a table may serve as an ironing board. On other occasions, the same children may use the same block of wood to represent a portable telephone or a miniature car, and the table might stand for a desk or garage.

In music, dance or the visual arts, children may also

represent events or play out scripts. Through the use of musical instruments, for example, they create sound stories that aurally depict a sequence of real or imaginary events, such as 'The fairies dancing'. Often children use instruments for dramatic effect, like crashing cymbals just as an exciting event occurs. They also enjoy playing instruments to support the drama of puppet plays or felt-board stories.

In dance and expressive movement, children symbolise objects and events through body movement and gesture. They stretch up on their toes and raise their arms by their sides, wiggling their fingers while moving to the fairy dance music. While drawing, painting, building with blocks or cardboard boxes, shaping clay or creating collages, young children also use visual images to symbolise objects and events. They imagine, fantasise and act out thoughts and feelings while fashioning their worlds in the plastic domain.

Partly dependent on developmental level, and partly dependent on purpose or reason, children may not always represent or symbolise in a direct way, or at least in a way that adults might recognise or understand. A three year old, for example, may draw circles and squares and label them 'potties' and 'windows', but if labels were not provided, we would not recognise these objects as such.

Kellogg (1969) and Smith (1983) provide us with a comprehensive description of the types of pre-symbolic and symbolic drawings that young children produce in the process of becoming users of visual symbols. Briefly, by the end of their third year, children begin to extend circles, squares and other geometric forms to create various combination shapes, such as circles divided into quarters or eighths, like a pie, which are called mandalas. The mandala and other forms, such as the 'sun', will eventually be used to represent objects that are recognisable to adults. The sun, for instance, will be drawn in the top corner of a picture to represent the sun in the sky and a mandala may be used for the windows of a house or a person's eyes. Six to 8-year-old children also symbolise objects and events in their artistic processes and products. A discussion of their work is presented later in the chapter in relation to play and school.

Creating for aesthetic pleasure

When preschool children 'scribble' or draw what appear to be non-representational shapes, such as circles and squares, they are not necessarily developmentally immature. Often children create visual images, such as patterns, simply for aesthetic purposes, particularly when they are experimenting with the physical properties of new materials (for example, felt pens compared to coloured pencils; play dough compared to clay). Likewise, young children might play musical instruments, sing or dance for the pleasure of the experience without 'being' anything. Such playful, kinesthetic experiences are to be encouraged as they help children appreciate the elements within each of the art forms — sound, movement, imagery, imagination.

To illustrate how children enjoy artistic expression, I will tell you about a four year old who enjoyed showing me the drawings she produced at childcare, often giving them a title or telling me a short story about them. She would go through her drawings one by one, holding them up and announcing, 'This is a picture of a boy riding a bike', or 'This is a fireman putting out a fire'. Occasionally, she would come to a picture that was clearly non-representational. At first she would uncomfortably make up some explanation and quickly discard it as unimportant and move on to the next 'real' picture. Because I find scribbles to be particularly aesthetic, usually balanced in colour and form, I would say, 'Hey wait Jessie, that's a very pretty picture. Can I just have a look at it please?' Then I would remark about the artistic features, such as colour, shape, pattern, balance or texture that were featured in the art work. Jessie would look at me somewhat doubtfully and continue showing and explaining her representational art works but discarding her scribbles until eventually I would say, 'Jess, you know sometimes I really like to just doodle or scribble pictures that aren't anything at all. Usually when I'm talking on the telephone or just sitting waiting for someone, I start to make circles and squiggly lines and things just because they look nice and because they are fun to make. Do you ever do that?' Then Jessie's eyes lit up and got really big, and she would just stare at me for about 30 seconds, seeing (I suppose) if I was going to change my mind or laugh or show in some other way that I was joking. After a moment, she picked up the next picture, which happened to be a scribble and holding it somewhat apprehensively, said 'and this is just a scribble'. Then I said, 'That's not just a scribble, that's a beauty! Look at all those looping, squiggling lines. And those red and blue blotches look really bright right next to each other, don't they?' She looked briefly at me, scanning my face to see if I was sincere, and from that point on would share all of her drawings with me, whether they were scribbles or representational pictures, on equal merit.

The equivalent of scribbling or doodling can be seen in other arts areas as well. In music, for example, children make up songs which are rambling little ditties consisting of nonsense syllables, or words that spontaneously come to mind. These aesthetic, play-like aspects of expression are important in all areas of the arts. Through artistic play, children use their bodies and voices to imagine and represent meaning through the integration of thought, the senses and symbols. Meaning comes when children make sense of personal, internal responses to their worlds. These responses are made through controlled attempts to explore, develop and express ideas and concepts. In other words, children make meaning from performing, making and doing (Alper, 1987; Smith 1980).

Some adults do not regard children's discoveries or creations as particularly distinctive. They might remark, 'What's so special about that? It looks to me just like any other 3-year-old's scribble'. While it might be true that most children in the process of normal development invent in a similar fashion, and that their products of invention may look similar, it is important for each of them to discover this process of invention through first-hand experience. A number of authors have acknowledged the significance of this process. John Holt talks about the importance of providing children with opportunities to turn their own reality into symbols (Holt, 1976). Piaget also said, '. . . in order to understand we have to invent, or that is, to reinvent, because we can't start from the beginning again. But I would say that anything is only understood to the extent that it is reinvented' (cited in Jennings, 1967). Gardner (1982) reasserted this point, saying 'as scientific or artistic creators, we do not solve the jigsaw puzzle of reality. Rather, we build endless realities out of Lego'.

Regardless of how we define this notion of reinvention, it is clear that it will occur most readily for young children through the processes of exploration, discovery learning, hands-on experiences, and play-like encounters, many of which may not involve language. Ideally, such experiences should be initiated by the child and supported or enhanced by the teacher through what is referred to as the child-centred approach to learning.

Child-centred arts education

The philosophy of child-centredness has been part of early childhood education for decades. Inspired by the beliefs of philosophers such as Dewey (1934), and educators such as Pestalozzi (1968) and Froebel (1895), early childhood educators espouse the view that children should learn through exploring, enjoying and discovering rather than inheriting knowledge from adults.

Child-centred learning experiences acknowledge the significance of play as an important means for children to learn about and understand themselves and their surroundings. It is also generally acknowledged that the arts are valuable media for children because they are similar to play (Swanwick, 1988). As discussed earlier, the arts provide opportunities for imagination, symbolisation and meaning making which can be sustained and extended beyond childhood.

Many artists and composers have described how they attempt to return to this state of childlike play behaviour to open up new artistic possibilities. Picasso described himself as having the ability to draw like Raphael as a child but then spent most of his adult life attempting to draw like a child again. Adult artists try to capture the freedom and grace of childhood, to start afresh with images, sounds and movement as if discovered for the first time. As Rosenblatt and Winner (1988) said, 'the preschooler lacks conventions, while the adult may reject them'. Freedom, grace and unconventionality are qualities that are inherent in the raw materials of play and can be enhanced in early childhood programs through a child-centred approach.

Through a child-centred approach, children are in charge of their own learning, in their own way, at their own pace. Through hands-on arts experiences they become involved in a number of processes that apply to all arts areas (see table 6.1). The processes outlined in table 6.1 do not imply a hierarchy. In other words, one process is not more important than another — each is important in itself. Yet there is an implicit order of complexity in which the processes are presented. Critiquing, for example, is a higher level skill than discovery, yet even young children demonstrate the ability to critique (Cole & Schaefer, 1990). With mastery, one process is not replaced by another. A child, or for that matter an adult, does not stop discovering once skills have been mastered. All processes might be considered part of a repeating spiral of learning, where each one is revisited time and again, regardless of developmental level.

Table 6.1: General artistic processes applicable to each of the arts domains.

Discovery involves observing, comparing, exploring options from a variety of perspectives, being open-minded, reinterpreting, making associations, finding alternatives, imagining, seeing possibilities, questioning, testing, finding purpose, taking initiative.

Pursuit involves entering into arts activities, focusing on a specific area, enjoying, being goal directed, staying on task, problem setting, problem solving, experimenting and risk taking with media, generating ideas, planning, carrying out a plan, selecting resources with artistic purpose, showing care and attention to detail, developing works over time or around personal themes.

Perception involves showing awareness of sensory experience, illustrating sensitivity to physical properties and qualities of materials and the environment, visualising, 'hearing inside the head', internalising movement, making fine discriminations, evidencing sensitivity to the variety of genres, cultures and historical periods, being able to understand another person's perspective.

Personal communication involves choosing artistic materials and elements with communicative intent, using symbols to represent and express ideas or feelings, using the imagination, creating stories or captions to artistic products.

Self-awareness and social interaction involve working independently, tapping into personal feelings, participating in preparation and clean up, recognising and working within personal capabilities, tolerating frustration, sharing discoveries, participating in group activities, cooperating, making suggestions, negotiating, empathising, appreciating other people's contributions.

Skill use involves manipulating materials, controlling muscular coordination and basic techniques, developing competency and mastery through experience and time, responding to different situations flexibly, using materials inventively, applying principles of the specific arts domain.

Analysis involves making choices, describing to others what is seen, heard, felt, thought or imagined, contributing own opinions, changing direction if necessary, appreciating, reflecting on process and product, relating learning to previous learning, changing attitudes.

Critique involves gaining insight and understanding, showing a sense of

Table 6.1 (cont.)

---

standards for quality, accepting and incorporating suggestions where appropriate, using the work of others for ideas and inspiration, articulating artistic goals, talking about own artistry and the works of peers and published artists, showing an interest in hearing and using arts terminology, using the processes of describing, interpreting and judging.

In order to understand and appreciate how children learn, early childhood teachers need to interpret the descriptors of the eight processes in ways that are appropriate for each child's ability. For example, exploring options has a different meaning to a two year old chewing on a crayon, a three year old discovering ways of making marks, and an eight year old exploring the different effects that can be achieved when drawing with crayon then painting over this with lightly tinted water.

In addition, each descriptor has meaning only when considered in relation to the learning environment, the teaching practices and methods used, and the organisation of the curriculum and content. For more information on curricular issues see *The Arts in Early Childhood* (Wright, 1991). At this point, a discussion of some general principles that support artistic development and learning in young children will be valuable. If young children are to enter into the artistic processes described in table 6.1, they require an appropriate learning environment which includes carefully selected artistic resources and materials, along with supportive guidance from adults.

The role of open-ended resources

The materials that provide opportunities for processes such as personal discovery and communication, perception, self-awareness and social interaction are those that can be called open-ended. Open-endedness means that the end result can be achieved in a number of ways; there is no one way that all explorers are expected to discover. By contrast, some experiences such as '2 + 2 = 4' involve an answer that everyone would agree is the correct answer. These latter experiences are referred to as convergent because the process converges or focuses on one specific point. In contrast, open-ended experiences branch outwards and several answers can be considered correct.

Earlier I gave the example of children using a block of wood to represent an iron in one instance and a portable telephone or a miniature car in others. Another example was a tea towel which was used by a child as a wedding veil. Both the block of wood and the tea towel can be, and often are, used by children in many ways and are therefore examples of open-ended resources. The wood might represent a sausage in 'kitchen play', while playing as a performing musician it might become a microphone, and when stacked with other blocks it could be built into numerous buildings, boats or cities. The tea towel, when used as head gear, can represent long hair, can be wrapped around the head when playing 'At the Beach', and can help a child become a nun, a princess or sheik. With a little imagination, it is possible for any object to be used as anything else.

When put in particular contexts, some objects are less likely to be transformed into something else because the imagination is not readily stimulated. If, for example, a child-sized, white tulle wedding veil were provided in all its glory, together with a fitted, sequin-studded headband, it would probably be used most regularly as just that. Because it is representational, it is largely a convergently oriented resource. This does not mean that children would not use the wedding veil when playing as a nun or a sheik, but it is less likely.

However, if children have access to various cloth pieces (including tulle, such as lace, cotton, hessian, satin or linen) in a variety of shapes and lengths, the qualities of the cloth — such as its weight, the way it drapes or floats and how it feels when worn — would stimulate the imagination and allow for a number of imaginative solutions. In addition, if the cloth is not shaped in a specific way (such as cut and sewn into a tutu), and not always to be fixed to a specific part of the body (such as the hips), it has further potential. The cloth can become part of a child's body and movement simply by being held, draped, looped or tied. If necessary, it can be fixed to the body through open-ended fasteners, such as scarves, belts, head bands, rubber bands, safety pins or spring paper clips.

Open-ended resources are available in all arts domains. In drawing, painting, collage, construction and clay, children are able to fashion their own worlds using paper, paints and brushes, boxes, glue, staplers, clay and cutting utensils. As with the cloth example, basic art materials can be presented in a way that limits children's ability to interpret their use. Colouring-in books, photocopied stencils and templates for products that all look alike and require step-by-step instructions (such as egg carton caterpillars), are classic examples of how art can be presented in a convergent way. Similarly, activities such as rolling marbles around in paint and then on paper or squirting or flicking paint onto paper from a distance involve random, chance-based results that may look interesting. However, they do not involve children in important meaning-making experiences or processes such as imagining, problem solving, reinterpreting, visualising, communicating thoughts or developing painting techniques.

Of all the arts, music is one area within the early childhood curriculum where children can be deprived of opportunities for play, freedom of expression and open-ended interpretation. While there are numerous resources (such as musical instruments and objects) that can be used to stimulate musical composition and dance, the focus of many early childhood programs is on a standard song repertoire, often accompanied with standard movements. Unlike art or pretend play, music and movement are often 'taught' at a set time of the day, include all children in the same room at the same time, and involve children in skills such as imitation and rote memorisation. Lessons often consist of playing musical instruments in a rhythm band context, based on the teacher's cues or some symbol chart to which she or he points. Movement generally involves children 'being' something suggested by the teacher, such as a plant growing from a seed, or a butterfly, even though many such images may have little or no meaning to some children. Meanwhile, children's spontaneous songs and dances go unnoticed.

Children can be encouraged to use their imaginations in music and movement through experiences such as the creation of sound stories, open-ended singing conversations or the use of musical instrument (Andress, 1980; Wright, 1991a). Likewise, they can use their imaginations and interpret movement suggestions offered by a teacher if they are more open-ended, and centre on physical states, such as 'light', 'heavy', 'strong', 'flowing', 'gentle', 'jerky' or 'stiff'.

The role of teachers

The role of teachers is significant in guiding children's learning and development. Resources are important for encouraging children's imaginative play, artistic processes and meaning-making, but teachers must also provide a learning atmosphere in which children feel comfortable enough to take intellectual risks. In other words, the learning environment should encourage children to experiment, to learn from both successful and unsuccessful attempts, and to be inspired to try again. Teachers can encourage children to ask questions, explore ideas and imagine new possibilities, and children must feel sure that they will receive support, guidance and respect from teachers and parents. Most importantly, the learning environment must be an atmosphere that encourages open-ended, process-oriented learning experiences.

However, no learning takes place in a vacuum. An early childhood curriculum based on children experiencing only their own art, dance, music and play would be like expecting them to acquire language by talking only to their own age group. Teachers can assist children in the process of artistic development and learning by setting the learning context and providing the appropriate materials. They can also observe children interacting with the resources and each other and, based on these observations, assist young people's spontaneous learning in a number of ways. Sometimes a teacher may simply observe children from a distance, offering moral support through comments such as 'I see', or by simply nodding, smiling, or winking. At other times a teacher might describe the children's processes or products using simple words which act as a form of encouragement to children, letting them know that what they are doing is valued and should be continued. At other times, a teacher may need to take a more active role, suggesting alternatives and initiating learning while trying to ensure that the child will then take the lead again.

As well as describing the eight artistic processes, table 6.1 provides a guide for helping teachers phrase supportive comments by focusing on the artistic processes in which children often engage. For example, under the discovery category a teacher might say the following for each part:

1. Observing — 'Tricia. I've been noticing that you have been looking at the spider's web for a long time. Sometimes I enjoy just looking at things that are pretty too.'

2. Comparing — 'You two boys have been thinking of and comparing a lot of different rhythms on your drums. That "boom, bim-bim" rhythm was very different to the one that went "diddle diddle boom".'

3. Exploring options — 'Mario has thought of an unusual way to make his puppet speak. I wonder if there are other ways.'

4. Being open minded — 'You know, Mariko, I'm with you. I can't see any reason why an elephant can't do a tap dance!'

5. Reinterpreting — 'That's a good version of that song.'

6. Making associations — 'Hisssss' (in response to a child who has just made a long, snake-like coil of clay, held it up and hissed at the teacher).

7. Finding alternatives — 'I've noticed you've tried it in

a lot of different ways — on your tip toes, on your tummy and with your elbow only.'

8. Imagining — 'You took your magic rug to the beach did you?'

9. Seeing possibilities — 'I wonder if this empty tissue box would work as a door?'

10. Testing — 'I don't know either. Why don't we try it out?'

11. Finding purpose — 'It's good to see that you two have found a use for that old boot!'

12. Taking initiative — 'That's great. I like it when someone can think of something interesting to play even when it's stinking hot.'

In the above examples the comments suggest how to reinforce (examples 1, 5 and 12), label (examples 2, 7), extend (3, 9, 10) and support (4, 6, 8 and 11). These interactions show the simple connections that a teacher can make between what a child has spontaneously enjoyed and the learning that has taken place, while still allowing for open-ended interpretation by the child. A multitude of similar comments could be made for other aspects of the eight artistic processes.

Influences opposing education through play

Schooling

As children progress beyond early childhood education into primary and secondary school, chances to play within a child-centred context seem to decrease. Fewer and fewer opportunities are provided for children to explore materials and create their own meaning through self-devised symbols. Instead, children's personal discoveries and understandings seem to be subordinated to the presentation of cultural knowledge and values. This transfer usually takes the form of teaching proficiency in relevant skills.

Rather than guiding children's learning and helping them develop their own symbols, the notion of teaching children symbols and symbol systems seems to take over. This usually involves teaching reading, writing and mathematical concepts. Yet meaning making through the creation of personal symbol systems also is a form of literacy development, although it is not the literacy usually associated with reading and writing or with numeracy.

In most school curricula, the symbols of the adult world seem to be deemed more relevant than those devised by children. In music, for example, children learn how to read music, which means mastering the ability to read and write traditional musical notation. In addition, they are taught folk or classical dance and learn specific, stylised movement to fingerplays and songs. Creative movement lessons often include experiences such as singing and moving to 'Hey dee hey dee ho, the great big elephant is so slow', where all children swing their arms like elephants' trunks while walking in a circle to the beat of the music. At school, the pretend play that had once been a large part of the preschool curriculum shifts in emphasis to a more structured experience called drama. In drama, children interpret and perform plays that other people, usually adults, have written. Finally, in the visual arts, children learn the accepted way to create images.

I am not suggesting that children be isolated from symbol systems of the adult world. Rather, I am arguing that children should have opportunities to learn about the culture, not only in the 'traditional' sense, but also to explore their world from a private and personal perspective.

The environmental aspect of schooling is but one factor that causes this shift of emphasis away from children's symbols and on to the symbol systems of the culture. The other factor is partly related to the biology of school-aged children. There is little doubt that children in their early school years have come to a stage in their development when they want to learn these 'big people literacies'. Not only do they want to learn how to read, write and do arithmetic, they also want to become literate in the arts. Wolf and Gardner (1980) described this period as one in which children want to learn how to use symbols competently so that they can become efficient communicators, or message-senders. Children are interested in refining their use of symbols so that everyone, even strangers, will be able to interpret their art works, dances, songs, poems and plays.

School-aged children's visual arts products often depict specific events, situations and stories that are important to them. For example, it is common that they will create hundreds of drawings on one theme, such as super-heroes, roller blading or fashion design. The amount of detail in the art work is focused on that aspect which was the inspiration for the drawing in the first place, such as the super-hero's challenges, the various stunts that roller blader's can perform, or the variety or detail in the various fashions that have been designed. Wilson and Wilson (1982) demonstrated how each art work may explore a different aspect of the same experience, and when the drawings are viewed as a collection, we get a broad profile of a child's understanding of the events being depicted.

In the realm of music, children in their early school years become interested in devising notations, like musical scores, that help them in skills such as remembering a song tomorrow that they created today. These notations show in summary form the pitch, rhythm and words of the song. In their sound stories (compositions about everyday or imaginary events), children enjoy thinking of symbols that will most clearly represent the sound they have created. Such symbols may be squiggly lines going up and down, followed by a star to represent the opening and closing of a squeaky door, or drawings of footprints with the addition of outward pencil strokes — like the rays of a sun — to show stomping feet. In play, children might draw pictures of the things they should make or collect in order to 'become' pirates or create the pirates' cave. These objects might include pirate clothing, eye patches, weapons, treasures, and cave lighting and furnishings.

Children's attraction toward creating notational symbols to help them keep track of objects and events has been referred to as second-order symbolisation (Gardner, 1991). Second-order symbolisation goes beyond simple symbolisation, such as gesture or picture drawing. It involves using a set of marks that itself refers to other symbolic events. For example, in the musical illustration earlier, children used the sound of loud, stomping feet to symbolise the spooky event of being pursued by a big heavy monster. These are first-order symbols. In addition, they drew pictures of the stomping feet to show the point in the sound story when we know the monster is coming. These set of marks are second-order symbols.

Such second-order systems of notation are central to many scholastic activities. They become the core of much of the school curriculum (for example, reading, writing and maths). Those children who are successful in learning and using second-order symbol systems are the ones who are classified as smart or successful. As Gardner (1991) phrased it, 'The capacity to engage readily in such meta-symbolic activities is certainly an aid to scholastic success; indeed, it is too often equated with it'.

My concern is that the schools are moving toward teaching children second-order symbolisation before they have had the opportunity to develop first-order symbolic learning through experiences such as play and experimentation with open-ended materials. For example, in Australia, many States have adopted the Kodály approach to music education which is directed largely toward helping children acquire musical literacy. Through a highly structured approach, children learn a sequence of musical skills that are developed through singing, reading music, and sight singing.

In comparison, the philosophy and practice of the Orff approach is to provide opportunities for children to experience musical concepts and skills through hands-on participation, and when understood at an intuitive level, the teacher labels this understanding for the children or shows them how the music can be notated. Other approaches to music education support the belief that symbolising music through notation should take place only after children have understood and applied first-order symbolisation. The authors of the Manhattanville Music Curriculum Program (commonly known as MMCP), a music education program that centres around personal expression and creativity have stated, 'All notation, whether it be devised by the student as his/her own performance resource or more formal in nature, should be approached with caution. Notes on paper can soon take the place of musical imagination' (Biasini, Thomas, & Pogonowski, undated).

Studies of children's musical ability have shown that when they have learned to notate music there can be a loss — at least temporarily — of important expressive qualities or details (Bamberger, 1991). In the school years, there seems to be a need to balance the scholastic aspects of musical and other artistic literacy with that of the creative, expressive aspects.

Culture

The importance given to the arts and the ways in which they are taught in schools depends on the value and meanings they are given by society. Intellectual, creative, expressive or other skills will develop only to the degree to which they are used and respected within the culture. Young children who grow up in a remote Australian Aboriginal community, for example, will develop a knowledge of their ancestry and spiritualism through a rich and ancient oral history and a spatial memory for the subtle variations in the contours and colours of the land (Klish & Davidson, 1984). Such traditions, experiences and forms of knowing are unlikely to be accessible to children living in a large, urban environment where they learn to navigate using road signs and landmarks, and acquire a great deal of their knowledge about life through books.

The particular symbol systems favoured, or not favoured, within a culture become the focus of what children learn in school. In China, for example, there is a uniform curriculum and national textbooks on how to teach arts education, with specific lessons outlined for each age (Winner, 1989). Winner commented that when observing art lessons in urban schools, she often saw the same lesson repeated almost without variation. While there may be some advantages to such an approach, Winner observed that children were not challenged to think visually or to solve visual problems; instead, they were given solutions in forms that are easy to master, and they were expected to master them. For instance, children were not expected to figure out by themselves how to draw something new; they were shown how to draw images step by step, line by line. She stated that the notions of art as process, as visual problem solving, or as innovation, are conspicuously absent.

While in Hungary I observed similar situations in relation to music education methods, and the song repertoire that the children learned. A sequential approach to visual arts education did not seem as apparent, although I did observe some lessons that were very teacher-, rather than child-oriented. In one class of six year olds, children were working with plasticine, making a cup and saucer through the step-by-step instruction of the teacher. Each child was instructed to divide their ball of plasticine into two: one part for the cup and one for the saucer. The teacher demonstrated how to reserve a small piece of plasticine to be used later for the handle, how to take one of the larger pieces and draw it upward and outward to shape the cup, how to roll and attach the handle to the side of the cup, and how to flatten out the second piece evenly to make the saucer.

While I was impressed with the ability of the children to duplicate the example presented by the teacher, I had a similar response to that of Winner in China. Where was the opportunity for children to visualise and create their own images? I photographed examples of the children's work to document the experience, and in the process asked if one of the children would sit beside his artwork

for another photo. The selection of this child was not because his product was better executed than that of the other children; in fact it probably wasn't as accurate as many. Rather, I was attracted to the fact that the boy had made a slightly smaller cup and saucer and had used the off-cuts and those collected from other children to create a snowman-like figure. He had found a way to comply with the wishes of the teacher by copying her example, but he also served his individual need to create his own image.

Compared to China and Hungary, Australian educators have historically espoused the practice of encouraging children to solve artistic problems through processes such as those outlined in table 6.1. However, it is possible that this tradition could change considerably in the next few years. Following the lead of English educators, Australians are now developing a National Arts Curriculum (Emery & Hammond, 1992) which should be implemented in the near future. The authors are defining sets and sub-sets of knowledge and skills that children are to acquire, along with statements of achievement levels. There is a fear among many in the arts that translating the processes of artistry into a written form may not only be difficult, but could overlook the aesthetic qualities that are inherent in the arts. As Boughton (1992) stated:

> The shortcoming here is the same as the problem associated with the behavioural objectives movement in the late Sixties. There is a very real danger that the standards that can be easily written, will be written, and that the complex, subtle, and tacit outcomes that are most valued in the arts will be ignored. Profile statements will trivialise the arts if the major effort in their writing is directed towards readily observable and assessable performance indicators at the expense of the more significant outcomes of arts learning.

Words do not easily capture the basic nature of the arts, particularly the way in which they function in young children's lives. An Australia-wide curriculum that defines what is to be learned along with achievement standards for particular age levels could shift the agenda away from imagination, artistic problem solving and the use of personal symbols, toward an approach which more closely resembles that of China.

In Australian arts education for young children, it is important that we value childhood as a period of development that should not be rushed. In early childhood education, children should be allowed to learn about and represent their world in their own way. 'The aim of the educator is not to mold children in the image of the adult, but rather to pose challenging problems so that children will eventually discover for themselves more cognitively advanced ways of understanding' (Winner, 1989).

Children need many opportunities to play with artistic resources throughout their school years. Through the process of play, they are free to use their imaginations to create or be anything. An educational emphasis on the teaching of competencies could rob children of the chance to make their own meaning, to comprehend themselves and their world through first-hand, internalised understanding. Such processes are at the heart of artistic experience, not only for children, but also for adults. We must value the open-ended, playful qualities of the arts if we are to encourage self-expression, intuition, reasoning, imagination and communication. If we value individuality, independence, uniqueness and creativity within our society, we must offer children opportunities to understand and interpret the world through artistic experiences — personal experiences that place the child at the centre of the learning.

One of the basic purposes of education is to transmit an understanding and appreciation of our culture to succeeding generations. The arts provide us with one of the most vivid ways of sharing our civilisation and, therefore, should be among the most fundamental areas of education. No-one who lacks basic knowledge and skills in the arts can claim to be fully educated.

References

Alper, C. D. (1987) 'Early childhood music education', in C. Seefeldt (ed.), *The early childhood curriculum: A review of current research*. New York: Teachers College Press.

Andress, B. (1980) *Music experiences in early childhood*. New York: Holt, Rinehart and Winston.

Bamberger, J. (1991) The mind behind the Musical Ear. Cambridge, Massachusetts: Harvard University Press.

Biasini, A., Thomas, R. & Pogonowski, L. (undated) New York: MMCP Interaction, Media Materials.

Boughton, D. (1992) Will the national arts curriculum be stillborn: Resuscitation through research or merciful euthanasia? Keynote paper presented at the AARE/NZARE Conference, Geelong, New South Wales.

Cole, E. S. & Schaefer, C. (1990) 'Can young children be art critics?' *Young children*, Vol. 45, No. 2, 33–8.

Corey, G. (1991) *Theory and Practice of Counselling and Psychology* (4 ed.). Pacific Grove, California: Brooks-Cole.

Davies, B. (1988) *Frogs and Snails and Feminist Tales*. Wellington: Allen & Unwin.

Dewey, J. (1934) *Arts as Experience*. New York: Academic Press.

Eisner, E. (1978) The role of the arts in the invention of man. Keynote address at the twenty-third World Congress of the International Society of Education through Art, Adelaide, South Australia.

Emery, L. & Hammond, G. (1992) National Curriculum Statement in the Arts: Formal Consultative Draft, University of Melbourne, Institute of Education, School of Visual and Performing Arts Education.

Froebel, F. (1985) *The Education of Man*. New York: Appleton.

Gardner, H. (1991) *The Unschooled Mind*. New York: Basic Books.

Gardner, H. (1988) 'On assessment in the arts: A conversation with Howard Gardner'. *Educational Leadership*, volume 1, 30–4.

Gardner, H. (1983) *Frames of Mind*. New York: Basic Books.

Gardner, H. (1982) *Art, Mind and Brain: A Cognitive Approach to Creativity*. New York: Basic Books.

Gardner, H. & Wolf, D. (1982) Waves and Streams of Symbolisation: Notes on the Development of Symbolic Capacities in Young Children. Paper presented at the International Congress on the Acquisition of Symbolic Skills, Keele, England.

Gutek, G. L. (1968) *Pestalozzi and Education*. New York: Random House.

Holt, J. (1976) *How Children Learn*. Harmondsworth, Middlesex: Penguin.

Jennings, F. C. (1967) 'Jean Piaget: Notes on learning'. *Saturday Review*, May 20, 83.

Kellogg, R. (1969) *Analyzing Children's Art*. Palo Alto, California: Mayfield.

Klish, L. Z. & Davidson, G. R. (1984) 'Toward a recognition of Australian Aboriginal competence in cognitive functions', in J. R. Kirby (ed.), *Cognitive strategies and educational performance*, New York: Academic Press.

Music Educators National Conference (1993) 'A vision for arts education'. *Soundpost*, Vol. 9, No. 3, 17–29.

Rosche, E. et al. (1976) 'Basic objects in natural categories'. *Cognitive Psychology*, Vol. 8, 382–439.

Rosenblatt, E. & Winner, E. (1988) 'The art of children's drawing'. *Journal of Aesthetic Education*, Vol. 22, No. 1, 3–15.

Simpson, A. (1988) 'Language, literature and art'. *Journal of Aesthetic Education*, Vol. 22, No. 2, 47–53.

Smith, N. (1980) Classroom practice: Creating meaning in the arts, in J. J. Hausman (ed.), *Arts and the Schools*. New York: McGraw-Hill.

Smith, N. (1983) *Experiences and Art: Teaching Children to Paint*. New York: Teachers College, Colombia University.

Swanwick, K. (1988) *Music, Mind and Education*. London: Routledge.

Tarr, P. (1987) Symbolic interactionism as a theoretical perspective for the study of children's artistic development. *Working Papers in Art Education*, Vol. 2, 69–77.

Vygotsky, L. S. (1962) *Thought and Language*. Cambridge: Massachusetts Institute of Technology.

Wilson, M. & Wilson, B. (1982) *Teaching Children to Draw: A Guide for Teachers and Parents*, Englewood Cliffs: Prentice Hall.

Winner, E. (1986) 'Where pelican kiss seals', *Psychology Today*, August, 25–35.

Winner, E. (1989) 'How can Chinese children draw so well?', *Journal of Aesthetic Education*, Vol. 23, No. 1, 41–63.

Wolf, D. & Gardner, H. (1980) Beyond playing or polishing: A developmental view of artistry, in J. J. Hausman (ed.), *Art and the Schools*, New York: McGraw-Hill.

Wright, S. (1991a) A child-centred approach to singing, movement and playing instruments in early childhood, in S. Wright (ed.), *The Arts in Early Childhood*. Sydney: Prentice Hall.

Wright, S. (1991b) Beyond a developmental approach to the arts, in S. Wright (ed.), *The Arts in Early Childhood*. Sydney: Prentice Hall.

Wright, S. (ed.) (1991) *The Arts in Early Childhood*. Sydney: Prentice Hall.

Wright, S. (1987) 'In Search of Creative Art in Young Children', *Australian Early Childhood Resource Booklet*, No. 4, 1–17.

SOCIAL DEVELOPMENT: PERSONAL IDENTITY AND SOCIAL COMPETENCE

Kym Irving

Ask parents of young children enrolled in early child-hood programs what their children gain from such programs and, undoubtedly, you will be told that along with intellectual and physical stimulation, their children benefit from the experience of interacting with others. It is generally assumed that by providing children with opportunities for social interaction their social development will be facilitated and, in large part, children do develop as individuals and group members in this way. However, when talking with both parents and educators, one also learns that there is a great deal of individual variation in young children's social development and behaviour. Discerning how and why these individual differences come about and what their implications are for educating young children is no simple task. Appropriate planning for young children requires an understanding not only of the major features and processes of social development from birth, but also of the complex interplay of cognition, affect and behaviour which underpins the social development of each child. In this chapter, we will explore a number of characteristics of social and personality development during early childhood.

Current theory in social development

In this first section we will examine several perspectives which provide a basis for understanding and facilitating young children's social development.

Psychoanalytic approaches

Psychoanalytic theorists like Freud and later Erikson brought attention to the role of the unconscious mind in development. Psychoanalysts believe that children are born with a number of basic instincts and that personality has three components. The *id* is responsible for instinctual desires and their gratification. As children begin to understand the demands placed on them for self-control and the delay of gratification, the *ego* is formed. It is responsible for rational thinking and the strategies which are necessary for dealing with reality. Finally, the *superego* is formed as children internalise the norms and standards of their culture and develop a moral conscience. Children develop through a number of stages each with a different bodily focus; from the oral and anal stages of early childhood, through the phallic stage of the school years to the genital stage of adolescence and adulthood. Today, most developmentalists reject Freud's theory because of its reliance on the interpretations of experiences of a small number of clinical patients and its lack of standardised, objective assessment. However, developmentalists do recognise the contribution Freud made to our awareness of the importance of early social relationships and to aspects of development such as attachment, aggression, morality and sex-role development.

Erikson's psychosocial theory, which retains Freud's notions of instinct and stage-like development of personality, draws attention away from sexual conflicts to the importance of social relationships and cultural contexts. Erikson described stages of development each with a focus on an unconscious dilemma. For infants, the dilemma is one of developing a sense of trust or mistrust through relationships with caregivers (trust vs mistrust). For toddlers, the focus is on balancing autonomy with feelings of shame and doubt (autonomy vs shame and doubt). Pre-schoolers show a sense of initiative which is kept in check through feelings of guilt (initiative vs guilt). During the school years, children are encouraged to work hard to achieve but through comparisons with others a sense of inferiority may develop (industry vs inferiority). Although Erikson's theory is appealing in that each of us can identify with issues such as developing trust and independence, it does not explain *how* or *why* children develop a sense of trust, autonomy, initiative or industry, nor does it provide a complete picture of development. However it does high-light important issues which are prominent at different ages, and many researchers are now using Erikson's description as a starting point before trying to explain how children achieve a range of goals, including those he outlined.

Evolutionary and biological approaches

Ethology is the study of the biological bases of behaviour, including evolution, causation, function and development (Cairns, 1979). The contributions of ethology and socio-biology provide us with insights into the nature of human beings as an animal species. According to these perspec-tives, innate tendencies have evolved over time because they enhance the survival of the species. Infants arrive in the world with certain behaviours 'wired in'. These preset tendencies are evident in the display of a range of human behaviours and emotions including attachment, empathy and aggression.

From the day of birth, humans are considered to be sociable creatures who initiate and maintain social encoun-ters. According to Bowlby (1973) and Ainsworth (1979), both caregivers and infants respond to cues which promote the development of an emotional bond between the two. Infants' cries attract caregivers who ensure that the infants' basic needs are met and, at the same time, encourage the establishment of important social and emotional bonds. Additionally, infants' sucking and grasping reflexes, reflex-ive and social smiles, following, proximity-seeking and spontaneous babbling, have positive effects on caregivers who perceive these behaviours as signals that children are happy and contented. Caregivers are biologically 'tuned in' to the signals emitted by infants.

Helping others may also be part of our biological make-up. According to Hoffman (1981), altruism (helping others without expecting a reward) is an inborn motive which helps ensure the survival of the species. By living together in cooperative groups, human beings are more likely to be protected from their enemies, have their needs met (for example, food and shelter), and successfully reproduce. Hoffman's research suggests that the first signs of altruism occur in infancy when babies cry in empathy to other babies' distress.

Currently, there is still much debate as to which human characteristics have evolutionary significance and whether there is empirical evidence for many of the claims of ethology and sociobiology. Recently there has been great interest in the role of genetics in development, particularly as attempts to map the DNA in the human genome gain momentum.

Behaviour geneticists study the interplay between hereditary predispositions and environmental influences. Of most interest has been the heritability of characteristics such as temperament, personality and mental health. For example, identical twins who share the same genes are much more alike in temperament and empathy than pairs of fraternal twins who are not identical (Eisenberg & Mussen, 1989). Additionally, temperament patterns appear fairly stable during the early childhood years. Thomas and Chess (1977) noted that there were groups of infants who shared similar temperament qualities. Infants with an *easy* temperament were even-tempered, happy children who reacted well to changes and new experiences. Infants with a *difficult* temperament were active, irritable, irregular in their habits, and vigorously disliked changes. Infants who were *slow to warm up* were moody, resistant to changes, and slow to adapt to changes and new circumstances. Scarr believes that children's heritable characteristics affect the behaviour of others towards them and, further, that these characteristics influence the environments that children prefer and seek out (Scarr, 1987; Scarr & McCartney, 1983). Infants with easy temperaments, for example, may gain more favourable attention from their caregivers than infants with difficult temperaments. Children who are less active may be more interested in passive activities such as reading and talking than children who are active or muscular. Although genetics play a part in the characteristics

children develop, the role of the environment is as important, and behaviour geneticists would agree that development is a product of the interplay between nature and nurture.

Social learning approaches

Social learning theory is the most prominent approach associated with social development and Albert Bandura is the most well-known social learning theorist. However, social learning approaches have undergone a number of transformations in the last 50 years. Historically, the theory grew out of an attempt by Dollard, Millard and colleagues during the late 1930s to 1950s to reinterpret psychoanalytic theory using concepts from learning theory. Learning theory suggested that behaviour could be the result of learned motives rather than the innate drives described by psychoanalytic theory. Changes in development could be the result of imitation and social reward, not just instinct. In the 1960s, Bandura and Walters shook off the psychoanalytic orientation and incorporated the concepts of *operant conditioning* and *reinforcement* from Skinner's behaviourist perspective. During the 1970s and 1980s, Bandura refined and elaborated the theory with concepts such as *observational learning*. More recently, Bandura has expanded his theory to encompass the role of children's thinking in the observation and imitation of others. Bandura's theory has therefore become a cognitive social learning approach and is now known as *social cognitive theory* (1989). The main elements of this theory are reinforcement (from behaviourism), imitation, observational learning, self-regulation and self-efficacy.

Children learn which behaviours to repeat and which ones not to repeat by their positive or negative outcomes (contingencies of *reinforcement*). For example, if a young child is rewarded by a group leader for sitting quietly during a story then the child is more likely to sit quietly during other storytelling sessions.

Children also learn from observing others and the consequences of their behaviour (*observational learning*). A 4-year-old child may learn that it is unwise to carve his or her initials into the top of a newly purchased coffee table by observing an older brother being punished for this behaviour. The child does not have to enact the behaviour to know what the consequences are and has therefore learnt vicariously (through the experience of her brother) that the behaviour is unacceptable. Similarly, children who see other children rewarded (with praise or an opportunity to play) for helping their teacher to move desks may be more likely to help the next time the teacher requires assistance. Observational learning requires a number of cognitive and behavioural skills, however. Children must first attend to the model and their attention may be influenced by how appealing or powerful the model is and by their ability to maintain attention and arousal. Once an event has been attended to, children must store this information in memory (retain it), convert it into appropriate actions, and finally be motivated to reproduce it. In the above example, the four year old may be quite capable of scratching her or his name into the coffee table (after having attended to the brother's actions and stored the image and actions in memory), but she or he is unlikely to be motivated to reproduce the behaviour if it is believed that she or he will be punished for it. According to Bandura, a great deal of learning takes place in this way.

Not only is behaviour influenced by the ability and motivation to attend, remember and replicate; it is also influenced by *self-regulation*. Bandura proposes that people set standards of achievement for themselves, then administer rewards to themselves when these standards are met and punishments when they are not. For example, in writing this chapter, I set a certain number of pages or themes to be completed on a daily basis. On days when this target was reached I felt satisfied with my progress (internal reward) and gave myself evenings off to read and listen to music (external reward). On days when I did not reach my standard, I felt disappointed (internal punishment) and usually worked into the evening to catch up (self-denial).

Children develop self-regulation through the standards that adults set, model and reward. Self-denial in order to achieve something worthwhile is usually rewarded by parents (piano practice instead of playing) and teachers (studying instead of going out). Self-regulation is a concept which has bearing on a number of areas of development, including social competence, as we shall see later.

In addition, Bandura (1982) suggests that each individual is constantly building up a picture of his or her strengths and weaknesses. These perceptions of *self-efficacy* influence the activities children and adults choose to pursue or avoid. For instance, if parents repeatedly tell their daughter that maths is a subject 'boys are much better at', the girl may become convinced to spend less time on maths than on her other subjects. A consequence of this might be lower maths grades, 'maths anxiety' or the perception that she is not very good at maths. Not feeling efficacious at maths, she may then choose to avoid taking further subjects in maths, statistics, and computer science, thereby excluding a number of career options that depend on well-developed mathematical skills (Shaffer, 1988).

Social-cognitive approaches

Other social-cognitive approaches focus primarily on children's thinking and include attribution theory and social information-processing perspectives. *Attribution theory* states that all people are constantly seeking explanations or causal attributions, for both their own and others' behaviour. All theories of attribution distinguish between internal and external causes of behaviour. Internal factors include attitudes, interests, efforts, desires and intentions, while external factors include such things as rewards and parental pressure. When children view their good behaviour as stemming from internal factors such as their character or internalised rules, they are more likely to behave in appropriate ways even when parents or adults are not present. When children see themselves as helpful and attribute their helpful behaviour to their own personal characteristics (for example, 'I'm a friendly boy who likes helping others'), they are likely to be helpful in a range of situations without adult prompting. Children who attribute their helpful behaviour to the fact that they will be rewarded for it (for example, 'I should help out because mum will let me watch TV if I do') are less likely to be helpful in situations outside those where a reward is offered.

According to attribution theory, one of the reasons why punishment is not effective in the long term and may have negative effects on children's development is that children learn to attribute their behaviour to external causes. When children are punished, they make the attribution 'I will do what mum or dad says because I will get hit if I don't'. Children who make this kind of attribution are likely to disobey parental rules when they think they will not be punished.

Dweck (1975, 1986) has applied attribution theory to the study of children's learning. She found that when children viewed their school failures as a result of internal causes such as lack of ability, they appeared to give up. These children did not attempt to solve problems, even those they could initially solve. Additionally, they tended to view their successes as related to unstable causes. They did well not because they had the ability but because they tried hard or they were lucky. These children developed *learned helplessness*, where instead of a sense of mastery and control they developed a sense of helplessness about their learning. The message to educators and parents from theories of attribution and learned helplessness is that children should be encouraged to attribute their successes to stable internal causes (ability) and their failures to unstable ones (not trying hard enough or not paying enough attention). Children who repeatedly get the message that they do not have the ability are likely to stop trying. Dweck and her colleagues have found that through attribution retraining children can learn to change their attributions and to respond to their failures by viewing them as something that they can overcome if they try harder.

Social information processing theories highlight the ways in which social information is attended to and processed. Dodge (1985, 1986) suggests that children's reactions to frustration, anger and provocation depend a great deal on the ways in which they process and interpret this information. Highly aggressive children may be aggressive because they expect peers to be hostile towards them; they therefore search for social cues which fit that expectancy. For example, when a child accidently knocks down the tower of a highly aggressive classmate, the aggressive classmate is more likely to interpret the behaviour as aggression and retaliate.

According to Dodge, children move through five steps in processing information about social events; *decoding, interpreting, response search, response decision* and *encoding*. Let's look at these five steps in an interaction between Sam and her friend Jo. While waiting for a drink, Sam is bumped by one of her classmates, Jo. Sam turns towards Jo to see what has happened (to *decode* the event). Rather than a look of concern, she sees a big grin on Jo's face (situational cue). Knowing that Jo is a friend who would not hurt her (consideration of past events), she *interprets* the bump as a friendly gesture. Jo considers what she can do in return (*reponse search*, for example, bump her back or smile or frown) and decides to grin back at Jo (*reponse decision*). Sam turns to Jo and greets her with a big smile (*encoding*). Social information processing models provide a useful approach to understanding children's thinking about a range of social situations.

The practical application of theory

What does each theory offer for educators of young children? Consider the following dilemma. A father of one of the children in your group approaches you with a concern about the selfishness of his child and asks, 'How can I encourage Michael to share his toys with the other children in his group?' Your response may fall under the umbrella of one of the theories just discussed or it may be an amalgam of those theories which offer you useful guidelines for changing the child's behaviour (if you believe this to be beneficial to the child).

Psychoanalytic perspective

Because Michael is four years old, Erickson's theory places him at the stage where there is a conflict between initiative and guilt. Children at this stage are making plans, setting goals, and showing persistence in order to gain a sense of purpose. Selfishness may be a consequence of Michael's single-mindedness at this stage. However, maturation also plays an important role in movement from one stage to the next and it may be that Michael is still dealing with the issue of control from the earlier stage of autonomy versus shame and doubt. He may want to maintain his control over toys and possessions as a means of expressing his sense of self. The focus of Erikson's theory is on the individual resolving each crisis, however if a conflict is unresolved at its appropriate stage, it may be returned to at a later stage. For Michael then, it may be a matter of maturation, or if his selfishness is part of the resolution of conflict associated with either initiative or autonomy, then when resolution occurs his behaviour may change. Can Michael's development of sharing behaviour be encouraged? Erikson's psychosocial theory emphasises the influence of culture and societal demands on children's development. If Michael lives in a culture where sharing is valued and expected of a four year old then sharing is more likely to occur. He is also more likely to develop sharing behaviour as he becomes aware of its importance to his social relationships.

Biological approaches

Some theorists propose that altruism is an instinctive part of human nature and that sharing behaviour derives in part from early infant-initiated interactions. Infants share what they find with others, through pointing and vocalising. As children develop, these behaviours develop into more complex patterns of reciprocity and sharing. However, as sociobiologists point out, these inborn tendencies are subject to environmental influence. In Michael's case, his sharing behaviour may have been inhibited by aspects of the environment or his relationships with others. Perhaps his behaviour is a result of adapting to the behaviour of his peer group who may also be less cooperative and sharing. Alternatively, there may be scant resources in his centre, leading him to retain his share rather than doing without. Temperament theorists might add to the discussion by pointing out that Michael may be less inclined to share with his peers because he is inherently less sociable than other children. Biological theories provide a description of how sharing behaviour may come about and why changes in behaviour may be the result of adaptation to changing circumstances. However, these theories generally describe behaviour while providing little information on how to alter it. To alter behaviour we need to turn to theories which examine behaviour and cognition; theories which, by the way, guide many of the interventions and therapies which are currently used by psychologists and therapists.

Social learning approaches

Social learning theorists would recommend the use of reinforcements and modelling to change Michael's behaviour. His actions would be carefully monitored for sharing behaviour and then rewarded with, perhaps, praise ('Good boy, Michael!'). As Michael's teacher and a powerful model, you may want to set an example by sharing your possessions with other adults or children and demonstrating the positive outcomes of being generous. You may also encourage Michael's observational learning by making sure that he observes other children being rewarded for sharing. Hopefully, Michael will come to view sharing as something which provides him with pleasure.

Social cognitive approaches

According to attribution theorists, social rewards are not enough to encourage Michael to be a generous person. He is likely to attribute his sharing behaviour to the rewards he receives and he may never come to perceive himself as a generous person or to view sharing as intrinsically satisfying. Instead, these theorists suggest that we need to communicate to him that he has behaved in a competent and responsible manner when he shares. Michael should be encouraged to make an internal attribution for his sharing ('I share because I am a good boy who knows how to treat his friends'). Encouraging children to view themselves as helpful, good-natured individuals is a powerful tool for developing children's prosocial orientations.

Social information processing approaches suggest that we need to understand how Michael processes and interprets sharing in order to understand his behaviour. How does he interpret sharing? Is there a fear of loss of the objects or of them not being returned? What has his past experience of sharing been? Perhaps Michael has lost his possessions to children who did not return them. In this model, we need to examine how Michael perceives sharing (in a positive or negative light), how he interprets the outcomes of sharing (whether or not they are beneficial), and whether he has accurately assessed the effects of not sharing. Using this information, we can then help him to develop more accurate perceptions of sharing and its benefits.

The development of personal identity

Social development during early childhood can be thought of as involving two complementary processes, individuation and socialisation. Individuation refers to the formation of an individual's personal identity or unique sense of who she or he is and includes personality characteristics, sex-role orientation, self-concept, and feelings of self-worth or self-esteem. On the other hand, socialisation is the process whereby an individual's standards, skills, motives, attitudes, and behaviours are shaped to conform to those regarded as desirable and appropriate within the individual's society. Socialisation involves the development of the abilities to establish and maintain friendships and relations with others, to become an accepted member of society and to regulate one's behaviour according to the rules and norms of that society (Damon, 1983).

Obviously, socialisation and individuation go hand in hand in development. For example, personal characteristics (such as caring and helpfulness) which are valued by a society or culture are more likely to be encouraged in developing children. Characteristics which are considered inappropriate (such as selfishness) are likely to be discouraged.

Personality and self-identity

A central component of identity development is personality. A range of definitions can be found for personality, however, I particularly like the one offered by Helen Bee (1989):

> Personality describes a broad range of individual characteristics, mostly having to do with the typical ways each of us interacts with the people and the world around us . . . and which tend to be persisting aspects of the individual.

Personality refers to those characteristics of an individual that demonstrate some stability across time and contexts. For example, we might come to the conclusion that a child is shy from observing his or her shy behaviour in preschool, at home, and on excursions, and from noting that he or she has demonstrated shyness from the beginning to the end of the year. There are a number of theoretical descriptions and explanations of the origins of individual differences in personality. Each of these theories is based on a set of assumptions about the nature of personality development and the mechanisms by which individual differences arise. Each perspective has contributed to our understanding of personality. For example, biological approaches have drawn attention to temperament, sociability and activity level; social-learning approaches to the learning of aggression and social skills; psychoanalytic approaches to the importance of attachment; and social-cognitive approaches to the development of self-concept.

Temperament and stability of traits

Personality depends on a complex interplay of inborn factors and experience; both heredity and environment. You may have heard people comment on similarities between various family members; 'He's as stubborn as his father' or 'She's very shy, just like her Aunt May'. The assumption seems to be that such characteristics are inherited. Do you agree? Most researchers would find it very challenging to say which personality characteristics are inherited.

A child's developing personality begins with the initial temperament of the child, although a range of environmental factors subsequently come into play. Temperament refers to *relatively consistent, basic dispositions inherent in a person that underlie and modulate the expression of activity, reactivity, emotionality, and sociability* (Goldsmith et al., 1987). *Activity* refers to the intensity and pace of a child's behaviour and speech. *Reactivity* refers to the intensity of a child's responses to stimulation and her or his tendency to approach or withdraw from objects and people. *Emotionality* refers to the frequency and intensity of a child's emotions. *Sociability* refers to the preference for being with others rather than being alone and the tendency to initiate and respond to social contacts. Individual differences in temperament can be seen in a range of behaviours and reactions during infancy. Some infants are shy and fearful of new situations. Others are sociable and smile readily at new acquaintances. Some infants are constantly on the move, thrashing about in their cribs or crawling on the floor, while others are more placid and calm. Some infants respond well to new foods, while others spit them out in seeming disgust. Additionally, children's reactions to stressful events appear to be influenced by temperament. After the pain of a vaccination, children with more difficult temperaments take longer to soothe and display more anger than children with easier temperaments (Izard, 1982).

Bee's definition of personality calls attention to the persisting nature of personality characteristics. How long across the lifespan characteristics can be traced is a matter of much debate. In the past, researchers found little evidence for the continuity of personality between infancy and later years. More recent longitudinal studies have indicated some stability for aggression and sociability. Additionally, some traits may continue because they are strongly reinforced, for example, dependence in females and aggression in males.

Currently there is much debate about the long-term consequences of being born with a *difficult* temperament. Some researchers suggest there is a link between difficult temperament at age three or later (rather than infancy) and future behavioural problems such as aggression (Bates, 1987). Importantly, the quality of caregiver-child interaction appears to influence the link between difficult temperament and later behavioural disorders. In one study, infants categorised as difficult at six months were followed up at two years of age (Lee & Bates, 1985). The mothers of these children had more conflicts with their children and used more intrusive control strategies than mothers who did not have children with difficult temperaments. It is possible that the difficult children responded to their mothers' control by demonstrating even more difficult behaviour. On the other hand, infants who have difficulty adapting to new routines may become much more adaptable if parents or caregivers remain calm, exercise restraint, and allow children to respond to novelty at a leisurely pace. Whether outcomes are favourable or unfavourable for children depends a great deal on the *goodness of fit* between child temperament and the demands of care-givers and the child-rearing environment.

Other studies have focused on the stability of character-istics such as inhibition and shyness. In a longitudinal project spanning from when the children were 21 months to seven and a half years, children's reactions to unfamiliar children and adults were found to be fairly stable across the years. Toddlers who stayed close to their mothers and didn't initiate play with unfamiliar children and objects were inhibited and shy in their approaches to unfamiliar children at age seven and a half (Kagan et al., 1984, 1988, 1989). Not all studies show stability of temperament over time, however, suggesting that environmental influences play a part in the unfolding of children's genotypes (genetic make-ups).

Aggression also appears reasonably stable from pre-school through early adolescence. Olweus's (1982) research on aggression and bullying in Sweden indicates that the amount of physical and verbal aggression at ages six to ten is a fairly good predictor of the tendency to threaten, insult, tease and compete with peers at ages ten to 14. Similarly, Lerner and her colleagues (1988) have found that children who expressed aggression and negativity in early childhood also showed these characteristics as adoles-cents. These studies, along with many others, suggest that it may be important to alter early aggressive behaviours through intervention programs.

Several longitudinal studies suggest that sociability is a reasonably stable attribute from about age two onward. Measures of sociability at two years predict sociability at age three and a half (Bronson, 1985) and sociability during the early school years has been found to predict sociability during adolescence and young adulthood (Kagan & Moss, 1962; Schaefer & Bayley, 1963).

In summary, a number of studies show that, for some children, characteristics that are apparent in early child-hood may continue throughout childhood and adolescence. Strongest evidence has accumulated for the stability of aggression and sociability. While these characteristics may have a biological basis, it is clear that environmental influences play a role in reinforcing and maintaining aggressive and sociable behaviours.

Differences between children

It is clear that children show differences along other personality dimensions. While there are many traits that could be discussed, in this section we will look at two dimensions which are particularly important because of their relationship to prosocial development, aggression and psychological health; self-control and resiliency. Some children appear much more able to tolerate frustration, resist temptation and delay gratification (wait for desired objects or events) than other children. Jeanne and Jack Block (1980) suggest that these abilities are part of a personality trait which guides behaviour across situations and time.

Ego-control and ego-resiliency

In 1968, the Blocks initiated a longitudinal study of 130 three years olds. Each year the children were comprehensively assessed using a number of psychological tests and procedures. The Blocks found that the children's behaviour could be described using the dimensions of ego-control and ego-resiliency (you can see the influence of psychoanalytic theory in these terms).

Ego-control (or self-control) refers to the ability to control impulses, feelings and desires. Children who overcontrol appear inhibited, show little expression of emotion and have limited interests. Undercontrollers, on the other hand, have difficulty delaying gratification, are distractible and move from activity to activity. Somewhere between the two is a healthy level of control. Interestingly, children who were undercontrollers at ages three and four more often used behaviours such as teasing, manipulation and aggression at age seven. On the other hand, the overcontrolled children were more often described as shy at age seven.

As the term suggests, *ego-resilience* refers to the ability to 'bounce back', to adapt and change to meet the demands of a situation. Children who show high resilience do extremely well throughout life. Perhaps you know a child (or an adult) who appears to cope well with traumas or setbacks or whose upsets never last long. In the Blocks's study, children who were resilient at age three became empathic, friendly seven year olds.

The Blocks suggest that these early individual differences may have developmental roots in a child's original temperament and in his or her home environment. In what ways can the home environment have an influence? Family environments which place a lot of emphasis on structure and order may promote ego-overcontrol. Families in which there is a lot of conflict and few rules and standards for behaviour may promote ego-undercontrol. On the other hand, ego-resilience appears to be fostered by families which demonstrate caring, competent relationships, open communication, and which have a clear set of moral values and standards.

Self-control takes some time to develop in children. Young children are often impulsive, find it difficult to resist temptation, cannot always control their emotions and experience stress if they have to wait for exciting events or objects. Some children have difficulty overcoming these early tendencies and learning to accommodate the demands of society. As the Blocks suggest, these differences appear very early in children and may be related to both temperament and parenting. More recently, researchers have identified the ways in which children come to develop self-control (Grusec & Lytton, 1988). First, children need to internalise a norm which stresses the value of self-control. Second, they need to develop the skills of self-control. Attempts to regulate infant behaviours start in many families when babies begin to explore their environment around eight or nine months. Parents begin to control their babies' actions and protect them from harm by exclaiming 'No, no!' or 'Don't touch!'. A little later, during the second year, children begin to regulate their own behaviour with comments such as 'Don't touch' when approaching a stove or electric outlet. Around eighteen months, children's activities are further organised through caregivers' requests for children to help tidy up or put away toys. Pointing and other non-verbal behaviours are often used to gain toddlers' attention and to point out things to be done and how to do them. By two to three years, children routinely respond to requests and show an ability to control their behaviour.

A number of factors underly this change from children's actions being governed by others to being under their own control. Children often use language to help control their behaviour. They may repeat words they have heard from their caregivers (for example, 'Don't touch!'). Self-instructions, such as tennis players' 'keep your eye on the ball', help individuals alter or improve their behaviour. A number of studies have shown that impulsive children can be taught to control their impulsivity through self-talk. The best strategy for helping preschoolers resist temptation and delay gratification is to have them either distract themselves by focusing on something else, such as a rhyme ('bananas in pyjamas are coming down the stairs'), or to focus directly on controlling their behaviour ('I must wait my turn'). Preschoolers have difficulty delaying gratification because they often do not know how to distract themselves or how to prevent their attention from focusing on the attractive qualities of objects or activities they desire. With younger children caregivers routinely distract and redirect children's attention for them. By verbally directing children's activities and attention, caregivers provide models and specific techniques that children can adopt.

The question of why some children show remarkable resilience even in the face of extreme adversity is one of great interest. Fascinating case studies of *resilient* children from a range of backgrounds and experiences have accumulated over the last few decades. They include survivors of the holocaust, children growing up in war (for example, Northern Ireland), children of divorce, children experiencing extreme poverty, children whose parents have abused them and children of parents who are psychologically disturbed. Resilient children do well academically and socially despite chronic poverty, traumatic stress, abuse or family disturbance (Garmezy, 1985; Rutter, 1987; Werner, 1982, 1984).

As infants, resilient children tend to elicit positive responses from family members and strangers. Generally, their temperaments could be described as easy. They are active, affectionate, cuddly, good-natured and easy to deal with. Resilient preschool children appear to be both independent and sociable. They are able to ask for help from adults and peers when they need it, but also show self-reliance and interest in new experiences. Often resilient children have a range of interests and hobbies that are not narrowly sex-typed. Usually, they are children who have established a close bond with at least one caregiver and have developed a basic sense of trust. Additionally, they have lived in households where there are clear rules and standards and responsibilities assigned to the children. Resilient children also find emotional support outside of the family. When life at home is stressful, they may make school a home away from home where favourite teachers become important models. In these schools their teachers provide ample praise and students are given positions of trust and responsibility. 'Early childhood programs and a favourite teacher can act as an important buffer against adversity in the lives of resilient children' (Werner, 1984). Interestingly, many resilient children have also been required to help others who have experienced distress or discomfort. Finally, chidren who are resilient have a positive attitude towards life and a confidence that things will work out.

These descriptions of the characteristics and lives of resilient children provide important information for educators of young children, and especially for those who work with children exposed to family disturbance or stressful life events. By supporting children, encouraging their interests and activities, providing responsibilities, modelling resilient behaviour and encouraging support networks for children, educators may help children to overcome the effects of stress and trauma. Additionally, giving children a positive view of the world and an attribution that they are confident, capable individuals is particulary important. It is worth emphasising that providing *all* children with these avenues of support and encouragement will facilitate optimal social development and psychological health.

Sex roles and gender concepts

There are quite a number of personality traits on which males and females are said to differ. These differences are highlighted by sex-role stereotypes which often rigidly categorise males and females without regard to individual differences and qualities. However, part of the process of individuation involves recognition of one's own gender and the attached set of expected behaviours, attitudes and duties (or sex roles). Damon (1983), noted:

> Well before age 3, the young child has been exposed to so much gender-related social feedback that any biologically 'pure' behavioural sex differences — if ever they existed — have long since been elaborated, shaped, discouraged, encouraged or otherwise modified by environmental influences. It is a simple fact, well documented in the psychological literature, that persons respond to boys and girls differently from birth onward.

According to social-learning theory, a vast system of social influences acts to produce sex differences in children's behaviours, activities and preferences. From birth on, children are *labelled* male or female and reacted to according to the stereotypes attached to these labels. In our culture many activities are structured in order to teach sex roles. This *structuring of activities* occurs across a wide range of contexts including the home, school, daycare, sport and recreational settings. For example, in some families, boys may be required to help dad mow the lawn while girls help with dishes and meal preparation. Additionally, males and females often provide very different behaviours for children to *model* or imitate. Children are more likely to display those behaviours which are *reinforced* or rewarded in some way. Obviously, they are less likely to imitate those which are not sanctioned. The behaviours which are sanctioned for boys are often quite different from those which are encouraged for girls. Children also learn about sex-appropriate behaviour by *observing* what happens to others.

Parents generally describe their sons and daughters in terms of stereotyped sexual characteristics from very early childhood. Research has shown that it is especially fathers who treat boys and girls differently. After birth, fathers are often more involved in the development of sons. As children grow older, fathers often stress achievement for sons and interpersonal interactions for daughters. Mothers, on the other hand, show less extreme differential treatment of sons and daughters. Fathers are also more likely to reward their children for playing with same-sex toys and to punish cross-sex play than are mothers (Fagot & Leinbach, 1987; Langlois & Downs, 1980).

Peer pressure for 'sex-appropriate' play also begins very early. Peers can be especially critical of children who play with toys associated with the other sex, often ridiculing offenders or disrupting their play (Langlois & Downs, 1980). Even 21- to 25-month-old boys have been observed to belittle or disrupt each other for playing with feminine toys or with a girl, and girls of this same age can be critical of other girls who choose to play with boys (Fagot, 1985).

Although there is now heightened awareness of the sex-typed content of children's books and programs, males and females are still often portrayed in a highly stereotyped fashion. Males are often the central characters who respond to emergencies, make important decisions, and assume positions of leadership. Females, on the other hand, are usually presented as passive, dependent, excitable, and lacking in ability (Kilbe & La Voie, 1981). When given roles of influence and power, they are more often the villains (Huston & Alvares, 1990). In television commercials, males are more often portrayed as experts on the advertised products who convince female consumers to buy the products. Exposure to stereotyped models on television has an effect on both children and adolescents. The more television children watch, the more they identify with sex role stereotypes and chose gender consistent toys (Frueh & McGhee, 1975; McGhee & Frueh, 1980). They are also more likely to view males and females in stereotyped ways.

Stereotyped behaviours for females and males are often the ones rewarded in schools. Even in preschool, teachers respond differently to boys and girls. Teachers may encourage boys to do things on their own while girls are encouraged to stay in close proximity. Additionally, boys appear to receive more detailed instructions from teachers than girls, who may be offered brief conversation, praise and assistance. These differences may influence girls' and boys' problem-solving and analytic abilities (Serbin & O'Leary, 1984).

While social-learning theorists have aided our understanding of why children behave in sex-typed ways, cognitive theorists have sought to explain children's thinking about their own gender. You may be aware that many preschool-aged children seem to go through a period of rigid adherence to sex-typed behaviour and play activity. Many adults and parents are confused by this, especially when they feel children have been provided with many choices and models of behaviour.

Kohlberg (1966), a cognitive theorist, proposes that children go through a number of steps in determining their own gender; gender identity, gender stability and gender constancy. Gender identity occurs by two or three years, when children understand that they are male or female. By four years, children realise that their gender is stable across time and cannot be changed (that is, girls grow up to be mothers not fathers). By six or seven, children are aware that gender is constant and cannot be changed as a result of changing appearance, behaviours, or desires. Putting on a dress does not change a boy into a girl. Kohlberg believes that once children have attained gender constancy, they are motivated to behave in sex-typed ways. Social-learning theorists disagree with Kohlberg and, as we have already seen, believe that reinforcements and models have an effect well before age seven.

Gender schema theory (Bem, 1981; Martin & Halverson, 1987) provides an alternate cognitive model to children's thinking about gender. Children first develop gender identity then develop two gender schemas or sets of rules about how girls and boys behave. The first one deals with how boys and girls differ, *same-sex/opposite-sex schema*. Children then develop a more complex *own-sex* schema which consists of detailed information about one's own sex role.

Once schemas are formed, children interpret the world and behave in ways that are consistent with them. If they come across contradictory information, they are likely to distort the information so that it fits with their current gender schemas. A study by Martin and Halverson (1983) provides an interesting example of how this distortion works. Five- to 6-year-old children were shown pictures of children behaving in gender-consistent ways (boy playing with a truck) and gender-inconsistent ways (girl chopping wood). One week later the children had more difficulty remembering the gender-inconsistent pictures and were more likely to change the character to be gender-consistent (boy chopping wood) (Martin & Halverson, 1983). Gender schema theory helps us understand how and why sex-typed orientations emerge and are often strongly maintained. Moreover, it tells us that gender schematic thinking is a reflection of the values and standards that society sets for men and women.

In summary, sex role development is a function of biology, socialisation pressure and children's own thinking. Additionally, gender-schema theory suggests that providing children with models of a range of behaviours may not be enough. Educators and parents need to actively discuss sex roles with children and provide opportunities for children's involvement in a range of activities. Providing children with a range of opportunities improves psychological health, self-esteem and resilience. Jeanne Block (1983) argues that providing girls and boys with equal activities and opportunities is an important step in making the sex roles of women and men more equal in society. Do you agree?

Self-concept, self-esteem and self-efficacy

If someone were to say 'Tell me about yourself' or if you were asked to write a short essay on 'Who am I?', your response would give an indication of how you perceive or define yourself. It would reveal something about your *self-concept*. Your description might include your age, sex, likes and dislikes, personality characteristics, personal philosophies, values and so on (some of which might be sex-typed). Similarly, children develop fairly definite and clear ideas about themselves and their qualities.

Although toddlers display self-recognition during the second year of life when shown their images in a mirror, they have a limited self-concept. By six or seven, however, children know if they are a girl or a boy, strong or weak, clumsy or coordinated, liked by others or not. During the preschool years (three to five years), children define themselves in terms of physical features (looks, age, sex, size) and actions and activities ('I help mummy'; 'I go to school'), while school-aged children include psychological traits (feelings, likes, characteristics) and family and group membership (cubs and brownies). Obviously, the ability to describe oneself and the types of descriptors used are closely linked to cognitive ability.

Self-concept has many dimensions and children may describe and evaluate themselves according to their academic, social, and physical abilities. Harter (1990) has developed scales for use with children from the preschool years through to adolescence. According to her research, young children (four to seven year olds) do not distinguish between the domains. It is not until the school years that *differentiation* occurs.

While self-concept refers to the descriptions we have of ourselves and our abilities, *self-esteem* can be thought of as

the positive or negative evaluations we make about ourselves. When our evaluations are positive then self-esteem
is said to be positive or high. When our evaluations are
negative then self-esteem is negative or low. Children's
self-esteem can be influenced by a number of factors,
including their experiences with success or failure, and
family relationships. Children who repeatedly experience
failure are likely to develop low self-esteem and poor self-
images. It is therefore important to provide children with
opportunities for success.

The self-esteem of preschool children appears relatively
robust and most preschoolers have very positive views of
their abilities. Although these children may be aware that
they cannot do things as well as others, they usually do not
express a great deal of concern about these differences.
However, in the early school years, as children become
more able to evaluate and make comparisons with others
and as their self-concept becomes more differentiated, self-
esteem may be influenced, particularly as demands to
achieve and succeed at school work increase.

Parenting styles exert a strong influence on self-esteem.
Parents who display an authoritative style of parenting are
likely to have children high in self-esteem. Authoritative
parents are warm and nurturing, yet firm and in control.
They have age-appropriate expectations for their children
and clearly communicate these expectations (Baumrind,
1972).

Self-esteem is also related to a feeling of control over
one's life or a sense of personal agency. We have already
encountered the term 'learned helplessness' which refers
to a lack of a sense of mastery or control. Parents and
teachers who use a suggestive style of interacting, such as
'Why don't you give this a try?' are more likely to foster a
sense of personal control in children than adults who use
more directive styles, such as 'Here, do this!' (Dweck &
Bush, 1976).

How important are these feelings of personal control
and mastery for social and personality development? Bandura suggests that our feelings of efficacy and control
influence many of our activities and the decisions we make

in life. Similarly, case histories of resilient children reveal that personal control, responsibility and a sense of mastery in the world help to overcome trauma and stress.

Recently, Seligman (1990), in his theory of 'learned optimism', has suggested that 'the manner in which you habitually explain to yourself why events happen . . . is the great modulator of learned helplessness'. He suggests that an optimistic *self-explanatory style* prevents helplessness, whereas a pessimistic self-explanatory style encourages helplessness, and that these styles are apparent from around age eight. Childrens' optimism and pessimism are related to their mothers' explanatory styles (optimistic or pessimistic), adult criticism (from teachers and parents) and children's life crises. Explanatory styles have three elements — permanence, pervasiveness, and personalisation. Children who give up easily believe that the causes of bad events are permanent, that bad events will always happen, that bad events will strike every aspect of life (pervasiveness) and that they are responsible for them (personalisation). Good events, on the other hand, are viewed as temporary, specific to certain situations, and caused by other people. Optimistic children show the opposite pattern — bad events are temporary, they are specific, and caused by others. Optimists believe that good events can always happen in all aspects of life and that they cause good things to happen. Children with low self-esteem usually believe that they are responsible for bad events ('I failed because I'm stupid'). Seligman suggests that by changing the way children see themselves, by providing positive models and appropriate attributions for their behaviour, children can become optimists. His recommendations fit well with the coping strategies of resilient children and the work by Dweck on children's achievement.

The role of educators

Educators of young children can do a great deal to foster children's developing personal identities. It is important to acknowledge children's temperamental idiosyncrasies and to allow them some experiences that challenge, but do not overwhelm, their coping skills. Educators should attempt to establish a goodness of fit between the environments they provide for children and children's temperament styles.

Children can be encouraged to develop a sense of responsibility and caring through the assignment of age-appropriate tasks and activities. Additionally, a special interest or hobby can serve as a source of gratification and self-esteem. By treating children's verbalisations as important and using their interests as a basis for discussion, children's feelings of self-worth are enhanced.

When children develop internal stable attributions about their abilities and are encouraged to view the world in optimistic ways, they are more likely to persist and succeed at tasks and develop a resilience in dealing with stressful situations. Providing children with opportunities for success and positive feedback about their competencies enables them to develop accurate perceptions of their abilities (self-efficacy).

In order to overcome the restrictions of sex-role stereotypes, children of both sexes should be offered a range of opportunities and activities. Discussion of the activities and tasks that can be undertaken by males and females will help children develop less narrow gender schemas.

In general, educators should be aware of the major principles of social learning and social cognitive theories and use these to create environments in which competent behaviours are expected, modelled, rewarded and discussed.

The development of social competence

Social competence involves the establishment and maintenance of relationships with others. In recent years, peer relationships have attracted increasing interest as children enter childcare and play groups at earlier ages and spend more time in contact with peers than ever before (Asher, 1990). Attempts to identify the nature of children's peer relationships and the skills which underly them have provided educators with a vast amount of information on which to base interventions and learning experiences.

Children's friendships

Children's friendships are important for a number of reasons. Friendships provide opportunities for social skills learning. In order to establish and maintain friendships, children need to communicate successfully, be able to put themselves in the other person's role (perspective-taking) and resolve conflicts (Rubin, 1980, 1983).

Friendships also facilitate social comparisons. In order for children to develop a valid sense of their own identity, comparisons with others are necessary; 'My picture is better than yours', 'Who can run faster — me or you?' 'You're bigger than me'. Friendships and peer contacts provide opportunities for children to develop a concept of self in relation to others. In addition, peer relations foster a sense of group belonging. Although children need to develop as separate and distinct individuals, they also need to feel part of a group. Finally, the ability to form relationships with peers during childhood has an influence on later relationships. According to Rubin, childhood is where we learn the basic skills of getting on with others.

While the interactions of infants and toddlers are not considered to be friendships, they do indicate that interest in peers begins very early. By six months, infants smile, squeal, touch and lean towards other infants. Older babies crawl towards one another and explore each other's facial features. As we have seen, individual differences exist between infants in sociability. In the second year, social exchanges with peers become longer and more coordinated. Two children will jointly manipulate toys and objects, each child taking a turn playing then offering the object to

their playmate. Toddlers also play simple games together such as hide-and-seek. By ages two and three, children's interactions with peers include giving attention, smiling, sharing and cooperating.

Young childrens' experiences with peers in childcare can encourage the development of competent peer relationships. Toddlers who spend a year or more with the same peers show more competent behaviour and cooperative play than children who are moved to a different group. The experience of being with peers helps children to master social skills (Howes, 1987).

Peer acceptance and status

Attempts have been made to identify those children who are popular and those who may be having difficulties forming friendships. The common approach to assessing *peer status* is a sociometric technique. Preschool and school-aged children are usually asked to nominate those peers they most (and least) like to play with. Five categories of peer status have been derived from this measure: average, popular, neglected, rejected and controversial (Coie, Dodge & Coppotelli, 1982). High status children are more outgoing, sociable, sympathetic and more likely to engage in prosocial behaviour than other children. Rejected and controversial children tend to be aggressive, start fights and are generally disruptive. Neglected children tend to be withdrawn (Coie, Dodge & Kupersmidt, 1990; Wasik, 1987). It has been found that children's peer status can be enhanced through modelling, reinforcement and direct training of social skills.

Children's names and appearances can influence whether or not they are accepted by peers. Even three to five year olds differentiate between attractive and unattrative children. Muscular or athletically built children are more readily accepted than overweight or thin children. Children who are overweight tend to be the least well accepted. In addition, children may respond adversely to unfamiliar or strange names.

Skills of friendship

How do children learn the skills of friendship? For some preschool children, it may be a difficult struggle, especially if they haven't had much previous experience interacting with peers. Usually children discover by trial and error which strategies work. They also learn by 'peer tutelage'.

An important set of skills revolve around children's attempts to gain entry into peer group activities. Popular preschoolers are particularly adroit at joining in play. Usually these children wait and watch the group, mimic the group's activities and then make a group-oriented statement. These children also engage in more cooperative play than other children (Ladd, Price & Hart, 1988).

Disliked children, on the other hand, tend to make irrelevant comments. Rejected children may try to disrupt the group's activities or make intrusive statements about themselves. Neglected children tend to sit and watch on the sidelines without making any attempt to join in (Black & Hazen, 1990; Dodge et al., 1983).

Group entry behaviours reflect children's knowledge of appropriate behaviours as well as their ability to implement them. Earlier, we examined Dodge's social information processing model. Not surprisingly, popular children are more skilful at each step of the model than unpopular children. Rejected children tend to offer inappropriate strategies for solving problems such as aggression and their repertoire of strategies is very limited.

Understanding friendships

Expectations about friendship and the reasons why children are selected as friends change as development occurs. Selman (1980, 1981) presents a stage approach to children's understanding of friends and friendships. He suggests that young children view friends as *momentary physical playmates*. A friend is someone to play with. Preschoolers may also think of friends as providing *one-way assistance*. Friends give you things and help you when you fall over. Not until the school years do children begin to see that friends may help each other. However, this is *fair-weather cooperation* and arguments can terminate friendships. For young children then, friendships have not developed into enduring relationships. Also, the physical attributes and activities of playmates, rather than psychological attributes, such as personal needs, interests or character traits, are emphasised in descriptions of friends. It is not until children are 11 or 12 that friends are seen as providers of support and intimacy.

Children's views of friendship provide insights into their world of relationships. But they do not provide a total picture. Consider Rubin's (1980) description of a preschool child who has lost friends through separation:

On my visit I immediately noticed that Ricky (about 5 years), once the most outgoing and popular boy in the class, seemed unusually quiet and subdued. Although he was playing with other children, he was engaged in activities that were beneath his usual level of sophistication — for example, jumping repeatedly on a plank — and he seemed to be playing with a lack of real involvement. I asked him whether anything was the matter, and he shook his head no. When I returned to school the next day though, Ricky came up to me and said sadly, 'Buddy Josh, Buddy Tony, Buddy David'. I asked Ricky why he was saying that. 'Those are my buddies' he replied, 'I miss them.'

It is clear that Ricky is experiencing strong feelings of sadness and loss at being separated from his friends. How children deal with such situations varies greatly, as do their reactions to rejection by friends. In the latter situation, responses may vary from withdrawal to attempting to win back the friend to immediately finding a replacement.

Parents and peers

Parents influence their children's social competence in a number of ways. Warm and supportive parents who set clear rules for social behaviour ('Be nice'; 'Play quietly'; 'Don't hit') are likely to have children who get on well with both adults and peers. Authoritative parenting which is democratic, age-appropriate and calls for a level of maturity helps children develop social competence (self-reliance, self-esteem, altruism, sociability, lack of aggression) (Baumrind, 1971; Damon, 1983). Popular children also have parents who smile and laugh a lot during their interactions with their children (Parke et al., 1988) This positive affect appears to 'rub off' on popular children who are likewise described as friendly and happy by their peers.

On the other hand, the children of permissive parents are often aggressive and unpopular with their peers and defy rules set by other adults and teachers. Similarly, parents who are very directive and controlling do not help their children develop good social skills. These parents have difficulty helping their children initiate play with unfamiliar children and use inappropriate methods such as disrupting children's play (Finnie & Russell, 1988; MacDonald & Parke, 1984; Putallaz, 1987).

Many parents recognise the importance of their children's friendships and often try to help their children establish and maintain rewarding friendships. They may influence their children's friendships by *setting the stage* (through their choice of schools and where to live), *arranging social contacts* (such as activities and visits), *coaching* (providing advice and guidance concerning friends), *providing models of social relationships* (by the way they interact with their own friends), and by *providing a home base* (secure, competent family relationships) (Rubin & Sloman, 1984; Parke et al., 1988). Parents who arrange opportunities for their children to meet with peers and who monitor but do not directly intervene in their children's interactions have children who are better liked by peers and who are rated as more competent by their teachers (Ladd & Golter, 1988). By increasing the number of experiences their children have with peers, these parents are providing opportunities for the development of social competence.

Can peers help children to be more competent? Observations of preschool and school-aged children show that the most frequent victims of aggression are those children who often reinforce their attackers by crying, withdrawing or giving in (Besag, 1989; Patterson et al., 1967). It is clear that children's social behaviours can be strengthened, maintained, or virtually eliminated by the reactions they elicit from peers. Educators, therefore, need to be aware of the powerful effects of peer interactions on children's behaviours and of the ways in which these interactions can be directed towards fostering competent prosocial behaviours.

Encouraging social competence

A good reason for intervening when children are experiencing peer problems, particulary rejection, is that these children are likely to continue to experience problems through childhood and adolescence. Rejected children may be at risk for a number of educational and psychological difficulties, including dropping out of school, psychopathology and criminality (Parker & Asher, 1987; Putallaz & Gottman, 1982). Children identified as rejected or neglected by their peers have become the focus of numerous training programs aimed at enhancing social knowledge and social skills (Asher & Renshaw, 1981).

Intervention programs usually focus on children's behaviour with peers, chidren's thinking about social problems, or both (see for example, King & Kirschenbaum, 1992).

In regard to children's thinking, Oden (1982) suggests a method for engaging children in learning to describe, propose and evaluate aspects of social interaction and relationship formation. This method fits well with problem-solving approaches to social dilemmas and the encouragement of the cognitive skills identified by Dodge. However, it must be remembered that modelling and reinforcing appropriate behaviours, along with building self-confidence (through the development of positive self-attributions) and self-control in children, are also important in helping them to become socially competent individuals. The steps in the model are:

1. Describe a problem or event (for example, teasing).
2. Describe the target child's feelings, behaviours, and perspective.
3. Consider the likely perspective of the other peer or peer group.
4. Discuss a number of strategies that are potential solutions to the problem.
5. Discuss the likely impact of a strategy for oneself and the peer/group.

In Australia, MacMullin et al. (1992) have developed a social problem-solving program for primary school children based on similar strategies (The Sheidow Park Problem Solving Program). This ten-week program begins with children identifying and becoming acquainted with a range of feelings. Next problems are identified and these may be based on the problems identified by a survey of the children's concerns (The Inventory of Problematic Situations for Children). In the third stage children are taught to consider the consequences of potential solutions and to review their choices and actions. A similar training program has been developed by Petersen and Ganoni (1989) for children and adolescents.

In programs which focus on children's thinking and behaviour, children are coached in skills such as how to offer support to peers, lead peers in play, and ask peers questions. They are then encouraged to try out these new ideas in games with peers. For preschool-aged children Mize and Ladd (1990) used two puppets to teach the following skills and concepts (details are provided in their reference):

- Leading peers. Preschoolers are often directive (but not bossy) in their attempts to get other children to play with them; 'Hey I be the cashier, and you come, you pretend you have to buy all these for your wife'. Children were asked to think about 'having a fun idea about something that both kids could do so that both have fun playing together'.

- Asking questions in a friendly or neutral tone.

- Commenting. Popular children often make comments about their play and activities; 'We're putting out the fire! We're putting out the fire!' Children were encouraged to think about 'just talking about what you and the other kid are doing'.

- Supporting peers through affection, giving help, and making positive comments. 'Doing something really nice that makes the other kid happy'.

Children were videotaped by the 'puppets' trying out the skills and then shown the videos. They were also enouraged to use self-evaluation and monitoring skills; to watch the videos and identify instances when they used a skill. The researchers found that the children's skills, particularly in leading and commenting, improved significantly. These efforts show that systematic approaches to the development of social skills can be employed with young children in an effective and appropriate way.

Although intervention to develop children's social skills can be warranted, Stocking and Arezzo (1979) point out that it is important to remember:

> The objective of social skills instruction is not to create 'popular' or 'outgoing' children but to help youngsters, whatever their personality styles, to develop positive relationships . . . with at least one or two other children.

Many of the social values held by the preschool teacher are 'built into the profession' (Adcock & Segal, 1983). Generally, the preschool period is viewed as a time when children can learn to take turns, to share, to respect the needs and desires of others, to make friends, and to learn to cope with stress and aggression in a positive way.

A teacher's style of managing children communicates to children the social values he or she most values. These expectations and values are often communicated by the rules set by a teacher; rules such as those to promote sharing, to reduce exclusion, for controlling aggression, and for maintaining order. For example, teachers often define or create special areas for various kinds of play, then set a limit on the number of children allowed in each area, thereby reducing opportunities for exclusion of children.

Educators also communicate their values in the emotional tone they set for children. Consider the different styles of the following teachers (from Adcock & Segal, 1983):

> Teacher A: (Holding a puppet called My Friend). Why are you so sad, My Friend? Your room is messed up? Don't worry, all these children will help you clean it up. Ben, can you help My Friend put the puzzles away? Ken, can you help with the blocks?

> Teacher B: (Holding the same puppet) Wow! Look at this room, My Friend. It's a mess. You need a giant clean up crew. O.K. crew, let's get to work. Ben, to the puzzle shelf; Ken to the blocks.

Teacher A appeals to the children's sense of empathy. The puppet is sad and the children can cheer him up by helping out. Teacher B focuses on the children's sense of group belonging and energetically assigns tasks to get the group going. Both teachers are effective in using their own personalities and styles to encourage the children's helping and tidying behaviours. It is important for educators to examine the values they bring to their work with children and to develop their own styles of fostering children's social competence.

References

Adcock, D. & Segal, M. (1983) *Making Friends: Ways of Encouraging Social Development in Young Children*. Englewood Cliffs, New Jersey: Prentice-Hall.

Ainsworth, M. (1979) Attachment is related to mother-infant interaction. In J. S. Rosenblatt, R. A. Hinde, C. Beer & M. Busnel (eds.), *Advances in the study of behaviour*, Vol. 9. Orlando, Florida: Academic Press.

Asher, S. (1990) Recent advances in the study of peer rejection. In S. Asher & J. Coie (eds.), *Peer rejection in childhood*. Cambridge: Cambridge University Press.

Asher, S. & Renshaw, P. (1981) Children without friends: Social knowledge and social skill training. In S. R. Asher & J. M. Gottman (eds.), *The development of children's friendships*. Cambridge: Cambridge University Press.

Bandura, A. (1982) Self-efficacy mechanism in human agency. *American Psychologist*, 37, 122–47.

Bandura, A. (1989) Social cognitive theory. In R. Vasta (ed.), *Annals of child development: Vol 6. Six theories of child development: Revised formulations and current issues*. Greenwich, CT: JAI Press.

Bates, J. E. (1987) Temperament in infancy. In J. D. Osofsky (ed.), *Handbook of infant development* (1101–49). New York: Wiley.

Baumrind, D. (1971) Current patterns of paternal authority. *Developmental Psychology Monographs*, 4, 1 (part 2).

Bee, H. (1989) *The Developing Child*. (5 ed.). New York: Harper and Row.

Bem, S. L. (1981) Gender-schema theory: A cognitive account of sex-typing. *Psychological Review*, 88, 354–64.

Besag, V. (1989) *Bullies and victims in schools: A guide to understanding and management*. Milton Keynes: Open University Press.

Black, B & Hazen, N. L. (1990) Social status and patterns of communication in acquainted and unacquainted preschool children. *Developmental Psychology*, 26, 379–87.

Block, J. H. & Block, J. (1980) The role of ego-control and ego-resiliency in the organisation of behaviour. In W. A. Collins (ed.), *Development of Cognition, Affect, and Social Relations* (Minnesota Symposium on Child Psychology, Vol. 13). Hillsdale, New Jersey: Lawrence Erlbaum.

Block, J. H. (1983) Differential premises arising from differential socialization of the sexes: Some conjectures. *Child Development*, 54, 1335–54.

Bowlby, J. (1973) *Attachment and loss*. Vol. 2. *Separation*. London: Hogarth Press.

Bronson, W. (1985) Growth in the organization of behaviour over the second year of life. *Developmental Psychology*, 21, 108–17.

Cairns, R. B. (1979) *Social development: The origins and plasticity of interchanges*. San Francisco: Freeman and Company.

Coie, J. D., Dodge, K. A. & Coppotelli, H. (1982) Dimensions and Types of Social Social Status: A cross age perspective. *Developmental Psychology*, 18, 557–70.

Coie, J. D., Dodge, K. A. & Kupersmidt, J. B. (1990) Peer group behavior and social status. In S. Asher & J. Coie (eds.), *Peer rejection in childhood*. Cambridge: Cambridge University Press.

Damon, W. (1983) *Social and Personality Development: Infancy through Adolescence.* New York: Norton & Co.

Dodge, K. (1985) A Social Information Processing Model of Social Competence in Children. In M. Perlmutter (ed.), *Minnesota Symposium on Child Psychology*. Hillsdale, New Jersey: Erlbaum.

Dodge, K. (1986) Social Information Processing Variables in the

Development of Aggression and Altruism in Children. In C. Zahn-Waxler, E. Cummings, R. Ianotti (eds.), *Altruism and Aggression*. New York: Cambridge University Press.

Dodge, K., Schlundt, D., Schocken, I. & Delugach, J. (1983) Social competence and children's sociometric status: The role of peer group entry behaviors. *Merrill-Palmer Quarterly*, 29, 309–36.

Dweck, C. S. (1975) The role of expectations and attributions in the alleviation of learned helplessness. *Journal of Personality and Social Psychology*, 31, 674–85.

Dweck, C. S. (1986) Motivational processes affecting learning. *American Psychologist*, 41, 1040–48.

Dweck, C. S. & Bush, E. S. (1976) Sex differences in learned helplessness: I. Differential debilitation with peer and adult evaluators. *Developmental Psychology*, 12, 147–56.

Eisenberg, N. & Mussen, P. H. (1989) *The roots of prosocial behavior in children*. Cambridge: Cambridge University Press.

Fagot, B. (1985) Beyond the reinforcement principle: Another step toward understanding sex-role development. *Developmental Psychology*, 21, 1097–104.

Fagot, B. I. & Leinbach, M. D. (1987) Socialization of sex roles within the family. In D. B. Carter (ed.), *Current conceptions of sex roles and sex typing: Theory and research*. New York: Praeger.

Finnie, V. & Russell, A. (1988) Preschool children's social status and their mothers' behavior and knowledge in the supervisory role. *Developmental Psychology*, 24, 789–801.

Frueh, T. & McGhee, P. (1975) Traditional sex-role development and amount of time spent watching television. *Developmental Psychology*, 11, 109.

Garmezy, N. (1985) Stress-resistant children: The search for protective factors. In J. Stevenson (ed.), *Recent advances in developmental psychopathology*. Oxford: Pergamon Press.

Goldsmith, H. H., Buss, A. H., Plomin, R., Rothbart, M. K., Thomas, A., Chess, S., Hinde, R. A. & McCall, R. B. (1987) Roundtable: What is temperament? Four approaches. *Child Development*, 58, 505–29.

Grusec, J. & Lytton, H. (1988) *Social development: History, theory and research*. New York: Spinger-Verlag.

Harter, S. (1990) Issues in the Self-Concept of Children and

Adolescents. In A. LaGreca (ed.), *Through the Eyes of the Child.* Boston: Allyn & Bacon.

Hartup, W. W. (1983) Peer relations. In E. M. Hetherington (ed.), *Handbook of child psychology: Vol. IV. Socialization, personality and social development.* New York: Wiley.

Hoffman, M. (1981) Is altruism a part of human nature? *Journal of Personality and Social Psychology,* 40, 121–37.

Howes, C. (1987) Peer interaction of young children. *Monographs of the Society for Research in Child Development,* 53, Serial No. 217.

Huston, A. C. & Alvares, M. M. (1990) The socialization context of gender role development in early adolescence. In R. Montemayor, G. R. Adams & T. P. Gullota (eds.), *From childhood to adolescence: A transitional period?* Newbury Park, California: Sage.

Izard, C. (1982) *Measuring emotions in infants and children.* Cambridge: Cambridge University Press.

Kagan, J. (1989) Temperamental contributions to social behavior. *American Psychologist,* 44, 668–74.

Kagan, J. & Moss, H. A. (1962) *Birth to maturity.* New York: Wiley.

Kagan, J., Reznick, J. S., Clarke, C., Snidman, N. & Garcia-Coll, C. (1984) Behavioural inhibition to the unfamiliar. *Child Development,* 55, 2212–25.

Kagan, J., Reznick, J. S. & Snidman, N. (1988) Biological basis of childhood shyness. *Science,* 240, 167–71.

Kilbe, R. & La Voie, J. (1981) Sex-role stereotypes in preschool children's picture books. *Social Psychology Quarterly,* 44, 369–74.

King, C. & Kirschenbaum, D. (1992) *Helping young children develop social skills: The social growth program.* Pacific Grove, Calif: Brooks/Cole.

Kohlberg, L. (1966) A cognitive-developmental analysis of children's sex-role concepts and attitudes. In E. E. Maccoby (ed.), *The development of sex differences.* Stanford: Stanford University Press.

Ladd, G. W, Price, J. M. & Hart, C. H. (1988) Predicting preschoolers' peer status from their playground behaviors. *Child Development,* 59, 986–92.

Langlois, J. & Downs, A. (1980) Mothers, fathers, and peers as socialisation agents of sex-typed play behaviours in young children. *Child Development*, 51, 1237–47.

Lee, C. & Bates, J. (1985) Mother-child interaction at age two years and perceived difficult temperament. *Child Development*, 56, 1314–25.

Lerner, J., Hertzog, C., Hooker, K., Hassibi, M. & Thomas, A. (1988) A longitudinal study of negative emotional states and adjustment from early childhood through adolescence. *Child Development*, 59, 356–66.

MacDonald, K. & Parke, R. (1984) Bridging the gap: Parent-child play interaction and peer interactive competence. *Child Development*, 55, 1265–77.

MacMullin, C., Aistrope, D., Brown, J., Hannaford, D. & Martin, M. (1992) *The Sheidow Park Social Problem Solving Program*. Bedford Park, SA: The Institute for the Study of Learning Difficulties, The Flinders University of South Australia.

Martin, C. & Halverson, C. (1983) The effects of sex-typing schemas on young children's memory. *Child Development*, 54, 563–74.

Martin, C. & Halverson, C. (1987) The roles of cognition in sex role acquisition. In D. B. Carter (ed.), *Current conceptions of sex roles and sex-typing* (123–38). New York: Praeger.

McGhee, P. E. & Frueh, T. (1980) Television viewing and the learning of sex role stereotypes. *Sex Roles*, 6, 179–88.

Mize, J. & Ladd, G. (1990) Toward the development of successful social skills training for preschool children. In S. R. Asher and J. D. Coie (eds.), *Peer rejection in childhood*. Cambridge: Cambridge University Press.

Oden, S. (1982) Peer relationship development in childhood. In L. G. Katz (ed.), *Current Topics in Early Childhood Education*, Vol. IV. Norwood, New Jersey: Ablex Publishing.

Olweus, D. (1982) Development of stable aggressive reaction patterns in males. In R. Blanchard & C. Blanchard (eds.), *Advances in the study of aggression* (Vol. 1). New York: Academic Press.

Parke, R. D., MacDonald, K. B., Beitel, A. & Bhavnagri, N. (1988) The role of the family in the development of peer relationships. In R. D. Peters & R. J. McMahon (eds.), *Social learning and systems approaches to marriage and the family*. New York: Brunner/Mazel.

Parker, J. G. & Asher, S. R. (1987) Peer Relations and Later Personal Adjustment: Are Low-Accepted Children at Risk? *Psychological Bulletin*, 102(3), 357–89.

Patterson, G., Littman, R. & Bricker, W. (1967) Assertive behavior in children: A step toward a theory of aggression. *Monographs of the Society for Research in Child Development*, Vol. 32 (5, Serial No. 113).

Petersen, L. & Ganoni, A. (1989) *Teacher's manual for training social skills while managing student behaviour*. Adelaide: Stop Think Do Ltd.

Putallaz, M. (1987) Maternal behavior and children's sociometric status. *Child Development*, 58, 324–40.

Putallaz, M. & Gottman, J. (1982) Conceptualizing Social Competence in Children. In P. Karoly & J. J. Steffen (eds.), *Advances in Child Behavioural Analysis and Therapy (Vol. 1): Improving Children's Competence*. Massachusetts: Lexington Books.

Rubin, Z. (1980) *Children's Friendships*. Glasgow: Fontana.

Rubin, Z. (1983) The skills of friendship. In Donaldson, M., Grieve, R. & Pratt, C. (eds.), *Early Childhood Development and Education*. Oxford: Basil Blackwell.

Rubin, Z. & Sloman, J. (1984) How parents influence their children's friendships. In M. Lewis (ed.), *Beyond the dyad*. New York: Plenum Press.

Rutter, M. (1987) Psychosocial resilience and protective mechanisms. *American Journal of Orthopsychiatry*, 57, 317–31.

Scarr, S. (1987) Three cheers for behavior genetics: Winning the war and losing our identity. *Behavior Genetics*, 17, 219–28.

Scarr, S. & McCartney, K. (1983) How people make their own environments: A theory of genotype/environment effects. *Child Development*, 54, 424–35.

Seligman, M. E. P. (1990) *Learned optimism*. Sydney: Random House.

Selman, R. L. (1980) *The Growth of Interpersonal Understanding*. New York: Academic Press.

Selman, R. (1981) The child as a friendship philosopher. In S. R. Asher & J. M. Gottman (eds.), *The development of children's friendships*. Cambridge: Cambridge University Press.

Serbin, L. A. & O'Leary, K. D. (1984) How nursery schools teach girls to shut up. In Fitzgerald, H. E. and Walraven, M. G.

(eds.), *Human Development — 84/85 Annual Editions*. Guildford, Connecticut: Dushkin.

Schaefer, E. S. & Bayley, N. (1963) Maternal behavior, child behavior, and their intercorrelations from infancy through adolescence. *Monographs of the Society for Research in Child Development*, 28, (Serial No. 87).

Shaffer, D. (1988) *Social and personality development, 2nd edition*. California: Brooks/Cole.

Thomas, A. & Chess, S. (1977) *Temperament and development*. New York: Brunner/Mazel.

Wasik, B. H. (1987) Sociometric measures and peer descriptions of kindergarten children: A study of reliability and validity. *Journal of Clinical Child Psychology*, 16, 218–24.

Werner, E. (1984) Resilient children. *Young Children*, November, 68–72.

Werner, E. & Smith, R. S. (1982) *Vulnerable but invincible: A study of resilient children*. New York: McGraw-Hill.

SOCIALISATION AND

FAMILY

RELATIONSHIPS

Donna Berthelsen

Introduction

Socialisation refers to the processes by which individuals acquire ways of behaving within a society, in order that they can function successfully within it. A child is born into a family which confers on the child a particular status within the community and the culture of which the family is a part. It is within the family, the community and the culture that a child experiences the social world and those features provide the framework within which socialisation occurs.

The family is by far the most significant social institution influencing the daily lives of most individuals. The family continues to hold the major responsibility for socialising children and it functions both as the first and the major reference group in which children develop and learn to understand the nature of social relationships. The manner in which the family functions as a system for interaction with a characteristic interactional style has very powerful effects on the social-emotional development of children. A child will derive from his or her 'family of origin' many of the patterns of behaviour, beliefs, attitudes and norms of social behaviour which will be carried throughout life.

This chapter focuses on aspects of theory and research about how the family influences the social-emotional development of children in early childhood (birth to eight years). Such knowledge is important for those who work with young children and their families in order to understand and so relate effectively to children and their parents. This chapter seeks to focus primarily on the social-emotional outcomes for children from family experiences but these same experiences may also have important implications for other developmental areas such as language or cognition.

Currently within developmental research, there is an emphasis on understanding the social contexts in which development occurs. Children's development has often been studied within 'laboratory' settings and/or was strongly reliant on maternal reports from structured interviews or structured questionnaires. However, families have another life outside of psychological experiments and there is a reappraisal occurring in social developmental research to ensure more ecological validity. There is more emphasis on using observational studies conducted in naturalistic settings and an acceptance of the legitimacy of using open-ended accounts of parents' and children's experiences within their families to ensure that perspectives other than the researcher's predetermined conceptions are taken into account. This is not to deny the continued, important place of experimental research but rather a recognition that a breadth of research methodologies will add to the nature and manner in which knowledge about developmental processes will be constructed. It is also important to realise that a great deal of psychological research on families has been focused on mother-child relationships and that mothers have been the sole respondents about family processes. While there has been increasing recognition of the roles of fathers within families, research still focuses strongly on mother-child interaction. As a result, there is much more known about mother-child relationships than about father-child relationships. There is also increasing interest in understanding the influences of siblings on the development of other children in families and through the 1990s this will be an important focus for research.

In this chapter systems theories of family development, in particular Bronfenbrenner's (1979) model of the ecology of human development, will be presented as a means for understanding the range of influences which affect families. Research areas of current interest in the social-emotional development of children which will then be addressed include the effect of temperament on parent-child relationships, the development of the early attachment relationship between child and parent, dimensions of parenting behaviour and parenting styles, parental belief systems and the intergenerational transmission of parenting behaviour. Finally, there will be a brief overview of the role of social support in parenting as families come under increasing stress in society and a review of the implications of non-parental care for young children.

The family as a context for development

Developmental theory and research have traditionally focused on the nature of individual development and on individual differences, without systematically accounting for how development is influenced by the social context in which the individual is embedded. Conventionally, the study of child development was approached from a framework which took the major bases of development as lying either within the child as conceptualised by psychoanalytic theory (Freud, 1957), or as primarily extrinsic to the child as in operant learning theory (Skinner, 1953). Such positions are the basis of the nature versus nurture debate about the relative effects of biological influences and environmental influences on development, which dominated developmental psychology until the 1960s. Increasingly, theory and research has sought to address the reciprocal influences of biology and environment on individual development, and to account for the impact on development of the contextual features in an individual's experience. Aspects of a child's family, community and cultural life which may or may not be experienced directly by the child are studied.

General systems theory

Von Bertalanffy (1968) proposed that the logic of general systems theory to explain the interactive, hierarchical functioning of biological systems could be extended to explain the functioning and interrelationships in personal and social systems. From this perspective the individual develops in interaction with her or his immediate social environment but aspects of the larger social context affect what goes on in her or his immediate settings. This

approach emphasises the interrelationships between different systems, for example the psychological and biological systems (the individual's psychological and physical conditions), the interpersonal systems (the relationships and interactions of the individual with others), the family systems (the interrelationships, traditions, values and norms of behaviour within the family) and the community/social-cultural systems. Key principles of a systemic perspective are that any system is an organised whole and that elements within the system are interdependent (Minuchin, 1985). Systems are conceptualised as being adaptive and self-regulating in order to achieve homeostasis after any internal or external change in or to the system. After major change, the system will reorganise itself to establish a new balance. This can be seen in the family system, with interdependent elements (the family members) and subsystems (the parent-child relationship or the marital relationship) adapting to the changes in the system which come with the birth of a second child. The birth brings adaptions to the nature and functioning of the subsystems in order to accommodate the new family member. Such changes will achieve new, differentiated relationships between the family members in order to maintain the system.

Developmental psychology generally acknowledges the validity of a systemic approach and an important conceptual contribution in applying a systems theory to human development has been made by Bronfenbrenner (1979) in his ecological theory of human development.

The ecology of human development

Human ecology is the study of the dynamic relationship between individuals and their unique set of environmental circumstances at a particular period of time. The assumption is that an individual's environment is the source of many developmental influences. The ecological viewpoint is a relational one in that it assumes that there are always both intrinsic and extrinsic influences on a developing child. It takes into account that both individuals and environments may change and that often changes in one bring about change in the other. The ecological approach in developmental research can be distinguished on the basis of two criteria. It includes the contexts of the child's life in the sphere of study and the child-context interactions are the objects of study.

Bronfenbrenner (1979) conceptualised the ecological environment of the individual as consisting of micro-systems, mesosystems, exosystems and macrosystems. The *microsystem* is the pattern of activities, roles and interpersonal relations experienced by a developing person in a given setting which has particular physical and material characteristics. The life of an infant is the pattern of feeding, sleeping, bathing, of playing primarily within the family setting and of interactions with parents, siblings and visitors. Increasingly, daycare settings are also a microsystem in which infants develop. Over time the number of physical and material settings, or microsystems, which a child experiences directly increases.

The *mesosystem* comprises the interrelations among two or more settings in which a developing person actively participates. Although the family is the principal context in which development takes place, other settings such as daycare centres or school do affect developmental processes directly as microsystems, but also in how they impinge on family life. Bronfenbrenner (1979) emphasises that the processes operating in different settings are not independent of each other. Events at home affect a child's development and progress in school and vice versa. The nature of the links between an individual's microsystems is the basis of the mesosystem. The number and quality of the links are important. A strong mesosystem with maximum links between the microsystems (such as home and daycare settings) is important for a child's development.

The last two systems in Bronfenbrenner's model are more removed from the child. The *exosystem* refers to one or more settings that do not involve the child as an active participant, but they are settings in which events occur that affect what happens in the microsystems. Exosystems may affect a child's development through their influence on family processes such as the work systems of the parents, parental social networks and community/government influences on family functioning. The impact of maternal employment on a child, the degree of social support which a mother has to ensure her wellbeing, and government decisions about family policies are examples of exosystems analyses.

The *macrosystem* refers to the consistencies in the form and content of the lower order systems (the microsystems, mesosystems and exosystems) that exist at the level of the subculture or culture in which an individual develops. This includes the belief systems or ideologies which are generally consistent within the culture. Macrosystems may reflect the lifestyles of particular groups and communities. For example, a macrosystem analysis could compare the differences between urban and rural lifestyles and how the lives of children vary within each lifestyle.

In later theoretical development, Bronfenbrenner (1986)

delineated *chronosystems* as a term for designating the influence on a person's development of changes at points in time or over time. The simplest forms of chronosystems are life transitions and their impact on a developing person. Two types of transitions have been usefully distinguished. Those that are normative such as school entry or puberty and those that are non-normative such as a severe illness in the family or moving to another city to live. Such transitions occur throughout the lifespan and often serve as direct impetuses for developmental change because they must be adapted to and accommodated.

The family: a microsystem

The study of family processes which affect socialisation and social-emotional development is an example of a microsystem analysis (Bronfenbrenner, 1979). The focus of study is the nature of the interactional behaviours and how those interactions foster or inhibit children's social-emotional competence. Within the family, children experience the first of their relationships with others and these relationships affect the course of children's development as differences in the nature and quality of relationships emerge.

The parent-child relationship has often been conceptualised as a process whereby parents influence children's behaviour, rather than as a system of interacting individuals in which children also affect parental behaviour (Bell, 1968). The unidirectional model is no longer tenable and the bidirectional nature of the child-parent relationship is now accepted in the study of family processes. To view the child-parent relationship as a subsystem within the family system is also important. Such a systematic framework also permits understanding of how an individual's regulatory power in the system changes over time (Minuchin, 1985). Undoubtedly, a parent drives many of the early interactional activities while his or her child is an infant, although the child is an active participant and is capable of influence on the system from the outset (Scarr, 1992). Over time, the child becomes a fully contributing member of the interactional system. From the emergence of focused attachment with the mother in the first year, the child gradually develops independence to negotiate other social relationships within and outside the family. As she or he becomes more active in exploration, in verbal abilities and in problem-solving, the mother-child interactions change in their nature and are structured to support the child in learning across many areas of development. Maternal intervention becomes less direct as the child becomes more competent across developmental areas, but the mother-child relationship continues to serve affective functions to regulate the child's feelings of security (Hartup, 1989).

There are many mechanisms by which a child develops and learns acceptable behaviours within the family so that he or she can function successfully within it. Parents model behaviours, manage environments, teach skills, act as a resource to facilitate learning and provide a supportive milieux (Clarke-Stewart, 1988). Socialisation may occur within the family by affective means which emerge from feelings and emotions expressed in person-to-person inter-action. For example, the development of attachment between a child and a significant other, usually the mother, is the first of many important emotional relationships that a child will form. The initial attachment to an adult figure helps a child to be responsive to learning in other domains, thus attachment is a mediator for optimising future inter-action and learning (Hartup, 1989).

Socialisation also occurs through a child's actions, so that she or he is the agent. Such social learning occurs through others' responses to the child's behaviours. This is referred to as operant learning (Skinner, 1953). If a child's behaviour receives a positive response from others then that behaviour is considered to be reinforced, and there is more likelihood that reinforced behaviours will recur. By positively reinforcing appropriate behaviours, parents teach children what behaviours are acceptable. If a behaviour does not receive attention and is ignored, then the likelihood of it being repeated is diminished. If a behaviour receives a negative response, then this is punishment, and the likelihood that it will be repeated is suppressed.

Within social-learning theory, Bandura (1973, 1977, 1986) proposes that a great deal of learning takes place through observing others, internalising this information, then imitating or modelling actions based on the internalised information. The models in a young child's social world include parents, siblings, extended family and peers. Social behaviours are learnt through cognitive processes as children are required to think about others' and their own actions, and these thinking processes mediate future behaviours. Adults help children to cognitively mediate their actions by giving instructions about expected behaviours and by explaining the standards they have for particular behaviours. If adults explain why certain behaviours are expected in certain situations then children learn to generalise about acceptable behaviours from one situation to another. They can then make decisions about how to behave in similar circumstances. Much of children's socialisation does occur through the intervention of adults, but at the same time children are cognitively dealing with their experiences.

At the social-cultural level, individuals are socialised through their membership of groups, in this case the family. Because individuals desire social approval they are subject to group pressures to adhere to the group's explicit and implicit rules and norms. In this way, conformity is achieved. Social-cultural values and behaviours also stem from traditions which set patterns for behaviour or for conducting interactions within families. A family may always conduct meal times in a certain manner, greet each other in a particular way, handle conflict in a characteristic style, have certain rituals for celebrations such as birthdays. Particular symbols or situations cue family members to the basis for behaviour expected on that occasion or in that interaction. In family therapy, it is recognised that understanding the traditions, rituals and symbols which a family uses and which may not always be explicit to its members is a key to helping it function more effectively (Berg-Cross, 1988).

Two major characteristics of families that influence socialisation are socioeconomic status and cultural background. Within Australian society, social stratification occurs primarily through achievement criteria such as education, occupation, income and place of residence. In other cultures, family lineage, sex or birth order may ascribe social status to an individual. Socioeconomic status may accord different opportunities and/or costs to a family and its members. For example, parents who have greater financial resources may offer their children more experiential learning experiences and environments which have more material resources. Generalisations about the influence of socioeconomic status on developmental outcomes need to be made cautiously as it is only one factor in a complex model of developmental influences. Through the 1970s a great deal of research was conducted on the effects of social class on parenting styles and the outcomes for children, but through the 1980s research moved beyond 'social-address' models of environmental influences to focus on a wider range of contextual features that affect children's socialisation within the family (Belsky, 1990). The cultural group to which a family belongs also imparts values and norms that set behavioural and role expectations for family members. The cultural background may determine how individuals within families relate to each other and the qualities families require of their children.

The influence of temperament on social-emotional development

As reciprocal processes characterise parent-child relationships (Bell, 1968), research has sought to identify which child characteristics influence parental behaviour. Important characteristics are a child's age, sex, physical health and temperament.

Temperament is a construct used to describe individual differences which are present from birth. Temperament has been defined as constitutionally based individual differences in reactivity and self-regulation (Rothbart, 1989) and as the tendencies to express primary emotions (Goldsmith & Campos, 1982). Temperament appears to be relatively stable over time from infancy to childhood, and affects how parents act towards their children (Bates, 1987). The effects however are dependent on the interaction of the parents' characteristics with the characteristics of each child (Clarke-Stewart, 1988). Thomas and Chess (1977) identified nine main dimensions of temperament. These are the activity level of a child; the regularity of bodily functioning including sleep, hunger and bowel movements; adaptability to changes in routine; response to new situations; level of sensory threshold to produce a response to external stimulation; intensity of responses to external stimulation; the general degree of positive or negative mood; the degree of distractability and the degree of persistence and attention span. On the basis of a profile on these dimensions, a child can be described by certain temperamental styles, such as easy or difficult (Thomas & Chess, 1977).

There are two propositions about the influence of temperament on parental behaviour. It is thought that parents are able to influence more easily children who have characteristics in the middle range of temperamental styles rather than those who have extreme styles. Differences in parental caregiving has been found to be greater for 'easy' children who are the norm, than for 'difficult' children (Buss & Plomin, 1984). A 'goodness of fit' theory proposes that if there is a match between parental behaviour and parents' expectations of an infant's temperament then parental behaviour is more likely to influence child behaviour (Lerner, 1986). For example, a difficult infant may do well with a parent who wants an energetic child and who can cope with the infant's demands, but that same infant might do poorly with a parent who lacks confidence in his or her parenting skills.

Temperament and attachment are considered related constructs in describing the characteristics of children, although the nature of this relationship remains controversial (Vaughn et al., 1992). Research has not determined how such constructs relate, since the construct of attachment is considered to be the organisation of an infant's psychological behavioural patterns over and beyond the specific behaviours on which the classification of temperament is based (Sproufe, 1985).

The development of attachment

The quality of attachment has been an important focus in the study of development within the family. Attachment is the close emotional bond between a child and a significant other person and is a relational construct rather than an individual attribute because it belongs to the child-caregiver relationship. The theories of John Bowlby (1969, 1973, 1980) used to explain the development of attachment stem from ethology and from psychoanalytic theory which emphasises the central role of affect in development and the importance of early experiences. Bowlby proposed that through early experiences with a primary caregiver a child develops an internal model about the responses of the significant other (most often the mother). This model is made up of certain expectations such as 'If I cry I will be picked up' of 'If that person yells at me he or she is angry with me'. Once formed this internal model resists change and becomes the basis on which the child interprets future affective experiences with others. It is the basis of a sense of self and lays the foundation for dealing with future intimate relationships including nurturing others and dealing with loss or separation (Sproufe, 1983).

A measure of attachment, called the Strange Situation

assessment, was designed by Ainsworth and her colleagues (Ainsworth et al., 1978). In this assessment, for brief periods of time, usually three minutes, children are subjected to mild social stress by exposure to an unfamiliar environment, an unfamiliar adult and by brief separations from the mother. About 70 per cent of the children tested using this procedure are classified as secure in their attachment to their mother. They are usually active in their exploration of the environment when their mother is present, are often but not always upset when their mother leaves them, and are easily soothed when she returns. About 20 per cent of children are classified as insecure-avoidant on the Strange Situation measure. These children do not appear to be overtly anxious when they are with their mothers, they do not always become upset when she leaves the room, but they avoid her on her return. About 10 per cent of the children tested are classified as insecure-resistant. These children appear anxious even when the mother is present, they are likely to be upset when she leaves and are either angry or resistant in their reaction to contact on her return. Main and Solomon (1986) have added another insecure attachment category to the original Ainsworth classification system. This is the classification of children as insecure-disorganised in their reactions. These children show no coherent strategy at 12 months for dealing with the stress of separation from or reunion with the mother.

Bowlby (1969) proposed that attachment develops as a result of mothers being responsive to their infants' physical and social needs. Differences in the quality of the attachment relationship is a function of mothers' sensitivity to children's signals. Belsky (1990) notes that research has found that security of attachment is related to prompt responsiveness to distress, moderate and appropriate stimulation, interactional synchrony, as well as warmth and involvement. Insecure-avoidant attachments are characterised by an intrusive and excessively stimulating interactional style on the part of the primary attachment figure, and insecure-resistant attachments result from an unresponsive, underinvolved parental style.

Ainsworth et al. (1978) suggest that the emergence of

attachment occurs in several steps. There is an initial pre-attachment phase during the first two or three months of life, followed by a phase where attachment is in the making. During this second phase, between three and six months, an infant begins to discriminate among adults and focuses a little more narrowly on familiar adults. The child does not show any anxiety on separation, usually from the mother. In the third phase of clear-cut attachment, from about six months of age, but more usually a little later, the child shows signs that he or she has formed a clear attachment, usually to a single person. Although some children have more than one attachment figure, under stress they usually show a preference for one person. Distress at separation from the attachment figure and fear of strangers is apparent during this period, most often between the ages of 10 to 18 months. There is evidence that father-child attachments have the same qualities as mother-child attachments but the classification of the mother-child attachment is unrelated to the classification of the father-child relationship within a family (Main & Weston, 1981). Studies of attachment using the 'Strange Situation' show consistency across cultural groups, although the timing of the appearance of clear attachment from child to child and from culture to culture varies slightly (Van Izendoorn & Kroonenberg, 1988).

The development of a clear attachment relationship is characterised by specific behaviours. The child uses the significant other person as a secure base from which to explore, when placed in new situations. This person becomes a source for clues and cues about new situations, because the child uses the person's non-verbal cues to assess situations. This is known as social referencing (Dickstein & Park, 1988). From about 18 months, the child has learned that physical contact with her or his mother is not essential and is content to play at greater distances from her and is comfortable if she is in sight. These developmental changes force some renegotiation of the relationship between the mother and child. Bowlby (1969) termed this the phase of goal-corrected partnership. Gradually, the mother's role involves less direct intervention in the child's activities and guidance is increasingly given by verbal instructions. At the same time, the child begins to understand things from his or her mother's point of view, begins to infer what feelings and motives are influencing her behaviour, and so a much more complex relationship develops between them.

Research evidence indicates that early mother-child attachment is associated with later child competence but this is assumed to be mediated by the quality of ongoing positive experiences which the child has with the mother and others. Stressful experiences can impinge on the child or the family and may disrupt the attachment relationship (for example, by prolonged separation). Secure attachment is associated with a range of social-emotional and cognitive competencies through early childhood so the quality of these early relationships appears to be an antecedent for ongoing, positive attitudes towards the self (Main, Kaplan & Cassidy, 1985). In contrast, infants who are insecurely attached at 12 months are likely to be hostile or socially isolated as children, but they can be helped to develop their sense of self if later supportive relationships are available (Sproufe, 1983).

Dimensions of parenting behaviour

A focus in the research on child-family relationships has been specifying the variations in parenting behaviour which are associated with desirable, socially competent behaviour in children. How should the important qualities of family environments that are optimal for the social-emotional development of children be conceptualised? Through the years the most frequently offered generalisation is that parental responsiveness is the important quality of 'good' family environments (Collins, 1984), and as already discussed this construct has also been proposed as the parental quality which is strongly associated with secure attachment. However, no single dimension of parenting can account for all the variability in social-emotional outcomes for children and only consideration of multiple dimensions of parenting makes the outcomes for children more predictable. Aside from responsiveness, other parental interactional behaviours which are considered important are control (discipline to ensure parental standards are met), maturity demands (expectations to perform competently socially, emotionally and intellectually), and clarity of the parent-child communication so that parents and children mutually understand expectations, actions and reactions. Parents who make explicit the behaviours they desire and the expectations they hold for their children's actions, then ensure that those expectations are met, can expect to have competent children provided this is combined with sensitivity and responsiveness to the children's needs. These dimensions of parental behaviour have repeatedly been found to be associated and influential characteristics which contribute to the social-emotional development of children (Collins, 1984).

The interaction between acceptance/emotional responsiveness and parental demand/control on continuums of high to low has been extensively studied and a typology of parenting styles which predicts different social-emotional outcomes for children has been developed. The classifications of parenting styles within this typology are authoritative, authoritarian, indulgent, and neglecting (Baumrind, 1972; Maccoby & Martin, 1983). Although no parent would use exactly the same style of parenting behaviour invariantly, parents do show some consistent pattern of behaviour or dominant style.

Parental behaviours and the outcomes for the children within this typology are:

- Authoritative parents are child-oriented. They are high in acceptance and responsiveness to their children and high in demand and control. They are accepting of, and responsive to, children's needs, desires and persuasive arguments, but they also set clear rules and standards for behaviour and make sure that these are met. Children of authoritative parents are generally self-reliant, self-controlled, socially competent and have high self-esteem.

- Indulgent parents are child-oriented. They are high in acceptance and responsiveness but low in demand and control. They do not place constraints on their children's behaviour and do not make demands for mature behaviour. Children of indulgent or permissive parents tend to be impulsive, aggressive, and they lack the ability to take responsibility.

- Authoritarian parents are self-oriented. They are low in acceptance and responsiveness but high in demand and control. They place strict limits on children's expression of desires, do not discuss rules and decisions, and suppress children's efforts to challenge authority. Authoritarian parents exert control by punishment and disapproval. Their children are more likely to be less socially competent and have lower self-esteem than the children of authoritative parents.

- Neglecting parents are self-oriented. They are low in acceptance and responsiveness and low in demand and control. They are not overly committed to their roles as parents and do not expend much time or effort on their parenting. They reject children, provide little guidance and only inconsistent discipline. Children of neglecting parents tend to be hostile and aggressive. They often have low self-esteem and show little regard for other people's rights.

An understanding of the patterns of parenting behaviour stemming from this research is useful but it must be kept in mind that it stems from a unidirectional model which emphasises that parents influence children's behaviour. It needs to be taken into account that children also contribute to the socialisation process. It has been proposed that authoritative parents are able to act reasonably and with firm control because their children too are reasonable, as well as compliant (Lewis, 1981). Bell (1977) proposed a 'control systems' theory. This theory proposes that both parent and child have sensitivities to the behaviour of the other and have certain, in-built tolerance levels for each other's behaviour. When a child has reached the upper limit of the parent's tolerance level, the parent's 'upper limit control' reactions, such as restriction or punishment, are activated. The child too shows control reactions to her or his parents when they exceed the 'upper limit' or 'lower limit' of her or his expectations. Parents and children thus display constant reciprocal adaption to each other's behaviour level.

Although it is a common assumption that child-rearing practices change over time as children mature, there is little research that explains how and what changes occur. Maccoby (1984) proposes that developmental changes in children alter the socialisation processes which parents can employ. Physical growth, language development, the decline of impulsivity, children's conceptions of others, children's conception of the self, the development of cognitive executive processes and increased striving for autonomy are child factors which have implications for change in the parent-child relationship and parenting practices. Maccoby (1984) notes that 'the development of the child constitutes a powerful force, enabling or even requiring parents and children to take on new joint agendas and to adopt increasingly mature forms of interaction with one another'. However, there will also be continuity over time in any family's interactional processes so that any changes in parenting practices as the result of children's development will depend on the nature and prior history of the parent-child interaction and the parent-child relationship.

The examination of disciplinary encounters has been a particular focus in the study of parent-child relationships, because such encounters provide a crucial context for learning strategies for controlling oneself (and for controlling others!). Patterson's research (1982) has been important in understanding the family processes involved in the development of aggressive and non-compliant behaviour in school-aged children. Parents are likely to use as much disciplinary pressure with their children as required to get the desired response. If children do not comply with parental requests then parents shift to higher levels of pressure, usually power-assertive techniques. Patterson has found that aggressive children do not desist from undesired behaviour as readily as cooperative children, thus parents are pressed towards increasingly stronger forms of discipline and so interactions become increasingly negative. Patterson's work has been influential in stimulating research into the origins of self-control, cooperation and compliance in younger children. If parents can do what is necessary early in a child's life to bring about cooperation and compliance, then the opportunity to be authoritative rather than authoritarian is more available as the child grows older. Diverse studies in this area indicate that parental behaviours which are consistent, proactive and indirect in the forms of control have children who are more compliant and cooperative than parents who simply react to difficult behaviour and use more direct control strategies such as physical punishment. A study by Pettit and Bates (1989) of proactive parental encounters with children using such strategies as anticipatory guidance, monitoring children's activities and expression of affection toward children, found that the absence of positive parental characteristics is as important to the subsequent development of behaviour problems as the presence of negative parental behaviours.

Parental characteristics

As mentioned earlier, responsiveness and sensitivity are very important aspects of parental behaviour, but implicit within these qualities demonstrated by competent parents are other personal resources. Belsky (1984) proposes that as individuals, parents need to be patient, to be able to decentre from a personal point of view as well as understand a child's immediate experience and developmental needs. They need the energy required to cope with the physical and emotional demands of parenting and they need a commitment to parenting in the sense of having a past, present and future investment in maintaining the patience and energy required to fulfil the parental role. Other personal resources for parenting included good communication skills, good physical health and access to social support (Belsky, 1984). The sources and the quality of social support help parents to cope effectively with their children, and support can come from the marital relationship, formal and informal social networks, employment status, and financial resources. Equal qualities of all these factors of personal resources and support are not necessarily present in all parents' lives, so a lack in one or more areas may be compensated for by the strong presence of factors in other areas. Parents may also be and feel less competent in their parenting if their own life history has limited the development of personal resources, or if a child's developmental problems have interfered with the development of the child-parent relationship.

Parental beliefs about parenting

A central feature regulating parental behaviour towards children is the beliefs they hold about what their children are like and why their children behave in particular ways (Dix & Grusec, 1985). Developing an understanding of parental beliefs has implications for professionals working with families, since a recognition that parents bring to any situation a personal set of beliefs about their role can provide a basis for communication about child-rearing issues. Everyone has a number of ideas, values, beliefs and attitudes which are relevant to the conduct of one's life and this knowledge is expressed through actions.

Attribution theories (Heider, 1958; Jones & Davis, 1965; Kelley, 1967) have provided a conceptual framework for understanding how parental beliefs are important determinants in the socialisation process. Attribution theories are information-processing approaches which emphasise that behaviour depends on the inferences a person makes about the causes of events, about the motives of those with whom they are interacting and about the properties of the social situations in which they are involved. Child-rearing practices are the expression of sets of attributions about why children behave as they do and about the characteristics of particular children. The attributional processes filter the information parents have about children's behaviour and determine the nature of parental reaction as they interpret and respond to children's actions. Parents develop their parental belief systems through their own socialisation experiences in being parented, from observing other parents, as well as from their 'on-the-job' training as parents. The belief systems are essentially cognitive structures but affect may influence the development of these beliefs and their expression. The belief systems may also be implicit rather than explicit and will include expectations and standards against which parents measure and respond to children's actions.

Consider how beliefs might mediate parental behaviour in the following example. A young child is at a large family gathering. She is talking to her older cousin and repeatedly swears. Her father asks her to stop several times. With each repetition, his voice grows louder as he becomes angry. However, the cousin keeps laughing and is therefore reinforcing the child's use of unacceptable language according to the father's standards. A particular series of belief/self-statements by the father might be:

- Children should not use bad language.
- Children should obey their parents, especially in front of other family members.
- She is not obeying me, therefore I must do something to ensure that she will not act this way again.

From his assessment of the situation, the father then decides what action he will take.

Parental attributions about child behaviour often stem from a position that a child is immature and so the behaviour is constrained by developmental limitations that are beyond the child's control. In this way, a child's behaviour is often attributed by parents to reflect his or her age, lack of experience and knowledge of the world, rather than his or her intentions or disposition (Dix & Grusec, 1985). Parents are enmeshed with children in a strong emotional relationship and therefore their children's behaviour has personal relevance. This causes parents to share emotionally their children's successes and failures and may exert an important influence on parents' perceptions and actions in reaction to their children's behaviours. Behaviours that arouse high emotion such as anxiety, anger or joy will elicit different attributions than behaviour which is neutral. High affect will increase the strength negatively or positively of the parents' evaluation, the extent to which children's behaviour is thought to be intentional or dispositional, and therefore the parental reaction to behaviour.

An illustrative research study in this area by Mills and Rubin (1990) addressed three questions:

1. When maladaptive social behaviours occur, how do parents believe they would react effectively?

2. To what causes do parents attribute problematic social behaviours?

3. What strategies do parents believe they would use to modify maladaptive social behaviours?

Parents in this study were asked to describe their likely reactions to hypothetical scenarios in which their young children acted aggressively or withdrew in social situations. Mothers and fathers reported similar emotional reactions, causal attributions and behavioural responses to the hypothetical situations. Both mothers and fathers had different reactions to situations involving aggression compared to withdrawal in social situations. Aggressive actions aroused stronger negative emotions such as anger, disappointment or embarrassment and age-related factors were used most often for the attribution of aggression. Parents chose high or moderate power strategies for disciplining aggression compared to the sort of strategies they would use for withdrawal in social situations. They inferred that social withdrawal was unmodifiable and was the product of a dispositional/temperamental factor within the child, rather than due to situational factors.

Bacon and Ashmore (1986) and Elias and Ubriaco (1986) found that competent child functioning was best predicted by flexible, well-differentiated parental belief systems. Parental beliefs which are narrow, poorly differentiated about what child behaviours should be encouraged or changed, organised too rigidly or without sufficient accommodation to situational determinants of behaviour, make it more likely that parents will not be able to act toward a child with flexibility or understanding, and this may have negative implications for the development of the child's social competence (Bacon & Ashmore, 1986).

The intergenerational transmission of parenting

A current research issue in developmental psychology is focused on how parents' experiences as children influence their values, beliefs, attitudes and behaviour towards their own children. This research attempts to understand the origin of parenting behaviours and the influence of personal childhood experiences on subsequent parenting behaviours in adulthood. Intuitively, the influence of personal experience as a child to subsequent parenting behaviour appears to be a reasonable proposition.

The intergenerational factors could include genetic factors whereby the transmission of genes from one generation to another influence how the next generation experiences their social and physical environment and therefore their behaviour as parents. Belsky (1990) notes that all the research on the influence of parenting on child development has this fundamental limitation in the confounding of genetic and environmental factors, but Van Ijzendoorn (1992) differentiates between those behaviours which may be genetically determined and those which are psychologically determined, and defines the intergenerational transmission of parenting as the process through which purposively or unintentionally an earlier generation psychologically influences the parenting attitudes and behaviour of the next generation. This definition also seeks to exclude the contextual factors in the intergenerational transmission of parenting since it focuses on psychological behaviours and attitudes which may be alike across generations. Contextual factors may be influential if the children of each generation are raised in the same physical and social circumstances so that such factors as living in the same house or the same town may stimulate intergenerational continuity. Any genetic transmission of parenting determinants combined with contextual factors may strengthen the intergenerational transmission of parenting attitudes and behaviours, but independently of the genetic and contextual influences there do appear to be psychologically determined influences stemming from a parent's own learning experiences as a child.

The mechanisms of transmission have been considered in a social-learning framework (Bandura, 1973, 1977, 1986) in which a child learns from the models which a parent provides, either by watching a parent interacting with other children or by the child's own experiences in interacting with the parent. As well as the social-cognitive framework, the intergenerational transmission of parenting behaviours has been interpreted through attachment theory. Adult attachment theory proposes that the degree of responsiveness that a parent received as an infant will in turn influence the degree of responsiveness that she or he will be able to exhibit towards her or his children (Main, Kaplan & Cassidy, 1985). Parents who experienced high degrees of responsiveness will be in turn more responsive to the signals of their own infant than parents who were rejected or treated ambivalently as infants. It is believed that parents who experienced rejection or ambivalence can restructure those experiences in later life through involvement in secure relationships or through counselling.

This line of research is still new and is likely to develop

extensively throughout the 1990s. Learning to be a parent may logically be an outcome of one's own experiences of being parented, but the research evidence is not strong enough as yet to ascertain the extent to which this might be so. It does seem plausible that the cognitive processes involved in internalising the parenting behaviour that was observed or experienced in one's family of origin, or through an attachment with a primary caregiver, may influence how an individual learns a certain parenting style.

Social issues and the effects of parenting

Parental support systems

Examining the sources of stress and social support in parenting is an example of exosystem analysis (Bronfenbrenner, 1979). Social support has implications for the developmental outcomes for children through indirectly mediating how parents cope with child-rearing responsibilities. Families are supported in their parenting by the social networks of which they are a part. Social networks are the relationships with friends, neighbours and relatives and support is information supplied through the social network that leads a person to believe that he or she is cared for, loved and esteemed and is a member of a network which has mutual obligations. Information that one is loved and esteemed provides emotional support and instrumental support is the availability of material items and services. Research has found that the quality of parental social networks and social support from spouse, family and friends for effective parenting are important for effective parenting (Homel, Burns & Goodnow, 1987; Weinraub & Wolf, 1983). However, it is by no means certain whether social support from significant others is a buffer to stress, or whether those that receive more social support and hence function more effectively are in fact just more socially skilled in relating to others than those who do not receive such support.

Families are embedded in social systems that are characterised by rapid social and technological change, and increasingly families are under stress. Social support can help them to cope with change and resultant stress. To be negotiated are developmental transitions such as the birth of a child, structural changes such as divorce, functional changes such as employment and socio-historical changes, for example through economic recession. Stressors such as unemployment, family violence and marital discord may have direct and indirect effects on children's behaviour, but the major impact of many of these stressors on children is mediated by change to the nature and quality of family interaction and child-rearing practices. For example, the changing economic circumstances in society have resulted in widespread unemployment. Edgar (1992) noted that some 700 000 Australian children have neither parent employed and that family support is essential to alleviate negative long-term effects. McLoyd (1989) has reviewed research in the United States on the effects of paternal job and income loss on children. Most of the effects are indirect and mediated by changes to the father's behaviour, such as increased irritability and pessimism, which result in less responsive and more punitive behaviour towards the children. Such changes in paternal behaviour increase children's risk of experiencing social-emotional difficulties. Job loss also increases the likelihood of other events impacting on children, such as divorce. However, strong maternal support and maternal expectations for mature and autonomous behaviour were found to be critical to children's resilience to the impact of paternal job loss.

Maternal employment and family life

As employment trends for women and men change, there is increasing recognition of the interdependence of work and family roles. Understanding the complexities in integrating work and parenting roles, childcare arrangements and family life has become prominent issues as maternal employment has increased. Hall (1972) suggested that while society expected wives and mothers to enact their various roles (employee, wife, mother) simultaneously, fathers and husbands were afforded the luxury of fulfilling these roles sequentially. This meant that when fathers were at work they were not expected to be concerned with family issues, while women were expected to always keep job-related and family issues in mind. Today, there is recognition that there is considerable overlap between work and family roles both for men and women but actual practice may not always allow women in the workplace the flexibility to deal with family issues. For instance, when a child is sick there is considerable stress on mothers to make arrangements that will not interfere with time at work (Ochiltree & Greenblat, 1991). Within a systems perspective, the return of the mother to employment is a major transition for the family. It originates outside the child but has a direct and indirect impact on the child, and there may be different effects over time as the result of this transition. For example, the initial period of the mother's employment has different effects compared to when the pattern becomes familiar, and stability and routine in the system is again established.

Because women have increasingly sought employment outside the home there has been extensive research on the effects of non-parental care on children. Empirical evidence of any differential outcomes for children of employed versus non-employed mothers has not been found (Hoffman, 1989). Although mothers who are employed spend less time with their young children, they tend to compensate for their absence in the proportion of direct interaction and in the amount of time spent with children during non-work hours (Hoffman, 1984). Studies of the quality of parent-child interaction between employed and non-employed mothers indicate that any differences are mediated by the mothers' level of education, role satisfaction and attitudes towards mothering, while dissatisfaction with full-time homemaking is likely to be particularly disruptive to mothers' responsiveness to young children (Hoffman, 1989). Employed mothers are also more likely to encourage independence in their young children, which is welcomed in families where both parents are working (Hoffman, 1979). Although most studies have found that mother-child attachment is secure in families where mothers are employed, there have been some indications in two studies that the proportion of insecure attachments in the employed group are higher than for the general population (Barlow, Vaughn & Molitor, 1987; Belsky & Rovine, 1988).

Despite a child's daily separation from his or her family, childcare does not mean separate socialisation but rather it becomes a second microsystem for development (Bronfenbrenner, 1979), so that in the ecological framework, the links between home and childcare (the mesosystem) are important for positive socialisation outcomes. Childcare can take many forms. Informally, families seek care for their children from other family members, commonly grandparents and formal care arrangements include daycare centres, family day-care arrangements and after-school care programs.

The research base on non-parental care has developed in a number of phases and stems primarily from the United States which has less uniform regulation than Australia on the conditions in care settings and less regulated industrial conditions for staff. This is important in the extrapolation of the research findings to the experiences of Australian children and families. In the 1970s, studies asked the question, 'What are the effects of non-parental childcare?'. These studies were mainly conducted in high-quality, university-based centres which may now be considered atypical, but it was generally found that day care did not affect children's security of attachment with their parents or their social-emotional development, although there were some indications that children in day care might be somewhat more aggressive and independent than children cared for at home by their mother. Further research began to specify some of the structural conditions for quality childcare to ensure optimal outcomes for children. These conditions included the group size of which a child is part, the nature and extent of the training of caregivers, and the caregiver-child ratio. Children in smaller groups where the child-staff ratio was smaller and where caregivers had education in child development and early childhood education were more cooperative and more emotionally secure (Phillips & Howes, 1987).

By the 1980s, as maternal employment increased and more day-care research was conducted, more specificity on effects was made. Primary factors affecting the development of children in childcare environments are the structural qualities of the care environment (such as group size and staff-child ratio), caregiver stability, timing of entry into non-parental care, and the length of time a child has been in non-parental care. Many of these studies indicated that children who had experienced day care before one year of age were at risk for insecure attachment and were more likely to be aggressive and non-compliant when aged three to eight (Belsky, 1988). Belsky's conclusions have been challenged on the grounds that much of this research lacked information about the quality of the care to which the children were exposed and that the children studied were not randomly assigned to care arrangements that varied systematically in quality. As a result, there was no way to adequately distinguish any negative effects of care (Clarke-Stewart, 1988). More recent longitudinal research indicates that when both age of entry and the quality of care are taken into account, children who enter a care situation in the first year of life and for whom the care quality is poor are more at risk for social-emotional difficulties (Howes, 1990).

Current research on non-parental care is focused on understanding the complex relationships between quality of care, family processes, parental work experiences and the outcomes for children. This is a focus on the complex ecology of care in which families, staff and operators of centres are all potential contributors to and stakeholders in the quality of experiences for children. Family variables which have been of interest in this research include parental wellbeing, parenting skills, family socioeconomic status and family structure, and these are being examined in relation to aspects of quality in the care situation and the outcomes for children. Evidence from such research indicates that the quality of care children experience depends on family circumstances. Family stress and limited psychological and financial resources are associated with poorer quality day care as these families are less able to seek out and afford quality care (Howes & Olenick, 1986; Howes, 1990).

As non-parental care becomes a fact of life for many children the factors which have traditionally been found to shape development for home-reared children may function differently or not at all for children who experience alternative care from an early age. For example, attachment security to a parent may not be as important as the nature of the attachment to alternative caregivers, or quality of day care may be more influential to development than particular family processes (Belsky, 1990). Belsky also proposes that child care experienced in the home and in day care may on one hand increase the accumulation of stress which impacts on a child or, on the other hand, it may offset single sources of vulnerability within a family system by providing other sources of support to the child.

Conclusion

The research on family processes and the social-developmental outcomes for children reviewed in this chapter provides strong evidence that many aspects of family life impact on children's development. There are direct experiences which impinge on children and also indirect experiences stemming from the fact that families are embedded in social systems. Central to an ecology of human development as proposed by Bronfenbrenner (1979) is the examination of systems of interaction that take into account environmental aspects beyond children's immediate situation and the need to view behaviour in context. A second theme which emerges from the systemic and ecological perspective that informs the analysis of parent-child relations is the reciprocal influences between parents and children as well as the reciprocal influences between developing individuals and the multiple contexts in which development takes place.

Research on family socialisation has looked for variations in how parents affectively respond to their children, interact with their children, discipline their children and how they think about their children. These variations will reflect different outcomes for children, however Scarr (1992) provides a reassuring final note for this chapter. She noted that 'children's outcomes do not depend on whether parents take children to the ball game or to the museum so much as they depend on genetic transmission, on plentiful opportunities, and having a good enough environment that supports children's development to become themselves'.

References

Ainsworth, M. D., Blehar, M. C., Waters, E. & Wall, S. (1978) *Patterns of Attachment: A Psychological Study of the Strange Situation*. Hillsdale, New Jersey: Erlbaum.

Bacon, M. K. & Ashmore, R. D. (1986) A consideration of the cognitive activities of parents and their role on the socialisation process. In R. D. Ashmore & D. M. Brodzinsky (eds.), *Thinking about the Family: Views of Parents and Children*. Hillsdale, New Jersey: Erlbaum.

Bandura, A. (1973) *Aggression: A Social Learning Analysis*. Englewood Cliffs, New Jersey: Prentice-Hall.

Bandura, A. (1977) *Social Learning Theory*. Englewood Cliffs, New Jersey: Prentice-Hall.

Bandura, A. (1986) *Social Foundations of Thought and Action: A Social and Cognitive Theory*. Englewood Cliffs, New Jersey: Prentice-Hall.

Barlow, P., Vaughn, B. & Molitor, N. (1987) Effects of maternal absence due to employment on the quality infant-mother attachment in a low risk sample. *Child Development*, 58, 945–54.

Bates, J. E. (1987) Temperament in infancy. In J. D. Osofsky (ed.), *Handbook of Infant Development* (2 ed.). New York: Wiley.

Baumrind, D. (1972) Socialisation and instrumental competence in young children. In W. W. Hartup (ed.), *The Young Child: Reviews of Research* (Vol. 2). Washington, D.C.: National Association for the Education of Young Children.

Bell, R. Q. (1968) A reinterpretation of the direction of effects in studies in socialization. *Psychological Review*, 75, 81–95.

Bell, R. Q. (1977) Socialization findings re-examined. In R. Q. Bell & R. V. Harper (eds.), *Child Effects on Adults*. Hillsdale, New Jersey: Erlbaum.

Belsky, J. (1984) The determinants of parenting: A process model. *Child Development*, 55, 83–95.

Belsky, J. (1988) The 'effects' of infant day care reconsidered. *Early Childhood Research Quarterly*, 3, 235–72.

Belsky, J. (1990) Parental and nonparental child care and children's socioemotional development: A decade in review. *Journal of Marriage and the Family*, 52, 855–903.

Belsky, J. & Rovine, M. J. (1988) Nonmaternal care in the first year of life and the security of infant-parent attachment. *Child Development*, 59, 157–67.

Berg-Cross, L. (1988) *Basic Concepts in Family Therapy*. New York: Haworth Press.

Bowlby, J. (1969) *Attachment and Loss, Volume 1, Attachment*. New York: Basic Books.

Bowlby, J. (1973) *Attachment and Loss, Volume 2, Separation: Anxiety and Anger*. London: Hogarth.

Bowlby, J. (1980) *Attachment and Loss, Volume 3, Loss, Sadness and Depression*. New York: Basic Books.

Bronfenbrenner, U. (1979) *The Ecology of Human Development: Experiments by Nature and Design*. Cambridge, Mass.: Harvard University Press.

Bronfenbrenner, U. (1986) Ecology of the family as a context for human development: Research perspectives. *Developmental Psychology*, 22, 723–42.

Buss, A. H. & Plomin, R. (1984) *Temperament: Early Developing Personality Traits*. Hillsdale, New Jersey: Erlbaum.

Clarke-Stewart, K. A. (1988) Parents' effects on children's development: A decade of progress? *Journal of Applied Developmental Psychology*, 9, 41–84.

Collins, W. A. (1984) Commentary: Family interaction and child development. In M. Perlmutter (ed.), *Parent-Child Interaction and Parent-Child Relations in Child Development: The Minnesota Symposia on Child Psychology*, Vol. 17. Hillsdale, New Jersey: Erlbaum.

Dickstein, S. & Park, R. D. (1988) Social referencing in infancy: A glance at fathers and marriage. *Child Development*, 59, 506–11.

Dix, T. & Grusec, J. E. (1985) Parental attribution processes in the socialisation of children. In I. E. Sigel (ed.), *Parental Beliefs Systems: The Psychological Consequences for Children*. Hillsdale, New Jersey: Erlbaum.

Edgar, D. (1992) Families in unemployment. *Family Matters*, No. 32, August, 1992.

Elias, M. J. & Ubriaco, M. (1986) Linking parental beliefs to children's social competence: Toward a cognitive-behavioural model. In R. D. Ashmore & D. M. Brodzinsky (eds.), *Thinking about the Family: Views of Parents and Children*. Hillsdale, New Jersey: Erlbaum.

Freud, S. (1957) On narcissicism: An introduction. In J. Strachey (ed. & trans.), *The Standard Edition of the Complete Psychological Works of Sigmund Freud* (Vol. 14). London: Hogarth Press.

Goldsmith, H. H. & Campos J. J. (1982) Toward a theory of infant temperament. In R. M. Emde & R. J. Harmon (eds.), *The Development of Attachment and Affiliative Systems*. New York: Plenum.

Hall, D. T. (1972) A model of coping with role conflict. *Administrative Science Quarterly*, 4, 471–86.

Hartup, W. W. (1989) Social relationships and their developmental significance. *American Psychologist*, 44, 120–6.

Heider, F. (1958) *The Psychology of Interpersonal Relations*. New York: Wiley.

Hoffman, L. W. (1979) Maternal employment: 1979. *American Psychologist*, 34, 859–65.

Hoffman, L. W. (1984) Maternal employment and the young child. In M. Permutter (ed.), *Parent-Child Interaction and Parent-*

Child Relations in Child Development. The Minnesota Symposia on Child Psychology (Vol. 17). Hillsdale, New Jersey: Erlbaum.

Hoffman, L. W. (1989) Effects of maternal employment in the two-parent family. *American Psychologist,* 44, 283–92.

Homel, R., Burns, A. & Goodnow, J. (1987) Parental social networks and child development. *Journal of Social and Personal Relationships,* 4, 159–77.

Howes, C. (1990) Can the age of entry and the quality of infant child care predict adjustment in kindergarten? *Developmental Psychology,* 26, 292–303.

Howes, C. & Olenick, M. (1986) Family and child care influences on children's compliance. *Child Development,* 57, 202–16.

Jones, E. E. & Davis, K. E. (1965) From acts to dispositions: The attribution process in person perception. In L. Berkowitz (ed.), *Advances on experimental social psychology.* (Vol. 2). New York: Academic Press.

Kelley, H. H. (1967) Attribution theory in social psychology. In D. Levine (ed.), *Nebraska Symposium on Motivation.* Lincoln: University of Nebraska Press.

Lerner, R. M. (1986) *Concepts and Theories of Human Development* (2 ed.). New York: Random House.

Lewis, C. C. (1980) The effects of parental firm control: A reinterpretation of findings. *Psychological Bulletin,* 90, 547–67.

Maccoby, E. E. (1984) Socialization and developmental change. *Child Development,* 55, 317–28.

Maccoby, E. & Martin, J. (1983) Socialization in the context of the family: Parent-child interaction. In E. M. Hetherington (ed.), *Socialisation, Personality, and Social Development.* In P. H. Mussen (ed.), *Handbook of Child Psychology,* Vol. 4, (4 ed.). New York: Wiley.

McLoyd, V. (1989) Socialisation and development in a changing economy: The effects of paternal job and income loss on children. *American Psychologist,* 44, 293–302.

Main, M. & Weston, D. (1981) The quality of the toddler's relationship to mother and father: Related to conflict behavior and readiness to establish new relationships. *Child Development,* 52, 932–40.

Main, M., Kaplan, N. & Cassidy, J. (1985) Security in infancy, childhood and adulthood: A move to the level of representation. *Monographs of the Society for Research in Child Development*, 50 (1–2, Serial 209), 66–104.

Main, M. & Solomon, J. (1986) Discovery of a new, insecure disorganised/disoriented attachment pattern: Procedures, findings and implications for the classification of behavior. In M. Yogman & T. B. Brazelton (eds.), *Affective Development in Infancy*. Norwood, New Jersey: Ablex.

Mills, R. S. & Rubin, K. H. (1990) Parental beliefs about problematic social behaviours in early childhood. *Child Development*, 61, 138–51.

Minuchin, P. (1985) Families and individual development: Provocations from the field of family therapy. *Child Development*, 56, 289–302.

Ochiltree, G. & Greenblat, E. (1991) Mothers in the workforce: Coping with young sick children. *Family Matters*, No. 28, April 1991.

Patterson, G. R. (1982) *Coercive Family Process: A Social Learning Approach*, Vol. 3. Oregon: Castalia.

Pettit, G. S. & Bates, J. E. (1989) Family interaction patterns and children's behavior problems: From infancy to 4 years. *Developmental Psychology*, 25, 413–20.

Phillips, D. & Howes, C. (1987) Indicators of quality in child care: Review of the research. In D. A. Phillips (ed.), *Quality in Child Care: What Does Research Tell Us?* Washington D.C.: National Association for the Education of Young Children.

Rothbart, J. M. (1989) Temperament in childhood: A framework. In G. A. Kohnstamm, J. E. Bates & M. K. Rothbart (eds.), *Temperament in Childhood*. New York: Wiley.

Scarr, S. (1992) Developmental theories for the 1990's: Development and individual differences. *Child Development*, 63, 1–19.

Skinner, B. F. (1953) *Science and Human Behaviour*. New York: Macmillan.

Sproufe, L. A. (1983) Infant-caregiver attachment and patterns of adaption in preschool: The roots of maladaption and competence. In M. Perlmutter (ed.), *Development and policy concerning children with special needs. Minnesota Symposia on Child Development*, Vol. 16. Hillsdale, New Jersey: Erlbaum.

Sproufe, L. A. (1985) Attachment classification from the perspective of infant-caregiver relationships and infant temperament. *Child Development*, 56, 1–14.

Thomas, A. & Chess, S. (1977) *Temperament and Development*. New York: Brunner/Mazel.

Van Ijzendoorn, M. H. & Kroonenberg, P. M. (1988) Cross cultural patterns of attachment: A meta-analysis of the strange situation. *Child Development*, 59, 147–56.

Van Ijzendoorn, M. H. (1992) Intergenerational transmission of parenting: A review of studies of nonclinical population. *Developmental Review*, 12, 76–99.

Vaughn, B. E., Stevenson-Hinde, J., Waters, E., Kotsaftis, A., Lefever, G. B., Shouldice, A., Trudel, M. & Belsky, J. (1992) Attachment security and temperament in infancy and early childhood: Some conceptual clarifications. *Developmental Psychology*, 28, 463–73.

Von Bertalanffy, L. (1968) *General Systems Theory: Foundations, Development Application*. New York: Braziller.

Weinraub, M. & Wolf, B. M. (1983) Effects of stress and social supports on mother-child interaction in single- and two-parent families. *Child Development*, 54, 1297–311.

THE 'WHOLE CHILD': LINKS AMONG AREAS OF DEVELOPMENT

Di Catherwood

Common themes

This book has presented current information and perspectives on development and learning in early childhood and considered the implications of this material for teaching. Each of the chapters in the book has dealt with different aspects of these issues, but there are many overlapping themes. Most important of all is the portrayal of young children as being actively engaged in their own development. It is clear that in all aspects of early learning, children apply an impressive repertoire of problem-solving skills aimed at acquiring and organising information about the world of people, objects and events. This theme is evident not only in the chapters dealing with cognitive development (chapters 2 and 3), but in every other chapter as well. Children's acquisition of language (chapter 4) displays a remarkable capacity to store, deduce and order information about the form and content of language. Even children's efforts to gain control over body movements (chapter 5) indicate a capacity to solve problems through the medium of the body itself. Likewise, early artistic development (chapter 6) reveals an ability to store, coordinate and apply information — in this case, through the channels of artistic expression. Finally, the chapters on children's social and emotional development (chapters 7 and 8) also reflect this perspective of young children actively exploring and testing the limits of social and interpersonal contexts.

Although each chapter focused on a different aspect of development, these aspects do not of course proceed in isolation from each other. There is a close interdependence among the various areas of development. An appreciation of this overlap is critically important for all early childhood teachers and caregivers. The impact of teaching strategies on the 'whole' child needs to be considered.

Some of the connections or links among the areas of development covered by the various chapters in this book are explored in the following discussion.

Links between cognitive development and other areas

There are obvious links between the material in chapters 2 and 3. Although these chapters focus on somewhat different age groups, there is a common view that cognitive growth consists of applying basic processes such as memory in the development of networks of knowledge or understanding. Cognitive development occurs with the elaboration or enrichment of these networks and with a corresponding increase in control over the use of short-term memory capacity during problem-solving or cognitive activity.

There are clear parallels between this view of cognitive development and the perspective on language acquisition presented in chapter 4. Cognitive and language development may often be out of step with each other, so that concepts can develop ahead of language or language can be incorrectly mapped onto underlying knowledge (see chapter 3 on 'animism' and chapter 4 on 'over-extensions'). However, language is inevitably tied to the content of cognition and much early language reflects children's attempts to name or verbally refer to some cognitive representation or concept. In turn, language can provide a powerful tool for developing cognitive skills. It offers an extra dimension to any underlying knowledge networks by serving to define or denote fuzzy representations or concepts. For example, a child may have a rich representation or knowledge of chocolate cookies, complete with sensory detail of the colour, shape, texture and taste of such objects. However, the added capacity to label or verbally symbolise this representation can significantly improve the ease with which the child can retrieve the information from long-term memory, deal with it in short-term memory, and apply it in problem-solving situations. Indeed, as described in chapter 4, even children's early 'telegraphic' speech is capable of conveying very complex ideas or knowledge.

Moreover, the process or pattern of language acquisition reveals clear similarities to cognitive development. For example, the systematic or organised way in which children acquire or deduce the rules of language resembles children's capacity to detect regularities in categories or concepts in general. Thus it may be that language and cognitive development draw on similar kinds of capacities in many regards.

There are also links between early cognitive development and motor learning (chapter 5). Both of these areas of early growth depend heavily on the intake of sensory information in the first instance. As explained in chapter 2, understanding the fundamental aspects of the world arises from children's capacity to process sensory information in a coherent and organised way. Likewise, mastery over the body's movements in our three-dimensional universe demands the coordination and application of information from the senses. Moreover, in developing this mastery, infants display a capacity to solve 'motor problems' (such as how to hold a spoonful of food or how to climb onto a chair) that reflects the same basic ability to store, retrieve and coordinate information that is evident in all problem-solving situations. All motor learning, regardless of whether it involves a simple action such as holding a cup, or very complex action sequences such as the movements involved in a dance routine, draws on these same basic capacities for dealing with information.

Motor development also influences cognitive development in a number of ways. Of particular importance is the enhanced capacity to use physical tools that comes through increasing fine motor control. Infants' ability to fully explore the properties of objects through touch is significantly improved with the development of effective grasping and manipulative movements of the hands and fingers, and coordination of hand movements and visual attention. Likewise, the capacity to solve problems involving objects can be aided by the motor ability to apply other tools to the task (such as using one object on top of another to reach the cookie jar on a shelf). Perhaps the most important aspect of early use of tools that engages both motor and cognitive processes is children's capacity to use the instruments of writing — namely pens and pencils, or perhaps computer keyboards. Similarly, the use of tools or media for artistic expression (chapter 6) such as brushes, pencils, clay and so on, require the mutual exercise not only of motor abilities but also cognitive and artistic capacities.

The development of artistry (chapter 6) obviously draws on the cognitive capacities discussed in chapters 2 and 3. In particular, children's use of symbols in various forms of artistic expression (body movements, drawings, clay sculpture, and so on) can be seen as reflecting the capacities for representation of some item and subsequent retrieval of stored information about that item from memory. In addition, the ability to form concepts or categories, described in chapter 2, can be seen in children's use of artistic symbols. For example (as explained in chapter 6), children's drawing or socio-dramatic play often reveals conceptual or 'prototypical' knowledge, rather than details about a specific item, event or person. In addition, the content of children's artistic symbols (drawings etc.) can reflect the same kinds of features involved in their cognitive representations or knowledge networks. For example, children's artistic work may reflect both sensory features, such as colours or movement, and information with a wider cultural meaning, such as a logo or word.

The social and interpersonal aspects of development are also closely tied to children's cognitive capacities. At a broad level, the contexts for early socialisation (the family, early childhood centre, and so on) serve to define or provide much of the 'meaning' or knowledge base for children's early cognitive and linguistic growth and for survival and success within those contexts. Children must not only acquire the appropriate language system, but

must also develop a knowledge base that reflects the values, beliefs and skills for those contexts. Children meet this challenge by applying the same basic cognitive skills described in chapters 2 and 3.

The nature of children's earliest social relationships or 'attachments' appears to have a profound impact on early cognitive development. As explained in chapter 8, a child who demonstrates evidence of a secure attachment to a caregiver is more likely to engage in sensori-motor exploration in the presence of the caregiver than a child displaying insecure attachment. It seems likely that a child who is preoccupied with social or emotional problems (as perhaps is the case for an insecurely bonded child) would have little spare energy for, or interest in, other problems or challenges presented by the environment.

Central to all aspects of development is children's growing self-identity (chapter 7). In regard to cognitive development, the relationship with self-identity is a mutual one. Cognitive activity can influence self-esteem or self-concept and vice versa, self-concept or esteem can affect cognitive growth. In regard to the former situation, children's self-esteem may be bolstered by the successful solution of a problem or task involving cognitive capacities, or alternately self-esteem may plummet in the face of persistent failure at some task. On the other hand, the degree of self-esteem or the nature of children's self-identity may influence cognitive activity. For example, children who strongly identify with a feminine gender stereotype may be unwilling to solve problems involving 'male' toys, or children with poor self-esteem may be so afraid of failing on some problem that they will not apply their full cognitive capacities to solving it. It is essential that all early childhood educators appreciate this close relationship between cognitive activity and self-identity, since it is likely that children's performance of 'cognitive' tasks will invariably intrude on their sense of self to some extent.

It would also seem that there is a close connection between children's cognitive and interpersonal skills in regard to the development of peer relationships (chapter 7). Many aspects of social competence demand problem-solving skills that require similar cognitive capacities to those needed for any other kind of problem. Facilitation of social competence can involve assisting children to develop effective cognitive strategies for dealing with interpersonal situations.

Other interrelationships

The links among the different areas are not of course restricted to those involving cognitive capacities per se. A number of other important overlaps or interdependencies should be mentioned.

The social dimensions of development impinge on all other aspects. Apart from the relationship with cognition already discussed, there is also a close link between social development and language acquisition. From its earliest emergence in the first year of life, language is used by children to communicate with other people. As described in chapter 4, children quickly perceive the power of language as a tool for eliciting attention and achieving goals in social and interpersonal contexts — that is, to solve problems in those contexts. Indeed, children's social relationships provide the basic material for language acquisition by offering children both a language sample and shared social or cultural meaning. Although children do not acquire language by simple imitation or modelling (chapter 4), it seems likely that effective language development requires not only exposure to the language of competent speakers, but also at least some focused attention or feedback from those speakers.

Social or interpersonal experiences also have a strong impact on children's development of artistry (chapter 6), with the former providing much of the meaning or content for the latter. For example, children's socio-dramatic play often reflects knowledge or concepts about social relationships or roles, while children's drawings or paintings may convey information about their feelings regarding themselves or their interpersonal experiences.

There may also be close links between children's social development or self-identity and performance of motor tasks. Many activities involving motor capacities are conducted within a social context (for example, sports or games such as tennis or football) and so necessarily make demands on children in social or interpersonal terms as well as purely physical or motor terms. One of the by-products of this situation is that children's motor performances are often compared. There are obvious implications of this for children's self-identity and self-esteem. Children who perform such tasks easily may incorporate motor competence into their self-concept, whereas children who experience difficulty in such tasks may develop low self-esteem in this area of their development, perhaps opting for alternative pursuits or interests.

Of course, most everyday activities and experiences involve multiple aspects of development. For example, children's development of reading skills involves: (a) perceptual processes to register the sounds and visual patterns of words, (b) cognitive processes for attending to and holding onto information in short-term memory, as well as retrieving knowledge from long-term memory, (c) language to enable the processing of the phonological, semantic and syntactic aspects of the reading material, (d) motor skills to permit the coordination of eye movements (and of vocal articulation if children are reading aloud), (e) social factors, if an adult is assisting or interacting with a child (f) emotional factors if the reading activity has implications for children's self-esteem or self-concept and (g) artistic activities, as might occur if children act out the reading material or engage in further creative processes as a result of the reading experience.

To use another example, a child who is learning to play the piano will not only call on aspects of artistic development in regard to creative expression or the application of musical symbols to that expression, but will also call on: (a) perceptual processes for registering and monitoring the sounds produced during playing or for conveying visual feedback regarding the position of the fingers on the keyboard, (b) cognitive processes for attending to and maintaining the musical sounds in short-term memory and for retrieving long-term memories enabling the recall of the musical composition, (c) language to deal with accompanying lyrics, (d) motor processes for coordinating and controlling the movement of the hands and fingers and (e) possibly social-emotional factors as well, if the child's self-esteem or interpersonal relationships are tied to the activity in any way.

The implications for early childhood education

One dominant theme regarding early childhood teaching emerges from all the chapters in this book. Learning is most effective when it engages children's interests and concerns and begins from a baseline of their knowledge or skill in a particular area of development. This highlights the importance of providing children with continuity between pre-existing knowledge frameworks and new information. It also reflects the need to consider not only the cognitive, linguistic, artistic or motor capacities required for a task, but also the social and emotional or motivational factors that may influence children's exercise of these capacities. The interconnectedness of the different facets of development has critical implications for early childhood teaching, regardless of whether this involves the formal classroom or the neighbourhood junior swimming team. Children's learning is not compartmentalised, but engages multiple capacities and aspects of development. There is a clear responsibility for all early childhood educators to reflect on the impact of any planned learning experience or activity on all these layers of early childhood experience and development. When these conditions are met and the 'whole child' is engaged, then the full capacity of the child to solve life's problems may emerge.

LIST OF CONTRIBUTORS

Gillian Boulton-Lewis is Associate Professor and Head of the School of Learning and Development in the Faculty of Education, Kelvin Grove Campus, QUT. She originally trained as a teacher in New South Wales, obtained a BA as an external student with the University of Queensland, an MEd from Canberra CAE and then a PhD from the University of Queensland. She has been a teacher, lecturer, senior lecturer, principal lecturer, and principal adviser in various States of Australia and in Papua New Guinea. Her main area of expertise and research is in the application of contemporary theories of learning to teaching, and in particular to mathematics education. She has published in this and related areas.

Di Catherwood is a Senior Lecturer with the School of Early Childhood, QUT and completed her doctoral work in cognitive development in the Department of Psychology at the University of Queensland. Her teaching and research expertise is in the area of perceptual and cognitive development in early childhood. In particular, she has been closely associated with the development of the Centre for Applied Studies in Early Childhood at QUT and is a member of the Australian Human Development Association.

Judith Bowey is a Senior Lecturer in the Department of Psychology at the University of Queensland. She obtained her PhD from the University of Adelaide in 1981. Judy's primary research interests are in children's reading and metalinguistic development. She is particularly interested in how specific language skills contribute to reading development. Judy has published in a number of areas, including children's oral reading, adult word recogni- tion, metalinguistic development, and phonological skills underlying children's word reading difficulties.

Carolyn O'Brien is a Lecturer in the School of Human Movement Studies at QUT. She graduated initially with a DipPhysEd from Sydney Teachers' College and taught physical education. On moving to Queensland in 1974 she completed Bachelors, Honors and Masters degrees in Human Movement Studies and a PhD in Human Movement Studies and Special Education. Her current research interests encompass development of advanced locomotor patterns in normally developing children and issues related to mainstreaming of disabled children in normal schools. She has had a book accepted by Chapman and Hall titled *Normal and impaired motor development: Theory into practice.*

Susan Wright is Associate Professor of Early Childhood in the Faculty of Education at QUT. She has a BEd and MEd from the University of Alberta and a PhD from the University of Newcastle, and has taught in early childhood programs and in tertiary education in both Canada and Australia. Her research interests include the study of children's use of metaphors in their drawings, and their perception of music via animated computer images, personal movement and open-ended discussion. She is currently investigating teachers', supervisors', and students' personal characteristics, pedagogical beliefs and practices with the aim to compatibly match these three groups. Her publications focus on the areas of creativity, the arts curriculum, and young children's learning and development in the arts.

Kym Irving is a Lecturer in the School of Early Childhood at QUT. She has a BA (Hons) and a PhD from the University of Queensland in the area of development psychology. She is also a member of the Centre for Applied Studies in Early Childhood and is a coordinator of the Centre's counselling and testing service provided for families of young children. Her research interests include the development of social competence, children's peer relationships, child care, sex role development and family relationships. She is currently involved in a longitudinal study of children's social development.

Donna Berthelsen is a Lecturer in Developmental Psychology in the School of Early Childhood in the Faculty of Education at QUT. She holds qualifications for primary teaching and special education, as well as a BA (Hons) and a Masters of Applied Psychology from the University of Queensland. She has worked as a teacher, counsellor, psychologist, and lecturer. Her research interests are in the areas of children's social development within the family, non-parental care of young children, and the psychological well-being of mothers with young children.